Blueprints Visual Scr
for Unreal Engine
Second Edition

The faster way to build games using UE4 Blueprints

Marcos Romero
Brenden Sewell

BIRMINGHAM - MUMBAI

Blueprints Visual Scripting for Unreal Engine
Second Edition

Copyright © 2019 Packt Publishing

Commissioning Editor: Kunal Chaudhari
Acquisition Editor: Ashitosh Gupta
Content Development Editor: Arun Nadar
Senior Editor: Jack Cummings
Technical Editor: Suwarna Patil
Copy Editor: Safis Editing
Project Coordinator: Manthan Patel
Proofreader: Safis Editing
Indexer: Manju Arasan
Production Designer: Arvindkumar Gupta

First published: July 2015
Second edition: August 2019

Production reference: 1230819

Published by Packt Publishing Ltd.
Livery Place
35 Livery Street
Birmingham
B3 2PB, UK.

ISBN 978-1-78934-706-7

www.packtpub.com

Contributors

About the authors

Marcos Romero is the author of the *Romero Blueprints* blog, which is one of the main references on the internet to learn about Blueprints. Epic Games invited Marcos to the Unreal Engine 4 closed beta program to experiment and collaborate with the evolution of the tools. He was also one of the first recipients of Unreal Dev Grants for Education. Marcos is a well-known figure in the Unreal community and, for Epic Games, he wrote the official *Blueprints Compendium* and *Blueprints Instructors' Guide*.

I would like to thank Tim Sweeney for creating the amazing Unreal Engine and for signing the greetings poster that was sent to me at the end of UE4 closed beta program. He has always been a great inspiration to me in my game programming career.
I'd also like to thank Luis Cataldi for recognizing my potential and giving me incredible opportunities to show my talents to the world.

Brenden Sewell is a creative director with a decade of experience leading teams in the development of compelling interactive experiences that entertain, teach, and inspire. Prior to joining E-Line, he explored the intersection of educational practice and industry game development culminating in his work as the principal game designer at the Center for Games and Impact. Here, he specialized in the development of immersive games for STEM education and teacher professional development. Since joining the E-Line team, he has led developments from concept, prototyping, and production, to release on a variety of projects ranging from a brain-training first-person shooter to a construction sandbox exploring the future of digital fabrication.

About the reviewers

Agne Skripkaite is an Unreal Engine 4 software engineer with a particular interest in **virtual reality (VR)** applications. Agne has a BSc physics degree with honors from the University of Edinburgh and became a full-time engineer partway through a physics PhD program at Caltech. Over the last few years, Agne has developed for room-scale and seated VR games as part of teams of various sizes, right from two-engineer teams to large development teams. Agne has also served as a user comfort and motion sickness mitigation expert for seated VR applications.

Matt Matte has over 10 years of experience in Unreal Engine and is the founder of Full Metal Jacket Games, whose *Tron*-inspired VR game was featured in Unreal Engine's Spotlight Projects. He is also the organizer of the world's largest Unreal Engine meetup with over 800 members in Seattle, and has published four games with Unreal Engine, including *Soldier Girl* and *Monkey Land 3D: Reaper Rush*.

Matt is an expert Unreal developer and technical artist who specializes in setting up characters, from rigging and creating animations to implementing AI behavior trees. He is particularly passionate about VR games. Full Metal Jacket Games has won top prizes in two Seattle VR Hackathons and a People's Choice Award for NASA's 2015 Space Apps Challenge.

Packt is searching for authors like you

If you're interested in becoming an author for Packt, please visit authors.packtpub.com and apply today. We have worked with thousands of developers and tech professionals, just like you, to help them share their insight with the global tech community. You can make a general application, apply for a specific hot topic that we are recruiting an author for, or submit your own idea.

Table of Contents

Section 4: Advanced Blueprints

Preface

Blueprints is the visual scripting system in Unreal Engine that enables programmers to create baseline systems that can be extended by designers.

This book will help you explore all the features of the Blueprint Editor and guides you through how to use variables, Macros, and Functions. You'll also learn about **object-oriented programming (OOP)** and discover the Gameplay Framework. In addition to this, you'll learn about how Blueprint Communication allows one Blueprint to access information of another Blueprint. Later chapters will focus on building a fully functional game by using a step-by-step approach. You'll start with a basic **First-Person Shooter (FPS)** template, and each chapter will build on the prototype to create an increasingly complex and robust game experience. You'll then progress from creating basic shooting mechanics to more complex systems, such as UI elements and intelligent enemy behavior. These skills developed using Blueprints can also be employed in other gaming genres. In the concluding chapters, the book demonstrates how to use arrays, maps, enums, and vector operations. Finally, you'll get insights into building a basic VR game.

By the end of this book, you'll have learned about how to build a fully functional game and have the necessary skills to develop an entertaining experience for your audience.

Who this book is for

This book is for anyone who is interested in developing games or applications with Unreal Engine 4. Whether you are brand new to game development or have just not had any exposure to Unreal Engine 4's Blueprint Visual Scripting system, this is a great place to start learning about how to build complex game mechanics quickly and easily without writing any text code. No programming experience is required!

What this book covers

Chapter 1, *Exploring the Blueprint Editor*, covers the Blueprint Editor and all the panels that are integrated into it. We will explore the **Components** tab, the **My Blueprint** tab, the **Details** tab, and the **Viewport** and **Event Graph** tabs. Then, we will go through what Components are and how to add them to a Blueprint.

Chapter 2, *Programming with Blueprints*, explains programming concepts that are used in Blueprints. We will learn about how to use variables, operators, Events, Actions, Macros, and Functions.

Chapter 3, *Actors and the Gameplay Framework*, teaches OOP concepts and explores the Gameplay Framework.

Chapter 4, *Understanding Blueprint Communication*, explores different types of Blueprint Communication, which allows one Blueprint to access the information of another Blueprint.

Chapter 5, *Object Interaction with Blueprints*, covers how to bring new objects to a Level to help build the world in which the game will be set. We will move on to manipulating materials on objects, first through the object Editor, and then by triggering during runtime via Blueprints.

Chapter 6, *Enhancing Player Abilities*, teaches you how to use Blueprints to generate new objects during gameplay, and also, to link actions in Blueprints to player control inputs. You'll also learn about how to create Blueprints that allow objects to react to collisions with our generated projectiles.

Chapter 7, *Creating Screen UI Elements*, demonstrates setting up a **Graphical User Interface** (**GUI**) that will track the player's health, stamina, ammo, and current objective. Here, you will learn how to set up a basic UI using Unreal's GUI Editor and how to use Blueprints to link the interface to the gameplay values.

Chapter 8, *Creating Constraints and Gameplay Objectives*, covers how to constrain the player's abilities, define the gameplay objectives for a Level, and track those objectives. We'll walk through setting up collectible ammo packs that will refill the ammo of the player's gun, as well as utilizing the Level Blueprint to define a win condition for our game.

Chapter 9, *Building Smart Enemies with Artificial Intelligence*, is a crucial chapter that covers how to create an enemy zombie AI that will pursue the player around the Level. We'll walk through setting up a navigation mesh on our Level and see how to use Blueprints to get enemies to traverse between patrol points.

Chapter 10, *Upgrading the AI Enemies*, teaches us how to create a compelling experience by modifying the zombie AI to have states, in order to give the zombies a little more intelligence. In this chapter, we'll set up the patrol, searching, and attack states for the zombies by using visual and auditory detection. Additionally, we'll explore how to make new enemies appear gradually, as the game is playing.

Chapter 11, *Game States and Applying the Finishing Touches*, adds the finishing touches that are required to make our game a complete experience before we finalize our game for release. In this chapter, we'll create rounds that will make the game increasingly difficult, game saves so that the player can save their progress and return, and player death to make the game's challenge meaningful.

Chapter 12, *Building and Publishing*, covers how to optimize graphics settings to get our game performing and looking at its best, and how to set up project information for distribution. Then, we'll learn about how to create shareable builds of the game to various platforms.

Chapter 13, *Data Structures and Flow Control*, explains what data structures are and how they can be used to organize data in Blueprints. We'll learn about the concept of containers and how to use arrays, sets, and maps to group multiple elements. This chapter shows other ways to organize data using enumerations, structures, and data tables. In this chapter, we'll also see how to control the flow of execution of a Blueprint by using various types of flow control nodes.

Chapter 14, *Math and Trace Nodes*, covers some math concepts needed for 3D games. We will learn the difference between world and local coordinates and how to use them when working with Components. This chapter shows us how to use vectors to represent the position, direction, velocity, and distance. The concept of traces is explained and various types of traces are presented. We'll see how to use traces to test collisions in the game.

Chapter 15, *Blueprints Tips*, contains several tips to increase the quality of Blueprints. We will learn about how to use various Editor shortcuts that speed up our work. This chapter shows some Blueprint best practices that will help you decide where and what types of implementation should be done. Finally, we'll learn about more useful Blueprint miscellaneous nodes.

Chapter 16, *Introduction to VR Development*, explains some VR concepts and explores the VR template. This chapter explores the functionalities of the pawn and motion controller Blueprints of the VR template. This chapter explains how to implement new objects that can be grabbed by the player using motion controllers, and we will learn about the Blueprint actions used to implement teleportation.

To get the most out of this book

Although some basic knowledge of the Windows OS or macOS is required, experience in programming or Unreal Engine 4 is not necessary.

This book is focused on Unreal Engine 4, which means you only need a copy of Unreal Engine to get started. Unreal Engine 4 can be downloaded for free from `https://www.unrealengine.com/` and comes with everything you need to follow along with this book.

Download the example code files

You can download the example code files for this book from your account at `www.packt.com`. If you purchased this book elsewhere, you can visit `www.packt.com/support` and register to have the files emailed to you directly.

You can download the code files by following these steps:

1. Log in or register at `www.packt.com`.
2. Select the **SUPPORT** tab.
3. Click on **Code Downloads & Errata**.
4. Enter the name of the book in the **Search** box and follow the onscreen instructions.

Once the file is downloaded, please make sure that you unzip or extract the folder, using the latest versions of the following:

- WinRAR/7-Zip for Windows
- Zipeg/iZip/UnRarX for Mac
- 7-Zip/PeaZip for Linux

The code bundle for the book is also hosted on GitHub at `https://github.com/PacktPublishing/Blueprints-Visual-Scripting-for-Unreal-Engine-Second-Edition`. If there's an update to the code, it will be updated on the existing GitHub repository.

We also have other code bundles from our rich catalog of books and videos available at `https://github.com/PacktPublishing/`. Check them out!

Download the color images

We also provide a PDF file that has color images of the screenshots/diagrams used in this book. You can download it here: `https://static.packt-cdn.com/downloads/9781789347067_ColorImages.pdf`.

Conventions used

There are a number of text conventions used throughout this book.

`CodeInText`: Indicates code words in the text, database table names, folder names, filenames, file extensions, pathnames, dummy URLs, user input, and Twitter handles. Here is an example: "Rename the Blueprint created to `RotatingChair`."

Bold: Indicates a new term, an important word, or words that you see on screen. For example, words in menus or dialog boxes appear in the text like this. Here is an example: "Click the **Unreal Engine** tab on the left-hand side."

Warnings or important notes appear like this.

Tips and tricks appear like this.

Get in touch

Feedback from our readers is always welcome.

General feedback: If you have questions about any aspect of this book, mention the book title in the subject of your message and email us at `customercare@packtpub.com`.

Errata: Although we have taken every care to ensure the accuracy of our content, mistakes do happen. If you have found a mistake in this book, we would be grateful if you would report this to us. Please visit `www.packt.com/submit-errata`, selecting your book, clicking on the Errata Submission Form link, and entering the details.

Piracy: If you come across any illegal copies of our works in any form on the internet, we would be grateful if you would provide us with the location address or website name. Please contact us at `copyright@packt.com` with a link to the material.

If you are interested in becoming an author: If there is a topic that you have expertise in, and you are interested in either writing or contributing to a book, please visit `authors.packtpub.com`.

Reviews

Please leave a review. Once you have read and used this book, why not leave a review on the site that you purchased it from? Potential readers can then see and use your unbiased opinion to make purchase decisions, we at Packt can understand what you think about our products, and our authors can see your feedback on their book. Thank you!

For more information about Packt, please visit `packt.com`.

Section 1: Blueprint Fundamentals

This section will explore the basic building blocks of Blueprints. You will gain a solid understanding of how Blueprints work and will be able to start creating your own games.

This section includes the following chapters:

- Chapter 1, *Exploring the Blueprint Editor*
- Chapter 2, *Programming with Blueprints*
- Chapter 3, *Actors and the Gameplay Framework*
- Chapter 4, *Understanding Blueprint Communication*

Exploring the Blueprint Editor

1

Welcome to the amazing world of game development with Unreal Engine 4. In this book, we will learn about how to develop games in Unreal Engine using the Blueprints Visual Scripting language, which was created by Epic Games for Unreal Engine 4.

The first step that is needed before we can learn about Blueprints is to prepare our development environment. Unreal Engine is free to download. We will learn about how to install Unreal Engine 4 and create a new project. After that, we will learn about some of the basic concepts of Blueprints and explore each panel of the Blueprint Editor.

In this chapter, we will cover the following topics:

- Installing Unreal Engine
- New projects and templates
- Blueprints Visual Scripting
- The Blueprint Editor interface
- Adding Components to a Blueprint

Installing Unreal Engine

To use Unreal Engine, you must first install Epic Games Launcher:

1. Access the website (https://www.unrealengine.com)
2. Register and download Epic Games Launcher
3. Install and start the launcher
4. Click the **Unreal Engine** tab on the left-hand side
5. Click on the **Library** tab that appears at the top of the screen
6. Click the **+** button next to **ENGINE VERSIONS** to add a version of Unreal Engine to the launcher

7. Click the **Install** button
8. Click the **Launch** button to start an already installed version:

It is possible to keep multiple versions of Unreal Engine. This book uses version 4.20.3, but the examples were tested in version 4.22.0 and worked well. Blueprint is already a stable technology. The examples created in this book should work without problems in later versions.

Creating new projects and using templates

After starting up Unreal Engine Editor, a two-tab window will appear. The **Projects** tab is used to open existing projects and the **New Project** tab is used to create a new project, as shown in the following screenshot. The **New Project** tab has templates that can be used for the creation of a project. There are templates made with **Blueprint** and templates made with the **C++** programming language. In this book, we will only use **Blueprint** templates:

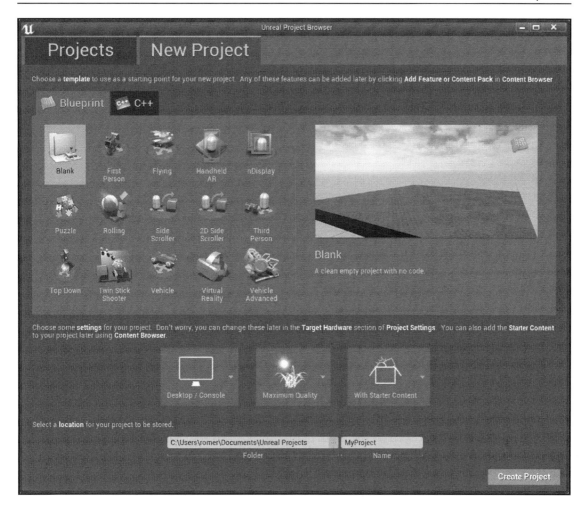

At the bottom of the preceding screenshot, there are three boxes with project configuration options. These options can be modified later in the project, and they are as follows:

- **Target hardware**: **Desktop / Console** or mobile/tablet
- **Graphical level**: **Maximum Quality** or scalable 3D/2D
- **Starter content**: With or without **Starter Content**

The starter content is a content pack with simple meshes, materials, and particle effects. The examples in this book assume that the starter content is being used.

The following are brief descriptions of each template:

- **First Person**: For games with a first-person perspective
- **Flying**: Contains a simple spaceship controlled by the player
- **Handheld AR**: For augmented reality applications
- **nDisplay**: For multi-display projects such as caves
- **Puzzle**: For puzzle games using a mouse or touchscreen
- **Rolling**: Contains a physics-based rolling ball controlled by the player
- **Side Scroller**: For 3D side-scroller games
- **2D Side Scroller**: For side-scroller games with 2D sprites
- **Third Person**: Contains a playable character with a camera that follows it
- **Top Down**: Contains a character controlled by a mouse with a camera at a great distance above it
- **Twin Stick Shooter**: Shows how to map the input to control movement and firing independently
- **Vehicle**: Contains a simple physics-driven vehicle controlled by the player
- **Virtual Reality**: Contains essential features for virtual reality games
- **Vehicle Advanced**: Contains a more complex vehicle with suspension

Select the **Third Person** template, choose **settings**, **location**, and **Name** of the project, and then click the **Create Project** button. After the project loads, the main screen of the Unreal Engine Editor will be displayed, as shown in the following screenshot:

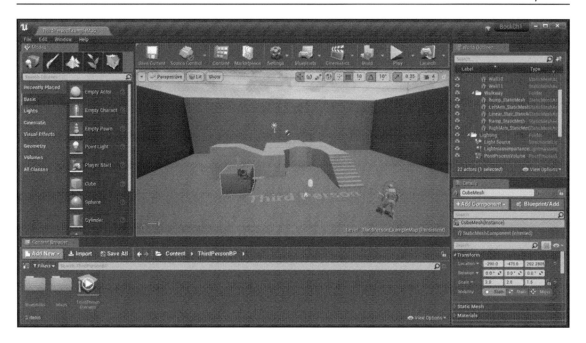

The main screen of the previous screenshot is also known as the Level Editor. These are the key panels of the Level Editor:

- **Toolbar**: Located at the top of the Level Editor. It contains buttons with commonly used operations. You can use it to save the Level, build the lighting, access other panels, and play the Level in the Editor.
- **Viewport**: Located at the center of the Level Editor. It shows the Level that is being created. You can use the **Viewport** panel to move around the Level and add objects on the Level.
- **Modes**: Located to the left of the Level Editor, the **Modes** panel can be used to change the editing mode of the Level Editor for a specialized interface such as **Landscape** mode.
- **Content Browser**: Located at the bottom of the Level Editor. It is used to manage the assets of the project. An asset is a piece of content of an Unreal Engine project. For example, **Materials, Static Meshes**, and **Blueprints** are all assets. If you drag an asset from **Content Browser** and drop it in the Level, the Editor creates a copy of the asset to place in the Level.
- **World Outliner**: Located to the right of the Level Editor. It lists the objects that are in the Level.
- **Details**: Located to the right of the Level Editor, below **World Outliner**. It shows the editable properties of an object that is selected in **Viewport**.

Blueprints Visual Scripting

The first question you should be asking is: what is a Blueprint?

The word Blueprint has more than one meaning in Unreal Engine. First, it is the name of a visual scripting language created by Epic Games for Unreal Engine 4. Second, it can refer to a new type of game object that was created using the Blueprint language.

There are two main types of Blueprints: **Level Blueprint** and **Blueprint Class**. Each Level of the game has its own **Level Blueprint** and it is not possible to create a separate **Level Blueprint**. On the other hand, **Blueprint Class** is used to create interactive objects for the game and can be reused at any Level.

Opening the Level Blueprint Editor

To open the **Level Blueprint** Editor, click on the **Blueprints** button, which is at the top of the main screen of the Unreal Editor. Then, select the **Open Level Blueprint** option, as shown in the following screenshot:

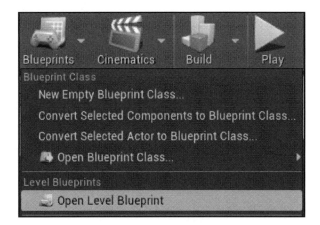

The Editor will open with **Level Blueprint** of the current Level. The **Level Blueprint** Editor is simpler than the **Blueprint Class** Editor because it has only the **My Blueprint** panel, the **Details** panel, and the **Event Graph** Editor. The following screenshot shows the **Level Blueprint** Editor:

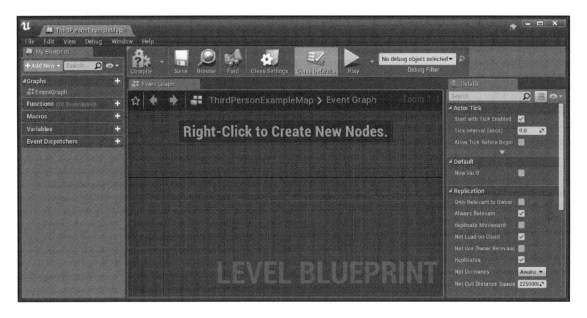

Creating a Blueprint class

Go back to the Level Editor window.

To create a new Blueprint class, click the green button of the **Content Browser**, labeled **Add New**, and select **Blueprint Class**:

On the next screen, you have to choose the parent class of the new Blueprint. For now, think of the parent class as the Blueprint type. The screen shows the most **Common Classes**, but if you need to choose another parent class, then just expand the **All Classes** option. After choosing the parent class, the Blueprint Editor will open:

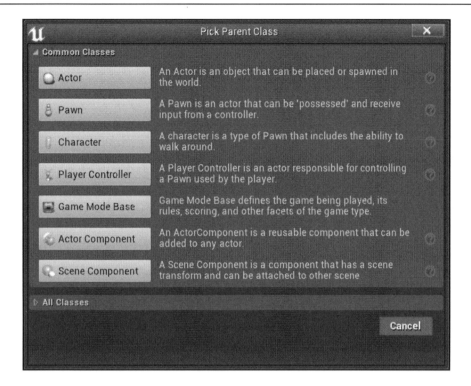

The Blueprint Editor interface

The Blueprint Editor contains several panels. Each panel is used to edit one aspect of a Blueprint. The main panels of the Blueprint Editor are listed as follows:

1. **Toolbar**
2. **Components**
3. **My Blueprint**
4. **Details**
5. **Viewport**
6. **Event Graph**

These panels can all be found in the following screenshot:

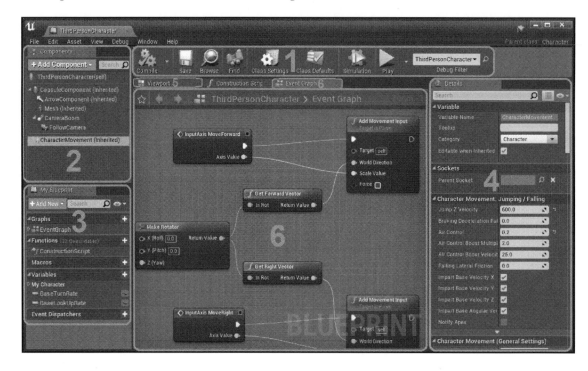

The Toolbar panel

The **Toolbar** panel is located at the top of the Blueprint Editor and contains some essential buttons for editing Blueprints:

The buttons are described as follows:

- **Compile**: Converts the Blueprint script into a lower-level format that can be executed. That means a Blueprint must be compiled before running the game or the changes made may not be reflected. Click this button to compile the current Blueprint. A green check icon will appear if there is no error.
- **Save**: Saves all changes made to the current Blueprint.
- **Browse**: Shows the current **Blueprint Class** in the **Content Browser**.

- **Find**: Searches nodes within a Blueprint.
- **Class Settings**: Allows editing of **Class Settings** in the **Details** panel. **Class Settings** contains some properties such as **Description**, **Category**, and **Parent Class**.
- **Class Defaults**: Allows editing of **Class Defaults** in the **Details** panel. **Class Defaults** are the initial values of the Blueprint variables.
- **Simulation**: Allows the execution to the Blueprint inside the Blueprint Editor.
- **Play**: Allows you to play the current Level.

The Components panel

The **Components** panel shows all the Components that are part of the current Blueprint:

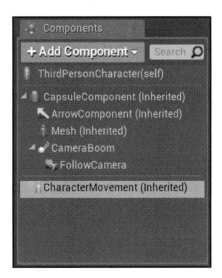

Components are ready-to-use objects that can be added to Blueprints. To do this, click on the green **Add Component** button of the **Components** panel. A Blueprint can be created with various features just by using Components.

The properties of a selected Component can be edited on the **Details** panel and the visual representation of some Components can be seen on the **Viewport** panel.

Static Mesh, lights, sounds, box collision, particle system, and camera are examples of Components found in the **Components** panel.

The My Blueprint panel

My Blueprint is a panel where we can create **Variables**, **Macros**, **Functions**, and **Graphs** for the Blueprint:

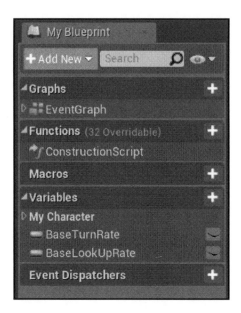

New elements can be added by clicking on the **Add New** button or clicking on the **+** button that is next to each category.

The properties of an element can be edited in the **Details** panel.

The Details panel

The **Details** panel allows you to edit the properties of a selected element of a Blueprint. The selected element can be a Component, Variable, Macro, or Function element. The properties shown in the **Details** panel are organized into categories.

The next screenshot shows the properties of a **Character Movement** Component. There is a **Search** box at the top of the panel that can be used to filter the properties:

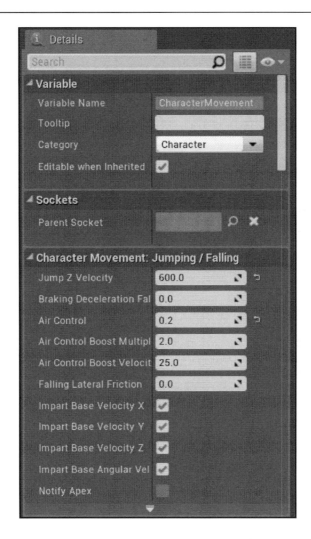

The Viewport panel

The **Viewport** panel shows the visual representation of a Blueprint and its Components. The **Viewport** panel has controls similar to the Level Editor, which you can use to manipulate the location, rotation, and scale of the Components.

The following screenshot shows the **Viewport** panel of the **ThirdPersonCharacter** Blueprint that is in the **Third Person** template. There is a **SkeletalMesh** Component that represents the player, a **Camera** Component that defines the view of the player, and a **Capsule** Component that is used for collision test:

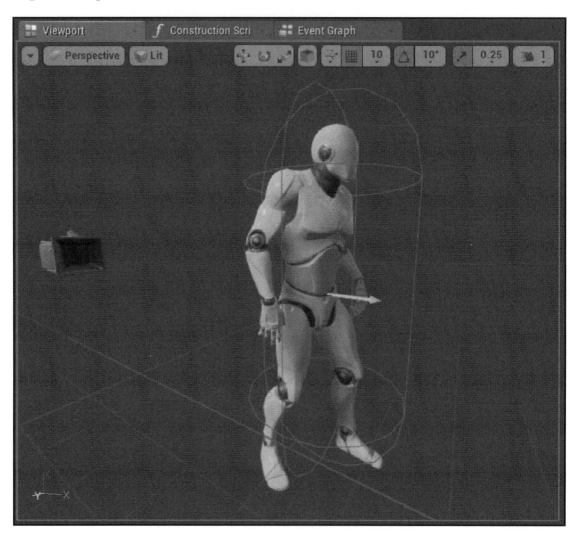

The Event Graph panel

It is in the **Event Graph** panel that we are going to program the behavior of a Blueprint. **Event Graph** contains **Events** and **Actions** that are represented by nodes and connected by wires.

An Event is represented by a red node and is triggered by gameplay Events. A Blueprint can have several Actions that will be performed in response to an Event. The next screenshot shows two Events: **InputAxis MoveForward** and **InputAxis MoveRight**. These Events are from the **ThirdPersonCharacter** Blueprint of the **Third Person** template:

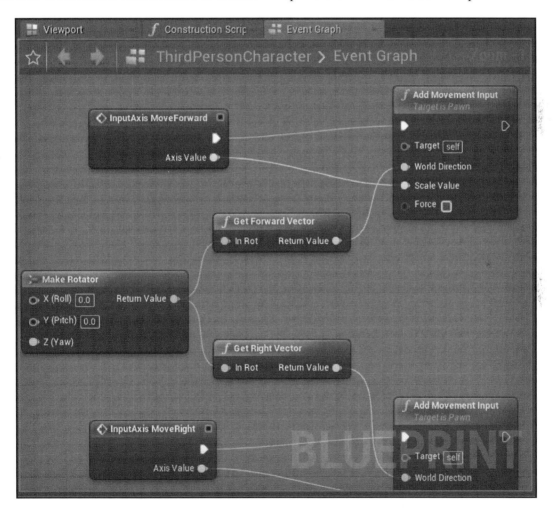

Adding Components to a Blueprint

Now, let's create our first Blueprint. It will be a very simple Blueprint that will only contain **Components**. For now, we will not use **Events** and **Actions**:

1. On the **Content Browser**, click the green **Add New** button and select **Blueprint Class**.
2. On the next screen, choose **Actor** as the parent class.
3. Rename the Blueprint created to `RotatingChair`.
4. Double-click this Blueprint to open the Blueprint Editor.
5. On the **Components** panel, click the green **Add Component** button and select **Static Mesh**, as shown in the following screenshot. This **Static Mesh** will visually represent this Blueprint:

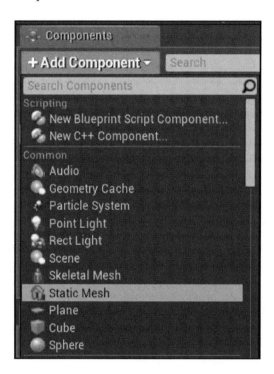

6. On the **Details** panel, there is a property named **Static Mesh**, which has a drop-down input. Click on the dropdown and select a **Static Mesh** named **SM_Chair**. This is a **Static Mesh** that is part of the starter content. The following screenshot shows the selected **SM_Chair**:

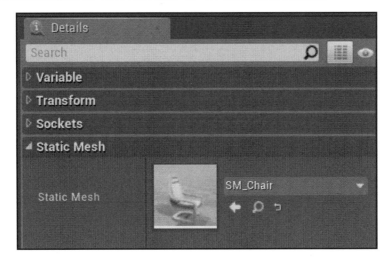

7. Let's add another Component. Click the green **Add Component** button and type `rotating movement` in the **Search** box.

8. Click on the **Rotating Movement** Component to add it. By default, this Component will rotate the Blueprint around the z axis, so we don't need to change its properties.

9. Click the **Compile** button and save the Blueprint.

10. On the Level Editor, drag the `RotatingChair` Blueprint from the **Content Browser** and drop it somewhere in the Level.

11. Press the **Play** button of the Level Editor to see the rotating chair.

Summary

In this chapter, we learned how to install Unreal Engine and create new projects using the available templates. We learned that there are two main types of Blueprints: **Level Blueprint** and **Blueprint Class**.

Then, we explored the different types of panels that are part of the Blueprint Editor. The familiarization with these panels will help when developing with Blueprints.

Finally, we have also created a simple Blueprint using only **Components**.

In the next chapter, we will learn how to program the behavior of Blueprints using **Events** and **Actions**.

Programming with Blueprints 2

This chapter presents the basic programming concepts used in Blueprints. Programming is essentially a way of writing instructions that will be understood and executed by a computer. Most programming languages are text-based, but Blueprint presents a different form of visual programming by using a node-based interface.

Some programming languages are known as scripting languages when they exist in a special environment or when they have a well-defined purpose. For example, Blueprints is the visual scripting language of Unreal Engine 4.

In this chapter, we will cover the following topics:

- Storing values in variables
- Defining the behavior of a Blueprint with Events and Actions
- Creating expressions with operators
- Organizing the script with Macros and Functions

Storing values in variables

A variable is a programming concept. It consists of an identifier that points to a memory location where a value can be stored. For example, a character in a game may have variables to store the value of its health, its speed, and the quantity of ammunition.

A Blueprint can have many variables of various types. The variables of a Blueprint are listed on the **My Blueprint** panel. Clicking the + button in the **Variables** category creates a variable:

Blueprint is a strongly typed language. This means that you must define the type of values that a variable can store, and this type cannot be modified during program execution.

When you create a variable, its attributes are displayed in the **Details** panel. The first attribute of a variable is its name, and the second attribute is its type. The various types are as follows:

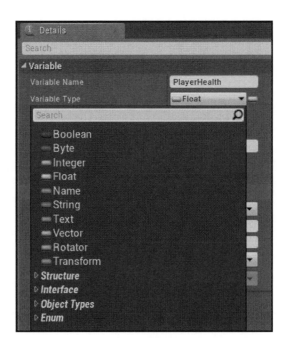

Each type is represented by a color. These are the types of variables:

- **Boolean**: Can only hold values of true or false
- **Byte**: Can store integer values between 0 and 255
- **Integer**: Can store integer values
- **Float**: Can store decimal values
- **Name**: Can store object identifiers
- **String**: Can store text
- **Text**: Can store text and can support language localization
- **Vector**: Contains the **X**, **Y**, and **Z** float values
- **Rotator**: Contains the **X (Roll)**, **Y (Pitch)**, and **Z (Yaw)** float values
- **Transform**: Can store location, rotation, and scale

There are also other types of variables related to **Structure**, **Interface**, **Object Types**, and **Enum**.

The following screenshot shows the **Details** panel with the attributes that can be modified in **Variable**:

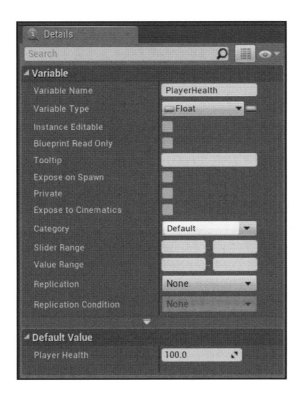

These attributes can be individually described as follows:

- **Variable Name**: This is the identifier of the variable.
- **Variable Type**: This is the type of values that can be stored.
- **Instance Editable**: When this box is checked, each copy of this Blueprint placed in the Level can store a different value in this variable. Otherwise, the same value is shared by all copies, called **instances**.
- **Blueprint Read Only**: If checked, the variable cannot be changed by Blueprint nodes.
- **Tooltip**: This contains information shown when the cursor hovers over the variable.
- **Expose on Spawn**: If checked, the variable can be set when spawning the Blueprint.
- **Private**: If checked, child Blueprints cannot modify it.
- **Expose to Cinematics**: If checked, this variable will be exposed to **Matinee/Sequencer**.
- **Category**: This can be used to organize the variables.
- **Slider Range**: This sets the minimum and maximum values that will be used by a slider to modify this variable.
- **Value Range**: This sets the minimum and maximum values allowed for this variable.
- **Replication** and **Replication Condition**: They are used in network games.
- **Default Value**: This contains the initial value of the variable. The Blueprint must be compiled before you can set the default value.

Defining the behavior of a Blueprint with Events and Actions

Most of the time, we will use Blueprints to create new Actors. In Unreal Engine, Actors are game objects that can be added to the Level.

Unreal Engine informs the state of a game for an Actor using Events. We define how an Actor responds to an Event by using Actions. Both Events and Actions are represented by nodes in the **Event Graph** panel.

Events

To add Events to a Blueprint, use the **Event Graph** panel. Right-click the **Event Graph** panel to open **Context Menu**, which has the list of available Events and Actions. If you need more space in the **Event Graph** panel, you can right-click and drag to move it to an empty area of **Event Graph**. **Context Menu** has a **Search** bar that can be used to filter the list of nodes. There is also the **Context Sensitive** checkbox that filters the possible Actions based on the node selected. The following screenshot shows **Context Menu** and some of the Events available:

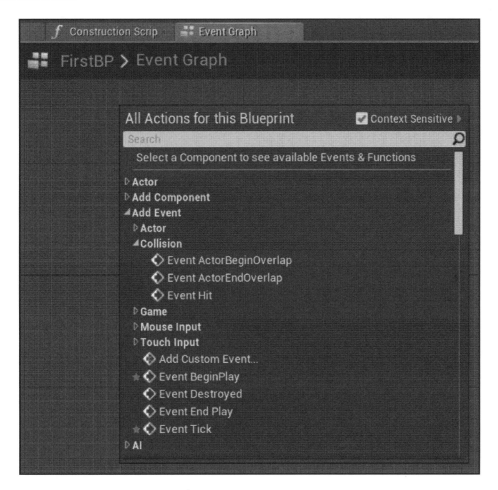

You can add several Events in the **Event Graph** panel, but you can add each Event only once. In addition to the Events provided by Unreal Engine, you can create new Events. These new Events are known as **Custom Events**.

These are some of the Events that are available:

- **Collision events**: These are executed when two Actors collide or overlap.
- **Input events**: These are triggered by input devices, such as the keyboard, mouse, touch screen, and gamepads.
- **Event BeginPlay**: This is executed either when the game is started for Actors already present on the Level Editor, or immediately after the Actor is spawned if that happens during runtime.
- **Event End Play**: This is executed when the Actor is about to be removed from the running game.
- **Event Tick**: This is called every frame of the game. For example, if a game runs at 60 frames per second, this Event will be called 60 times in a second.

Actions

When an Event is triggered, we use Actions to define how a Blueprint will react to this Event. You can use Actions to get or set values in the Blueprint variables or call Functions that modify the state of a Blueprint.

The following screenshot shows **Event BeginPlay** of a Blueprint. In this example, the Blueprint has a string variable named **Bot Name**. The **SET** action assigns the **Archon** value to the **Bot Name** variable. The next action, **Print String**, displays the value that is received on the **In String** pin on the screen. These values that are passed to the Functions are known as parameters. The **In String** pin is connected to a **GET** node of the **Bot Name** variable that returns the value of the **Bot Name** variable and passes it to the **Print String** Function:

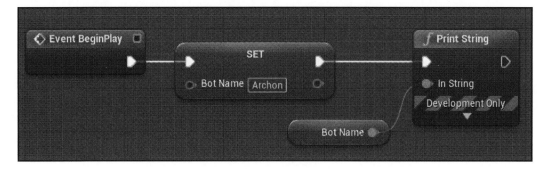

To add the **GET** and **SET** Actions of a variable to **Event Graph**, simply drag and drop the variable in **Event Graph** to show the **GET** and **SET** options. Other Functions such as the **Print String** are added from **Context Menu** that appears when you right-click on the **Event Graph** panel. The **GET** and **SET** Actions can also be searched in **Context Menu**.

The white lines that connect the Actions are also known as the execution path.

Execution path

The white pins of nodes are called **execution pins**. The other colored pins are the **data pins**. The execution of the nodes of a Blueprint starts with a red Event node, and then follows the white wire from left to right until it reaches the last node.

There are some nodes that control the flow of execution of the Blueprint. These nodes determine the execution path based on conditions. For example, the **Branch** node has two output execution pins named **True** and **False**. The execution pin that will be triggered depends on the Boolean value of the **Condition** input parameter. The following screenshot shows an example of the **Branch** node:

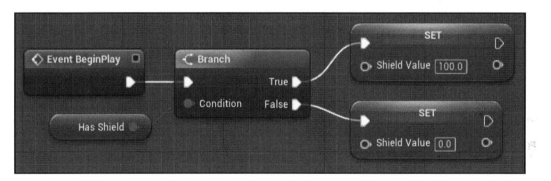

In this example, when **Event BeginPlay** fires, the **Branch** node evaluates the value of the **Has Shield** Boolean variable. If the value is **True**, then the **True** pin will be executed and will set the value to 100.0 in the **Shield Value** variable. If it is **False**, the value 0.0 will be set in the **Shield Value** variable.

Creating expressions with operators

Operators are used to create expressions using variables and values. These operators are found in **Context Menu** within the **Math** category separated by the variable type.

The main types of operators are arithmetic, relational, and logical.

Arithmetic operators

The arithmetic operators (+, -, *, and /) can be used to create mathematical expressions in Blueprints. The following screenshot shows the equivalent nodes in Blueprints. These operators receive two input values on the left and give the operation result on the right. The + and * operators can have more than two input parameters; just click on the **Add pin** button on the node to add another input parameter. The input values can be obtained from a data wire or entered directly in the node:

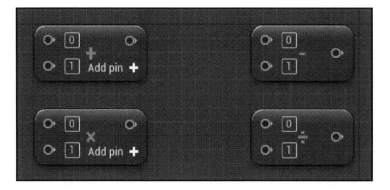

 The * symbol is the multiplication operator in programming languages. Blueprints also recognize * as the multiplication operator but use the letter X as the label of the multiplication node. You need to use the * symbol when searching for multiplication nodes in the Context Menu.

The following screenshot shows a simple arithmetic expression. The numbers on the screenshot show the order of execution of the nodes. The execution starts with **Event BeginPlay**. The **SET** node assigns a new value to the **Magic Points** variable, but this value must be obtained using the data wire that is connected to the output of a multiplication node, which will need to get the value of the **Willpower** variable using another data wire to multiply by 20.0:

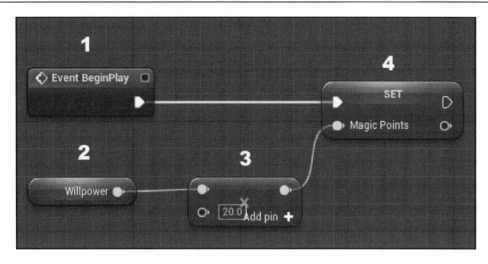

Relational operators

Relational operators perform a comparison between two values and return a Boolean value (**True** or **False**) as a result of the comparison. The following screenshot shows the relational operators in Blueprints:

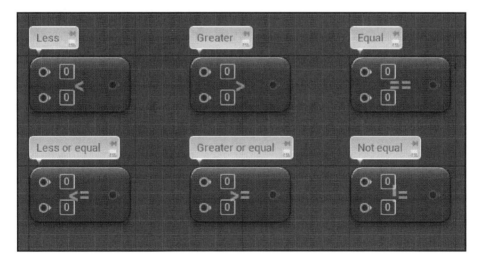

The following screenshot shows an example with a relational operator, assuming these Actions are performed when a game object receives damage. A **Branch** node is used to test whether the **Health** variable value is less than or equal to 0.0. If it returns **True**, then this game object will be destroyed:

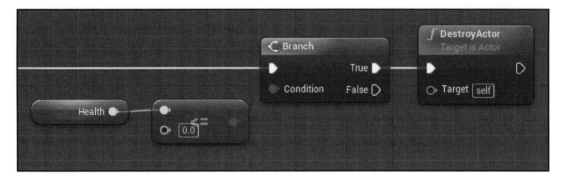

Logical operators

Logical operators perform an operation between Boolean values and return a Boolean value (**True** or **False**) as a result of the operation. The following screenshot shows the main logical operators in Blueprints:

These are the descriptions of these operators:

- **OR**: Returns a value of **True** if any of the input values are **True**
- **AND**: Returns a value of **True** only if all input values are **True**
- **NOT**: Receives only one input value, and the result will be the opposite value

The following screenshot shows an example of using the **AND** operator. The **Print String** node will only be executed if the **Health** value is greater than 70.0 and **Shield Value** is greater than 50.0:

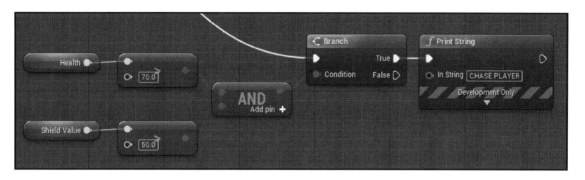

Organizing the script with Macros and Functions

When we are creating Blueprint scripts, sometimes, a group of Actions is used in more than one place in Blueprint. These Actions can be converted into Macros or Functions, simplifying the initial script because this group of Actions will be replaced by only one node. Also, if you need to change something in this group of Actions, this change will only be implemented in the Macro or Function rather than having to search every location where this group of Actions was used. This is a good programming practice to use as it simplifies code and debugging.

Creating Macros

To create Macros, use the **My Blueprint** panel and click the + button in the **Macros** category. The following screenshot shows the **My Blueprint** panel with a Macro named `SetupNewWave`:

The attributes of a **Macro** are displayed in the **Details** panel. In this panel, you can define input and output parameters. Input parameters are values passed to **Macros/Functions**. Output parameters are values returned from **Macros/Functions**. The following screenshot shows the **Details** panel of the SetupNewWave Macro with two input parameters and one output parameter. In **Macros**, the execution pins are defined as parameters:

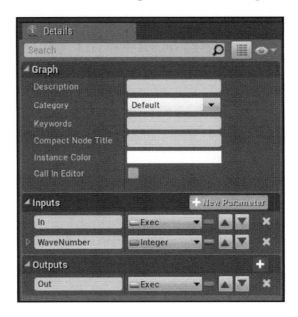

The following screenshot shows the contents of the SetupNewWave Macro. The idea of this Macro is to set some variables for the next wave of enemies in a game. It receives the current **WaveNumber** as an input parameter, stores this value in the **Current Wave** variable, and determines the number of enemies by multiplying the current **Wave Number** by 5:

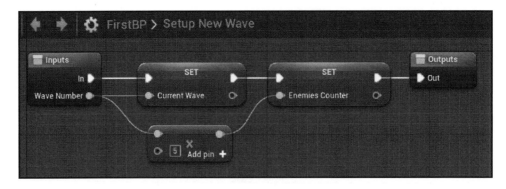

To add the Macro to **Event Graph,** drag the name of the Macro from the **My Blueprint** panel and drop it in **Event Graph,** or look for it in **Context Menu**. When the Macro is executed, the Actions that are in it will be executed. The following screenshot shows the `SetupNewWave` Macro being called in **Event BeginPlay** with a value of 1 in the **Wave Number** input parameter:

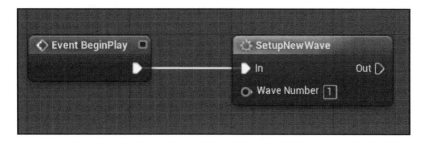

Creating Functions

One of the advantages of **Functions** is that a Function created in one Blueprint can be called from another Blueprint. To create Functions, use the **My Blueprint** panel and click the **+** button in the **Functions** category. The following screenshot shows the **My Blueprint** panel with a Function named `CalculateWaveBonus`:

As with **Macros**, the attributes of the Function are displayed in the **Details** panel, where input and output parameters can be defined. The following screenshot shows the **Details** panel of the `CalculateWaveBonus` Function, with two input parameters and one output parameter:

When creating a Function, we can define whether it will be **Pure**. To do this, check the **Pure** attribute shown in the previous screenshot. A **Pure** Function has no execution pins; therefore, it can be used in expressions. **Pure** Functions should not modify the variables of its Blueprint, so they are mostly used as get-type Functions. The following screenshot shows the visual difference between a standard Function and **Pure Function**:

The following screenshot shows the contents of the `CalculateWaveBonus` Function. This Function calculates **Bonus Points** of a wave based on **Wave Number** and **Time Left**. The value found is returned via the **Bonus Points** output parameter:

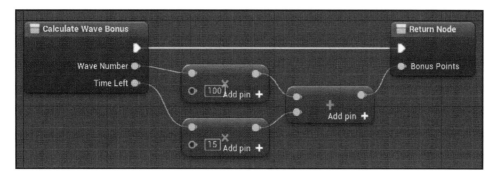

The following screenshot is of the node that represents the `CalculateWaveBonus` Function. It can be added to the **Event Graph** panel from **Context Menu** by right-clicking **Event Graph** or by dragging the Function name from the **My Blueprint** panel and dropping it in **Event Graph**:

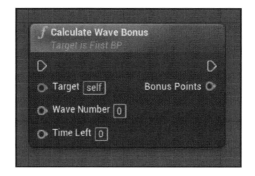

Macros versus Functions versus Events

Sometimes, it is not clear when to create a Macro, a Function, or a Custom Event, since they have several characteristics in common. The following table shows a comparison between them to help you to choose the most appropriate for your requirements:

	Macros	Functions	Events
Input parameters	Yes	Yes	Yes
Output parameters	Yes	Yes	No
Execution paths (input/output)	Any number	One	One
Callable by another Blueprint	No	Yes	Yes
Latent Actions (for example, delay)	Yes	No	Yes
Timeline nodes	No	No	Yes

Summary

In this chapter, we learned about how to store values in the variables of a Blueprint and how to use Actions to define the response of a Blueprint to an Event. After that, we saw how to create expressions with operators and organize our script with Macros and Functions. These are the key elements needed to define how a Blueprint should act within a game.

In the next chapter, we'll learn about how to use the Gameplay Framework.

3
Actors and the Gameplay Framework

Blueprints are based on the principles of **object-oriented programming (OOP)**. One of the goals of OOP is to bring programming concepts closer to the real world. In OOP, we define classes with variables and Functions that are used as templates in the creation of new objects.

Unreal Engine has some essential classes that are used in the development of games. These classes are parts of the Gameplay Framework. The main class of the Gameplay Framework is called an **Actor**.

In this chapter, we will learn about the following topics:

- OOP concepts
- Managing Actors
- Exploring the Gameplay Framework classes

OOP concepts

Let's learn about some elementary concepts of OOP, such as classes, instances, and inheritance. These concepts will help you learn about various elements of Blueprints Visual Scripting.

Classes

Many real-world objects can be classified by the same type, even though they are unique. As a very simple example, we can think of a person class. In this class, we can have attributes such as name and height, and Actions such as move and eat. Using the person class, we can create several objects of this class. Each object represents a person with different values in their name and height attributes.

When we create a Blueprint, we are creating a new class that can be used to create objects in the Unreal Engine. As the following screenshot shows, the option that appears when creating a new Blueprint asset is **Blueprint Class**:

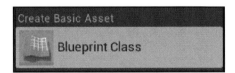

There is another concept, known as **encapsulation** that consists of hiding the complexity of a class. The variables and Functions of a Blueprint class can be **private**, which means that they can only be accessed and modified in the Blueprint class where they were created. The **public** variables and Functions are those that can be accessed by other Blueprint classes.

Instances

An object created from a class is also known as an **instance** of that class. Each time you drag a Blueprint class from **Content Browser** and drop it into the Level, you create a new instance of this Blueprint class.

For example, imagine that a Blueprint was created to represent a character type in a game. The following screenshot shows that three instances of this Blueprint class were added to the Level:

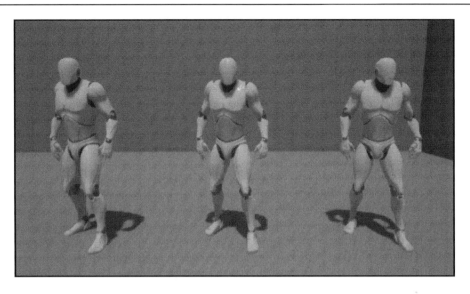

Inheritance

In OOP, classes can inherit variables and Functions from other classes. When we are creating a Blueprint, the first thing we have to do is choose the parent class of this Blueprint. A Blueprint class can only have one parent class, but can have several child classes. The parent class is also known as the **superclass**, while the child class is known as the **subclass**.

As an example of using inheritance, imagine that we are creating several Blueprints that represent different types of weapons in a game. We can create a base Blueprint class called Weapon with everything that is common to all weapons in the game. Then, we can create the Blueprints that represent each of the weapons using the Weapon class as the parent class. The following diagram shows the hierarchy between these classes:

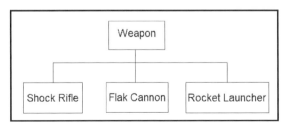

Inheritance is also used to define the class type of a class since it accumulates all the types related to its parent class. For example, we can say that an instance of the Shock Rifle class is of the Shock Rifle type and also of the Weapon type. Because of this, if we have a Function with a Weapon input parameter, it can receive instances of the Weapon class or any instances of its child classes.

Managing Actors

The Actor class is the base class that's used for objects and can be placed or spawned in a Level. Most of the Blueprints that we'll create will be based on the Actor class or the Actor's child classes. Therefore, the features we will look at in this section will be useful for these Blueprints.

Referencing Actors

Variable types such as integer, float, and Boolean are known as primitive types because they only store simple values of the specified type. When working with objects or Actors, a variable cannot store all the data of an Actor because it is a complex type. Instead, the variable just points to a memory location where the data of the Actor is stored. This type of variable is known as an **Object Reference**.

For example, the following diagram represents instances of two Blueprint classes in memory. The instance of the BP Barrel Blueprint class has an integer variable named Hit Counter, with a current value of 2. The other variable, named BPFire, is an Object Reference, which is referencing an instance of **Blueprint Effect Fire**. We can access the public variables and Functions of a Blueprint using an Object Reference variable:

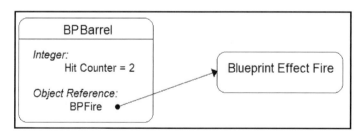

In a Blueprint, we can create variables that reference objects/Actors. First, create a variable. Then, click on the drop-down menu of the **Variable Type** parameter. The **Object Types** category lists the classes that are available in Unreal Engine and the Blueprints classes that we created in the project. Just click on one of the classes and then choose the **Object Reference** option that appears in the submenu. The following screenshot shows the creation of a variable called BPFire. It will be used to reference objects/instances of the **Blueprint Effect Fire** class, which is part of the starter content:

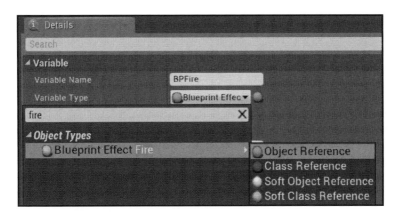

The default value of an **Object Reference** variable is **None** (also known as null), which means that the variable is not referencing any instances. We can assign an instance to this variable in the Level Editor. To do this, check the **Instance Editable** attribute of the variable so that it is accessible in the Level Editor. Drag the Blueprint from the **Content Browser** and drop it into Level. In the **Details** panel, you can select an Actor of the Level that is of the same type as the variable.

Object Reference variables can also refer to instances that are created at runtime.

Spawning and destroying Actors

There is a Function called **Spawn Actor from Class** that creates an Actor instance. This Function receives the class of the Actor and the Transformation that will be applied, as input parameters. The Transformation defines the location, rotation, and scale that will be used by the new Actor. Another input parameter, called **Collision Handling Override**, defines how to handle the collision at the time of creation. A reference to the new instance is available in the **Return Value** output parameter and can be stored in a variable.

To remove an Actor instance from the Level, use the **DestroyActor** Function. The **Target** input parameter indicates which instance will be removed. The following screenshot shows an example of using the **Spawn Actor from Class** and **DestroyActor** Functions. Pressing the *1* key creates an instance of **Blueprint Effect Fire** using the same Transformation of the Blueprint instance that contains this script. The reference to the new **Blueprint Effect Fire** instance is stored in the BPFire variable. When you press the *2* key, a test is done using the **Is Valid** Macro to check whether the BPFire variable is referencing an instance. If the value of BPFire is **None**, then it is not valid. If it is valid, then it calls the **DestroyActor** Function that receives the BPFire variable as the **Target** input parameter and destroys the **Blueprint Effect Fire** instance that was previously created:

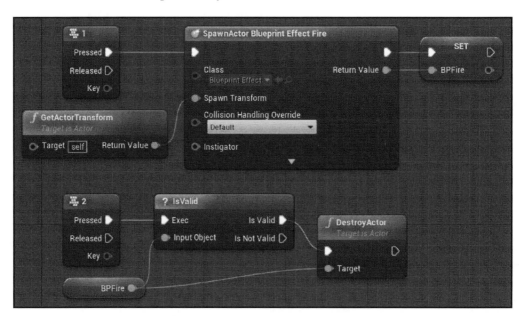

Construction Script

One of the panels in the Blueprint Editor is called **Construction Script**, and is shown in the following screenshot. **Construction Script** is a special Function that all Actor Blueprints perform when the Blueprint is first added to the Level, when a change is made to its properties in the Level Editor, or when an instance is spawned at runtime:

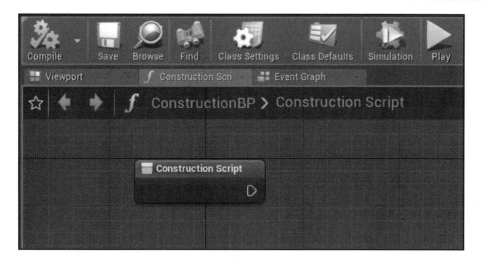

Construction Script is very useful for creating flexible Blueprints that allow the Level Designer to configure some features of an instance of these Blueprints within the Level Editor.

As an example, let's create a Blueprint with an **Instance Editable Static Mesh** so we can choose a different Static Mesh for each instance of the Blueprint that is on the Level:

1. Create or use an existing project that has the starter content.
2. Click the **Add New** button in **Content Browser** and choose the **Blueprint Class** option.
3. On the next screen, choose **Actor** as the parent class.
4. Name the Blueprint ConstructionBP and double-click it to open the Blueprint Editor.
5. Click the **Add Component** button in the **Components** panel and choose the **Static Mesh** Component. Rename the Component StaticMeshComp, as shown in the following screenshot:

6. In the **My Blueprint** panel, create a new variable named **SM_Mesh**. In the **Details** panel, click the **Variable Type** drop-down menu and search for Static Mesh. Hover over **Static Mesh** to display a submenu and then choose **Object Reference**. Check the **Instance Editable** attribute, as shown in the following screenshot:

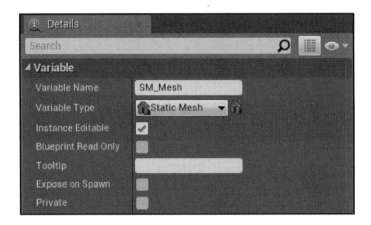

7. Press the **Compile** button on the toolbar. Let's define an initial Static Mesh for the **SM_Mesh** variable at the bottom of the **Details** panel. Click the drop-down menu of the **Default** value attribute and choose the **SM_TableRound** Static Mesh.

8. Click the **Construction Script** panel. Drag the StaticMeshComp Component from the **Components** panel and drop it into the **Construction Script** graph to create a node.

9. Click on the blue pin of the StaticMeshComp node, then drag and drop in the graph to open the **Context Menu**. Search for set static mesh and choose the Function with this name, as shown in the following screenshot:

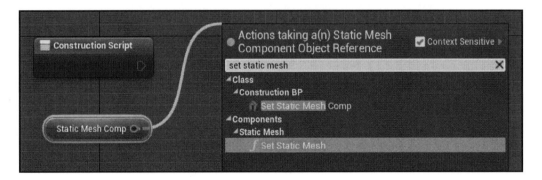

10. Drag the **SM_Mesh** variable from the **My Blueprint** panel, drop it into the **Construction Script** graph, and choose the **Get SM_Mesh** option in the menu that appears. Connect the **SM_Mesh** node pin to the **New Mesh** pin of the **Set Static Mesh** Function. **Construction Script** should look similar to the following screenshot. When **Construction Script** executes the **Set Static Mech** Function, it gets the Static Mesh from the **SM_Mesh** variable and sets it on the **Static Mesh Comp** Component:

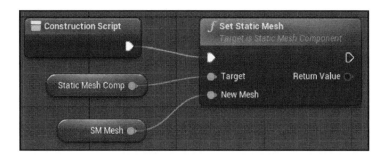

11. Compile the Blueprint. In the Level Editor, drag ConstructionBP from **Content Browser** and drop it into the Level to create an instance. Drag and drop the ConstructionBP again to create one more instance. Select one of the instances on the Level and, in the **Details** panel of the Level Editor, check that the **SM_Mesh** variable is visible and editable, as shown in the following screenshot:

12. Click the drop-down menu of the **SM_Mesh** variable and choose another Static Mesh, such as the **SM_Couch**. The Construction Script will immediately execute and change the Static Mesh of the instance that was selected. The following screenshot shows two instances of the `ConstructionBP` class. The instance on the left of the screenshot is using the default Static Mesh, but the instance on the right had its Static Mesh modified to **SM_Couch**:

Exploring the Gameplay Framework classes

One of the first steps of creating a new Blueprint is choosing the parent class that will be used as a template. The following screenshot shows the panel that is displayed for choosing the parent class. The classes that are displayed on the buttons are known as **Common Classes** and are part of the Gameplay Framework. To use another class as the parent class, expand the **All Classes** category and search for your desired class:

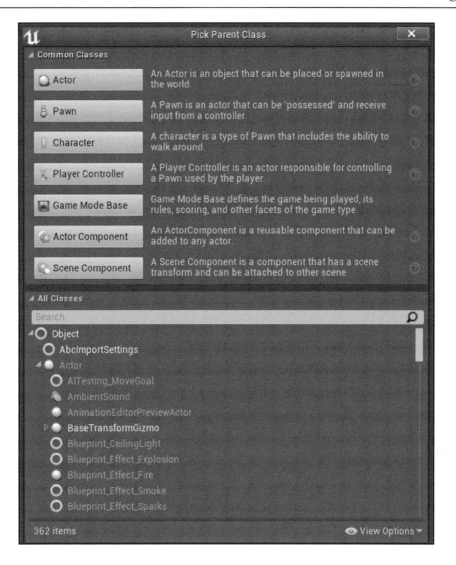

The following diagram shows the hierarchy of **Common Classes**. In Unreal Engine, there is a base class called **Object**. Classes inherit the characteristics of the class above it, which is their parent class. Based on the inheritance concept of OOP, we can state that an instance of the **Character** class is a **Pawn** class, and is also an **Actor** class:

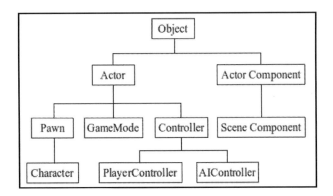

By analyzing this hierarchy, we can see that the **Actor Component** and **Scene Component** classes are not Actors. These classes are used to create Components that can be added to Actors.

Let's take a closer look at some of the **Common Classes**.

Pawn

Pawn is a child class of **Actor**. A **Pawn** class is an **Actor** class that can be possessed by a **Controller**. The **Controller** class represents a player or AI (artificial intelligence). For each instance of the **Pawn** class, there is an instance of the **Controller** class. Conceptually, the **Pawn** class is the physical body, while the **Controller** class is the brain.

Create a Blueprint based on the **Pawn** class and click the **Class Defaults** button to display it on the **Details** panel. The parameters that are inherited from the **Pawn** class are shown in the following screenshot. These parameters show that the **Pawn** class can use the rotation values of the **Controller** class that is possessing it, thus indicating how a **Controller** class possesses a **Pawn** class:

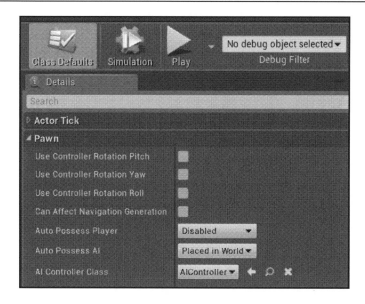

The two main child classes of **Pawn** are **Character** and **WheeledVehicle**.

Character

The **Character** class is a child class of the **Pawn** class; therefore, it can also be possessed by a **Controller** class. This class was created to represent characters that can walk, run, jump, swim, and fly.

A Blueprint based on the **Character** class inherits the following Components:

- **CapsuleComponent**: This is used for collision testing.
- **ArrowComponent**: This indicates the current direction of the character.
- **Mesh**: This Component is a Skeletal Mesh that visually represents the character. The animation of the **Mesh** Component is controlled by an animation Blueprint.
- **CharacterMovement**: This Component is used to define various types of character movements, such as walking, running, jumping, swimming, and flying.

These Components are shown in the following screenshot:

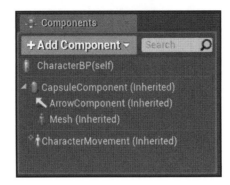

The **CharacterMovement** Component handles movement as well as replication and prediction in multiplayer games. It contains a lot of parameters that define various types of movements for the character:

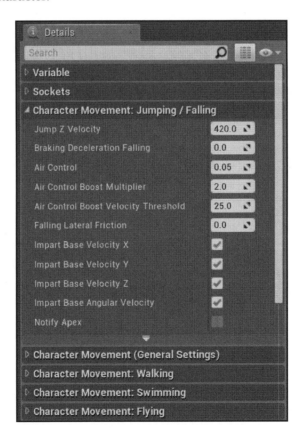

PlayerController

The **Controller** class has two main child classes: **PlayerController** and **AIController**. The **PlayerController** class is used by human players, while the **AIController** class uses AI to control the Pawn.

The **Pawn** and **Character** classes only receive input Events if **PlayerController** is possessing them. Input Events can be placed on **PlayerController** or **Pawn**. The advantage of putting the input Events in **PlayerController** is that these Events become independent of the **Pawn**, making it easier to change a **Pawn** class that is being possessed by the **Controller** class.

The following screenshot shows how to change a **Pawn** possessed by **PlayerController** in-game, and shows the use of the **Possess** Function. In this example, there are two characters in the Level that can be controlled by the player by pressing the *1* or *2* keys. Only the **Character** class currently being possessed receives the **PlayerController** commands:

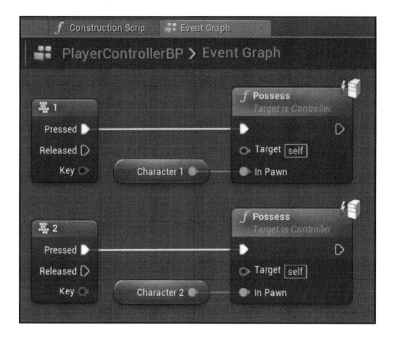

Game Mode Base

Game Mode Base is the parent class for creating **Game Mode**. A **Game Mode** class is used to define the rules of the game and specifies the default classes used for the creation of **Pawn, PlayerController, GameStateBase, HUD,** and other classes. To change these classes in **Game Mode**, click the **Class Defaults** button to display them on the **Details** panel, as shown in the following screenshot:

To specify the default **Game Mode** class of a project in the Level Editor, click **Edit | Project Settings...** Then, in the **Project** category, select the **Maps & Modes** option. Choose **Game Mode** in the **Default GameMode** property's drop-down, as shown in the following screenshot. In the **Selected GameMode** category, you can override some of the classes that are used by **Default GameMode**:

Each Level can have a different **Game Mode**. The **Game Mode** of a Level overrides **Default GameMode** of the project. To specify **Game Mode** of a Level, click the **Settings** button in the Level Editor and choose the **World Settings** option. Choose **Game Mode** in the **GameMode Override** property's drop-down, as shown in the following screenshot:

Game Instance

Game Instance is not one of **Common Classes**, but it is important to know about the existence of this class. The **Game Instance** class and its data persist between Levels because an instance of the **Game Instance** class is created at the beginning of the game and is only removed when the game is closed.

All Actors and other objects in a Level are destroyed and respawned each time a Level is loaded. So, the **Game Instance** class is an option to use if you need to preserve some variable values in the Level transition.

To assign the **Game Instance** class for use in your game, modify the project's settings by going to **Edit** | **Project Settings** | **Maps & Modes** on the Level Editor, as shown in the following screenshot:

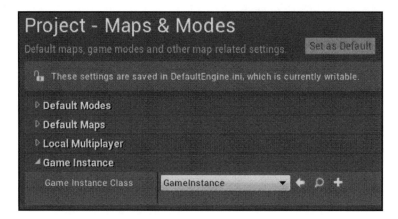

Summary

In this chapter, we learned about some of the principles of OOP that aid our understanding of how Blueprints work. We learned about how the Actor class is the base class that's used for objects that can be placed or spawned into a Level.

We also saw that the Gameplay Framework contains classes that are used to represent some game elements and learned about how to create Blueprints based on some **Common Classes**.

Our next step is to learn about how our Blueprints can communicate with each other, which we will cover in the next chapter.

4
Understanding Blueprint Communication

This chapter presents **Blueprint Communication**, which allows one Blueprint to access information from, and call the Functions and Events of, another Blueprint. This chapter explains **Direct Blueprint Communication** and shows how to reference Actors on a Level Blueprint. The concept of casting is explained in depth because it is an essential part of Blueprint Communication. We are also going to learn about **Event Dispatchers**, which enable communication between Blueprint classes and the Level Blueprint, as well as how to bind Events.

For each of these topics, we will do step-by-step examples to facilitate our understanding of the concepts and practice the creation of Blueprint scripts.

The following topics will be covered in this chapter:

- Direct Blueprint Communication
- Casting in Blueprints
- Level Blueprint Communication
- Event Dispatchers
- Binding Events

Direct Blueprint Communication

Direct Blueprint Communication is a simple method of communication between Blueprints/Actors. It is used by creating an object reference variable that stores a reference to another Actor/Blueprint. Then, we can call Actions using this object reference variable as the **Target** input parameter of these Actions.

As an example, let's create a Blueprint called BP_LightSwitch. The initials of BP_ are a naming convention used to facilitate the identification of a Blueprint asset. BP_LightSwitch has an object reference variable of the **Point Light** type that references a **Point Light** placed in the Level. When the player overlaps the BP_LightSwitch Blueprint on the Level, it toggles the visibility of the **Point Light**.

Follow these steps:

1. Create or use an existing project that contains starter content.
2. Click the **Add New** button in the **Content Browser** and choose the **Blueprint Class** option.
3. On the next screen, choose **Actor** as the parent class.
4. Name the Blueprint BP_LightSwitch and double-click it to open the Blueprint Editor.
5. Click the **Add Component** button in the **Components** panel and choose the **Static Mesh** Component. In the **Details** panel, choose the **SM_CornerFrame** Static Mesh, as shown in the following screenshot. This Static Mesh is a simple visual representation of our light switch. Also, change **Collision Presets** to **OverlapAllDynamic** so that Static Mesh will not block the player's movement:

6. In the **My Blueprint** panel, create a new variable named Light. In the **Details** panel, click the **Variable Type** drop-down menu and search for Point Light. Hover over **Point Light** to display a submenu and then choose **Object Reference**. Check the **Instance Editable** attribute, as shown in the following screenshot:

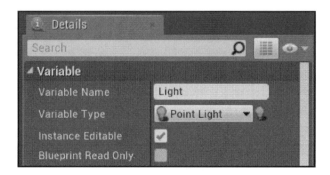

7. Drag the `Light` variable from the **My Blueprint** panel and drop it into the **Event Graph**. Choose the **Get Light** option to create a node. Drag from the blue pin of the **Light** node and drop in the graph to open **Context Menu**. At the top of **Context Menu**, there is a checkbox named **Context Sensitive**. If checked, the list of nodes is filtered to Actions that can be used in the current context, which, in this case, are the Actions that can be used with a **Point Light** object reference. Search for `toggle` and choose the Function named **Toggle Visibility (PointLightComponent)**, as shown in the following screenshot:

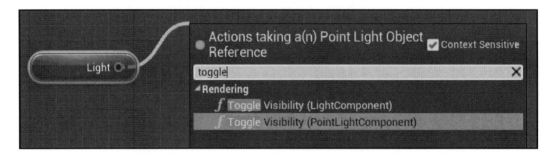

8. Right-click **Event Graph** and add **Event ActorBeginOverlap**. Drag from the blue pin of the `Light` node, drop it in the graph to open **Context Menu**, and add the **Is Valid** Macro, which is the one with the white question mark. This Macro is used to test whether the `Light` variable is referencing an instance. Connect the nodes, as shown in the following screenshot. Compile this Blueprint:

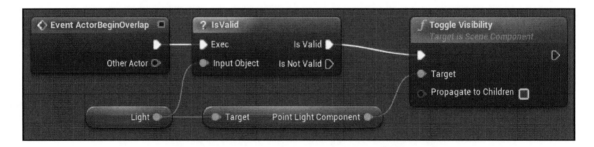

9. In the Level Editor, look at the **Modes** panel on the left. **Point Light** is in the **Basic** category, as shown in the following screenshot. Drag **Point Light** and drop it somewhere in the Level to create an instance. In the **Details** panel, change the name of the **Point Light** instance to `Lamp` and set the **Mobility** attribute to **Movable**:

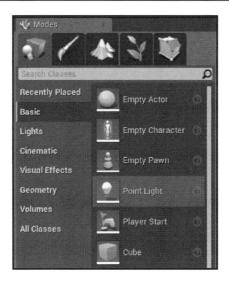

10. Drag the `BP_LightSwitch` Blueprint class from **Content Browser** and drop it in the Level in a place near the **Point Light** instance that we added to the Level. The next screenshot shows the **Details** panel of `BP_LightSwitch`. The `Light` variable appears in the **Details** panel because we checked the **Instance Editable** attribute. Click the drop-down menu of the `Light` variable to show all **Point Light** instances that are in the Level and select the **Point Light** instance that we renamed to `Lamp` in the preceding step. Essentially, this is Direct Blueprint Communication. `BP_LightSwitch` has an object reference to another Actor/Blueprint and can call its Actions:

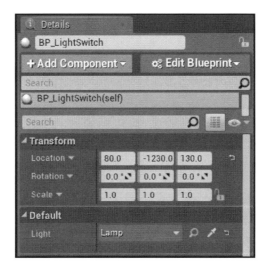

11. Click the **Play** button to see the BP_LightSwitch Blueprint in Action. Every time your character overlaps the instance of BP_LightSwitch, it toggles the visibility of the selected **Point Light**. The following screenshot shows an example using the **Third Person** template. The **Point Light** variable is on the wall, and the BP_LightSwitch Blueprint is on the floor:

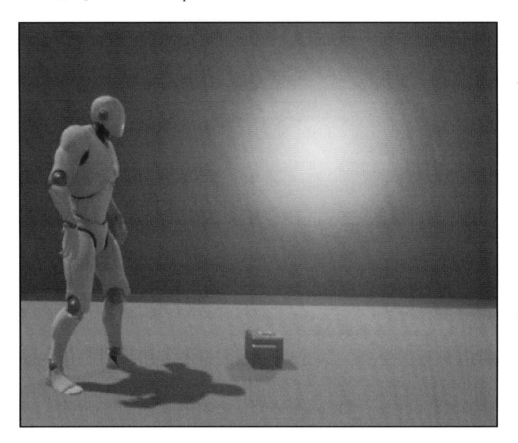

Casting in Blueprints

There is a node named **Cast To** that tries to convert reference variable types to new specified types. To understand casting, it is necessary to remember the concept of inheritance between classes, as we covered in Chapter 3, *Actors and the Gameplay Framework*.

The following diagram represents a Blueprint called `BP_GameModeWithScore`. **Game Mode Base** is the parent class of this Blueprint. Based on the inheritance concept, we can use a variable of the **Game Mode Base** object reference type to reference an instance of `BP_GameModeWithScore`. However, this variable is unable to access the variables and Functions that were defined in the `BP_GameModeWithScore` Blueprint:

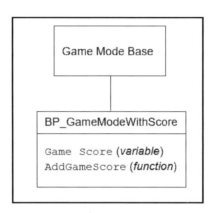

Therefore, if we have a **Game Mode Base** object reference, we can try to cast this reference using the Function `Cast To BP_GameModeWithScore`. If the instance is of the `BP_GameModeWithScore` type, then `Cast To` will succeed and return a `BP_GameModeWithScore` object reference that we can use to access the variables and Functions of `BP_GameModeWithScore`.

Let's do this example in the Blueprint Editor:

1. Create or use an existing project, based on the Third Person template, with the starter content.
2. Click the **Add New** button in the **Content Browser** and choose the **Blueprint Class** option.
3. On the next screen, choose **Game Mode Base** as the parent class.
4. Name the Blueprint `BP_GameModeWithScore` and double-click it to open the Blueprint Editor.
5. In the **My Blueprint** panel, create a variable named `GameScore` of type integer and create a Function named `AddGameScore`.
6. In the **Details** panel of the `AddGameScore` Function, add an **Input Parameter** named `Score` of type integer. This Function is used to add points to the `GameScore` variable.

7. In the graph of the Function, add the Actions shown in the following screenshot. To add the **GET** and **SET** nodes of the **Game Score** variable, simply drag the variable, drop it into the graph, and choose either **GET** or **SET**. The **Print String** Function is used to display the current value of the **Game Score** variable on the screen:

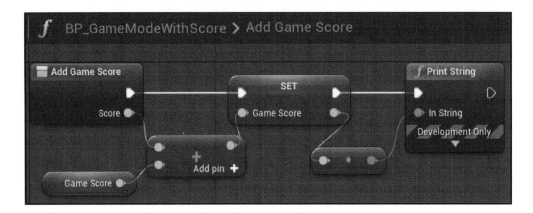

 The node that is between **SET** and **Print String** is a converter. To create it, simply connect the **SET** output parameter to the **In String** input parameter of **Print String**. Because the parameters are of different types, the converter is created automatically.

8. Compile and save the BP_GameModeWithScore Blueprint. The next step is to set the Level to use BP_GameModeWithScore as **Game Mode**.

9. In the Level Editor, click the **Settings** button and choose **World Settings**. In the **GameMode Override** attribute, click the drop-down menu and choose BP_GameModeWithScore, as shown in the following screenshot:

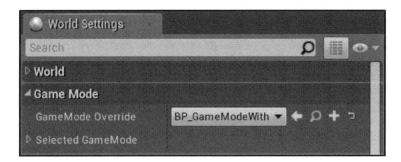

10. Create a Blueprint and use **Actor** as the parent class. Name it `BP_Collectable` and open it in the Blueprint Editor.

11. Click the **Add Component** button in the **Components** panel and choose the **Static Mesh** Component. In the **Details** panel, choose the **SM_Statue** Static Mesh and in **Materials**, go to **Element 0** and choose **M_Metal_Gold**. Also, change **Collision Presets** to **OverlapAllDynamic**, as shown in the following screenshot:

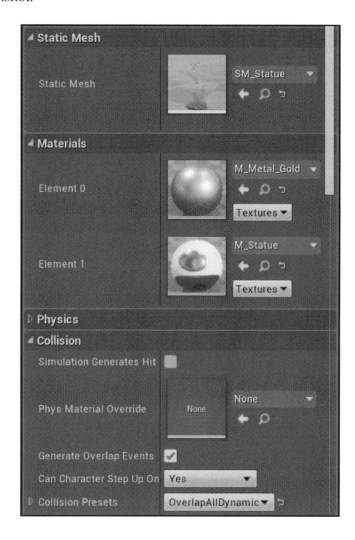

12. Right-click **Event Graph** and add **Event ActorBeginOverlap**. **Other Actor** is the instance that overlaps the `BP_Collectable` Blueprint. Drag from the blue pin of **Other Actor** and drop in the graph in order to open **Context Menu**. Choose the **Cast To ThirdPersonCharacter** Action, as shown in the following screenshot. **ThirdPersonCharacter** is the Blueprint that represents the player in the Third Person template. We are using the **Cast To** Action to test whether the instance referenced by **Other Actor** is the player:

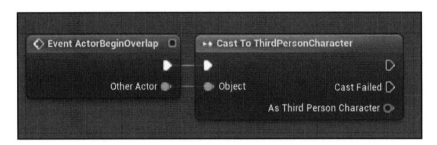

13. Right-click **Event Graph** and add the **Get Game Mode** Function. Drag from the blue pin of **Return Value** and drop it in the graph in order to open **Context Menu**. Choose the **Cast To BP_GameModeWithScore** Action. Drag from the blue pin of **As BP Game Mode With Score**, drop it in the graph, and choose the **Add Game Score** Action in the **Context Menu**. Type 50 in the **Score** input parameter. Right-click **Event Graph** and add the **DestroyActor** Function. Connect the white pins of the nodes. The content of **Event ActorBeginOverlap** is shown in the following screenshot:

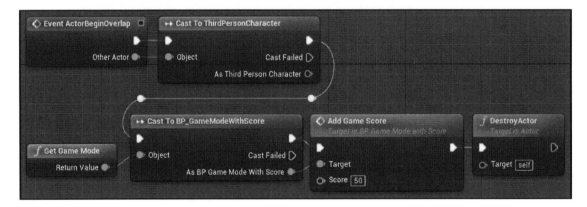

The **Get Game Mode** Function returns a reference to **Game Mode** used by the current Level. But the type of the return value is **Game Mode Base**. By using a variable of this type, we were unable to access the **Add Game Score** Function. Therefore, it was necessary to use **Cast To BP_GameModeWithScore**.

14. Compile BP_Collectable. In the Level Editor, drag and drop some instances of BP_Collectable in the Level. Click the **Play** button to test the Level. Use your character to collect the statues.

The two white connection pins that appear in the previous screenshot are called **reroute nodes**. They can be added from **Context Menu** and are used to aid in the organization of the Blueprint.

Level Blueprint Communication

Unreal Engine 4 has a special type of Blueprint called **Level Blueprint**. Each Level of the game has a default Level Blueprint. They are useful for creating Events and Actions that only happen at the current level. To access the Level Blueprint, click the **Blueprints** button at the top of the Level Editor and choose the **Open Level Blueprint** option, as shown in the following screenshot:

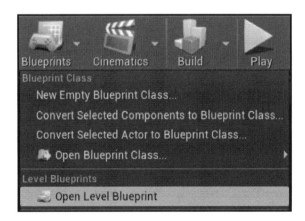

In the Level Blueprint, we can easily create references to Actors that are on the Level. To see this in practice, let's create an example where **Box Trigger** is added on the Level. When an Actor overlaps the trigger, **Blueprint_Effect_Sparks** is activated, producing the effect of a spark:

1. Create or use an existing project based on the Third Person template with the starter content.

2. In the Level Editor, look at the **Modes** panel on the left. In the **Basic** category, there is a **Box Trigger**, as shown in the following screenshot. Drag the **Box Trigger** and drop it somewhere in the Level:

3. Resize and place the **Box Trigger** in a location in the Level through which the player must pass. The following screenshot shows an example. The **Box Trigger** is hidden in the game:

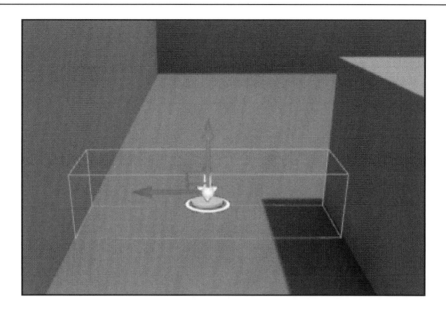

4. Confirm that the **Box Trigger** is selected and open the Level Blueprint by clicking the **Blueprints** button at the top of the Level Editor and choosing **Open Level Blueprint**.

5. Right-click **Event Graph** and add the Event labeled **Add On Actor Begin Overlap** that is within the **Add Event for Trigger Box 1** category, as shown in the following screenshot:

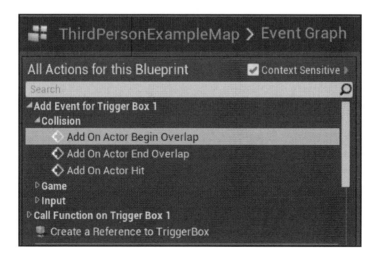

6. Return to the Level Editor. In **Content Browser**, Content | StarterContent | Blueprints folders, open **Blueprint_Effect_Sparks**. On the **Components** tab, select the **Sparks** Component and in the **Details** tab, search for the auto activate attribute and uncheck it, as shown in the following screenshot. Compile **Blueprint_Effect_Sparks**:

7. In the Level Editor, drag **Blueprint_Effect_Sparks** from **Content Browser** and drop it in the Level near the **Box Trigger** to create an instance.

8. Confirm that **Blueprint_Effect_Sparks** is selected and open the Level Blueprint. Right-click on **Event Graph** and select **Create a Reference to Blueprint_Effects_Sparks**, as shown in the following screenshot:

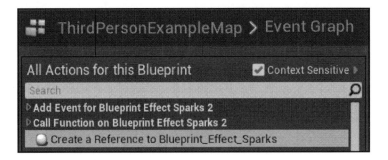

9. Drag from the **Blueprint_Effect_Sparks** blue pin of the node and drop it in the graph in order to open **Context Menu**. Search for `activate` and choose **Activate (Sparks)**. Connect the white pin of the **OnActorBeginOverlap (TriggerBox)** Event to the white pin of the **Activate** Function, as shown in the following screenshot:

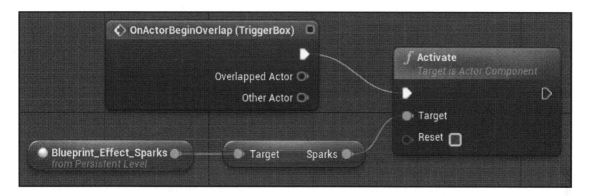

10. Compile the Level Blueprint and click the **Play** button of the Level Editor to test the Level. Move your character to the location of the **Box Trigger** in order to activate the sparks.

In this example, we saw how to add references and Events to Actors in the Level Blueprint. This is the essence of **Level Blueprint Communication**.

Event Dispatchers

An Event Dispatcher allows a Blueprint to inform us when an Event happens. The Level Blueprint and other Blueprint classes can listen to this Event, and they may have different Actions that run when the Event is triggered.

We create Event Dispatchers in the **My Blueprint** panel. As an example, let's create a Blueprint named BP_Platform. When an Actor overlaps the BP_Platform Blueprint, it calls an Event Dispatcher called PlatformPressed. The Level Blueprint is listening for the PlatformPressed Event and spawns an explosion when this Event is triggered:

1. Create or use an existing project that contains the starter content.
2. Create a Blueprint and use **Actor** as the parent class. Name it BP_Platform and open it in the Blueprint Editor.

3. Click the **Add Component** button in the **Components** panel and choose the **Static Mesh** Component. In the **Details** panel, choose the **Shape_Cylinder** Static Mesh and change the **Z** value of the **Scale** attribute to 0.1. Also, change **Collision Presets** to **OverlapAllDynamic**, as shown in the following screenshot:

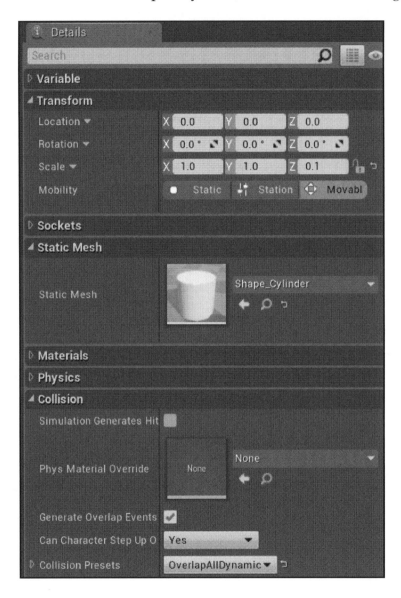

4. Compile the Blueprint. In the **My Blueprint** panel, create an Event Dispatcher and name it `PlatformPressed`. An Event Dispatcher can have input parameters. Let's create one to send a reference to the `BP_Platform` instance that was overlapped. In the **Details** panel, create a new parameter in the **Inputs** category, name it `BP_Platform`, and use it as a `BP Platform` type object reference, as shown in the following screenshot:

5. Right-click **Event Graph** and add **Event ActorBeginOverlap**. Drag the `PlatformPressed` Event Dispatcher and drop it in **Event Graph**. Choose **Call** in the submenu. Right-click **Event Graph**, search for `self`, and select the **Get a reference to self** Action. The **Self** Action returns a reference to the current instance. Connect the Actions, as shown in the following screenshot:

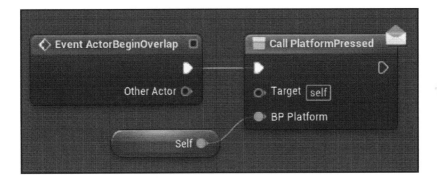

6. Compile the Blueprint. In the Level Editor, drag `BP_Platform` from **Content Browser** and drop it in the Level to create an instance. Click the **Blueprint** button at the top of the Level Editor and choose **Open Level Blueprint**. Right-click **Event Graph** and select **Add Platform Pressed**, as shown in the following screenshot:

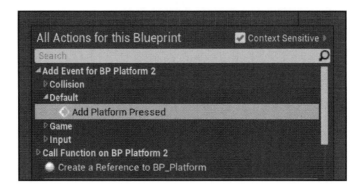

7. Right-click **Event Graph**, search for `spawn actor`, and select **Spawn Actor from Class**. Click the drop-down menu in the **Class** parameter and select **Blueprint Effect Explosion**. Drag from the blue pin of the **PlatformPressed (BP_Platform)** Event, drop it in the graph in order to open **Context Menu,** and choose the **GetActorTransform** Action. Connect the nodes, as shown in the following screenshot:

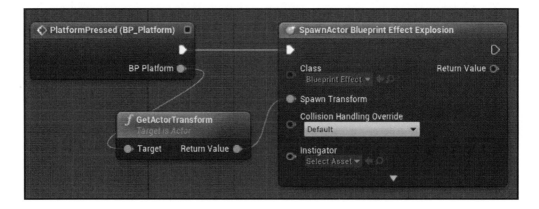

8. Compile the Level Blueprint and click the **Play** button of the Level Editor to test the Level. Move your character to the location where `BP_Platform` is. When your character overlaps it, the Level Blueprint will spawn an explosion at the same place.

Binding Events

There is a **Bind Event** node that binds one Event to another Event or to an Event Dispatcher, which can be in another Blueprint. When an Event is called, all the other Events that are bound to it are also called.

As an example, let's create a child Blueprint class of **Blueprint_Effect_Sparks**. This new Blueprint binds an Event to the PlatformPressed Event Dispatcher of the BP_Platform Blueprint that we created in the previous example:

1. Open the project used in the example of Event Dispatcher.
2. Create a Blueprint, expand the **All Classes** menu, and search for **Blueprint_Effect_Sparks**, which we'll use as the parent class. Name it BP_Platform_Sparks and open it in the Blueprint Editor.
3. In the **My Blueprint** panel, create a variable named BP_Platform of the BP_Platform type object reference. Check the **Instance Editable** attribute.
4. Drag the BP_Platform variable from the **My Blueprint** panel and drop it in **Event Graph**. Choose the **GET** option to create a node.
5. Drag from the blue pin of the **BP Platform** node and drop it in the graph to open **Context Menu**. Add the **Bind Event to PlatformPressed** Action.
6. Drag from the red pin of the **Bind Event** node, drop it in the graph, and choose **Add Custom Event**.
7. Drag the **Sparks** Component from the **Components** panel and drop it in the graph. Drag from the blue pin of the **Sparks** node, drop it in the graph, and choose **Activate**.
8. Connect the nodes, as shown in the following screenshot, and compile BP_Platform_Sparks:

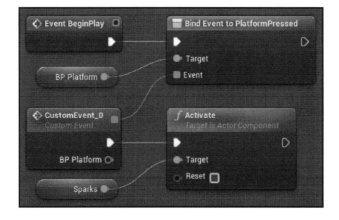

9. Add an instance of `BP_Platform_Sparks` near the instance of `BP_Platform` that is already on the Level. On the **Details** panel of the Level Editor, click the drop-down menu of the `BP_Platform` variable and select one instance.

10. Click the **Play** button of the Level Editor to test the Level. Move your character to the location of `BP_Platform`. When your character overlaps it, the `PlatformPressed` Event Dispatcher is triggered, and the Custom Event of `BP_Platform_Sparks` is executed, activating the sparks.

Summary

This was a practical chapter. We created step-by-step examples for each Blueprint Communication. We learned about how a Blueprint can reference another Blueprint using Direct Blueprint Communication and how to reference Actors on the Level Blueprint. We saw how to use casting to access variables and Functions of a child class, and how to test whether an instance reference is of a certain class.

We learned about how to use Event Dispatcher to inform us when an Event happens, and how to respond to this Event Dispatcher in the Level Blueprint. We also saw that we could bind an Event of another Blueprint to an Event Dispatcher.

This chapter concludes section 1. We have now learned about the Blueprint fundamentals necessary to start scripting games and applications in Unreal Engine 4.

In section 2, we will start to build a first-person shooter from scratch with step-by-step tutorials. In the next chapter, we will create the project, add objects to the Level, manipulate the Materials of the objects, and add movement.

Section 2: Developing a Game

2

In this section, you will start to build a first-person shooter from scratch with the help of step-by-step tutorials. Blueprints will be used to develop the gameplay mechanics and user interface.

This section includes the following chapters:

- Chapter 5, *Object Interaction with Blueprints*
- Chapter 6, *Enhancing Player Abilities*
- Chapter 7, *Creating Screen UI Elements*
- Chapter 8, *Creating Constraints and Gameplay Objectives*

5
Object Interaction with Blueprints

When setting out to develop a game, one of the first steps toward exploring your idea is to build a prototype. Fortunately, Unreal Engine 4 and Blueprints make it easier than ever to quickly get the essential gameplay functionality working so that you can start testing your ideas sooner. We will begin by prototyping simple gameplay mechanics using some default assets and a couple of Blueprints.

In this chapter, we will cover the following topics:

- Creating a new project and a Level
- Placing objects in a Level
- Changing an object's Material through Blueprints
- Using the Blueprint Editor and connecting Blueprints together
- Compiling, saving, and playing our game
- Moving objects in the world with Blueprints

Creating a project and the first Level

Before we can begin setting up gameplay elements, we need to create a project that contains the content of our game. To access Unreal Engine 4 and begin setting up our project, we must first open the Epic Games launcher. From Epic Games launcher, click on the tab labeled **Unreal Engine** and click on the **Launch** button to open the engine.

Setting a template for a new project

Once you click on **Launch**, you are presented with the Unreal Engine project browser. This, by default, takes you to the **Projects** tab, which shows you a thumbnail view of all the projects you have created, as well as any sample projects you might choose to install. For our purposes, we want to start a new project, so click on the tab labeled **New Project**.

From the **New Project** tab, you can select a template that gives you the initial assets to use for your game; alternatively, you can choose to start a blank project. You can see two subtabs under the **New Project** tab, labeled **Blueprint** and **C++**. Creating a project from the content within the **Blueprint** tab starts your project with a basic set of behavior that is built using Blueprints. The **C++** tab is used to create projects where at least some of the core types of behavior of the game are going to be built using the C++ programming language. Since we want to get a prototype first-person shooter up and running quickly, without having to build the basic controls from scratch, we should ensure that we have the tab labeled **Blueprint** selected. Then, we choose the **First Person** template, as shown here:

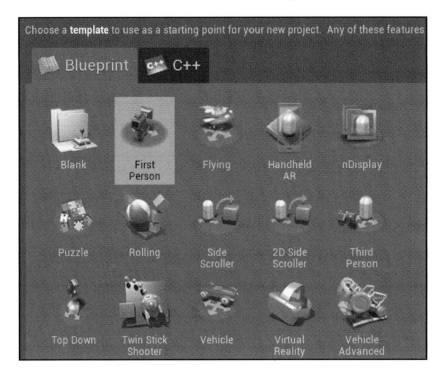

Making sense of the project settings

The next step is to adjust the project settings to our liking. The three gray boxes below the template selector allow us to select the class of hardware we are targeting (desktop/console or mobile/tablet), the graphics scalability, and whether we want to create our project with or without starter content. Leave these settings at their default values (**Desktop / Console**, **Maximum Quality**, and **With Starter Content**). Below these, you can see a folder path field used to designate where you would like to store your project on your hard drive, as well as a name field to input the name by which your project will be known. I named the project BlueprintScripting and stored it in the default Unreal Projects folder, as shown in this screenshot:

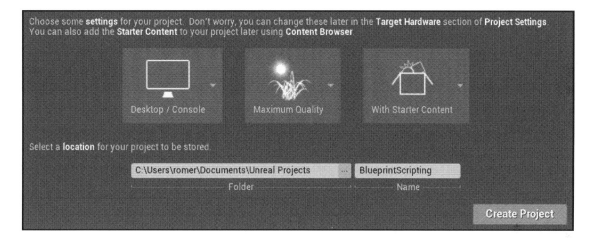

Creating the project

Now that we have a template selected and the project settings set up the way we like, we can create the project. To do so, click on the green **Create Project** button. After the engine is done with initializing the assets and setting up your project, Unreal Editor will open Level Editor, where you can create and view Levels, place and modify objects, and test your game as you modify it.

Pressing the **Play** button—as shown in the following screenshot, located in the toolbar—allows you to try the default gameplay that is built into the **First Person** template. This includes player movement, shooting a simple projectile, and using projectiles to apply force to primitive box objects. In play mode, the **Play** button will be replaced with a **Pause** button and a **Stop** button. You can press the **Pause** button to temporarily halt the play session, which can be useful when you want to explore the properties of an interaction or Actor that you have just encountered during gameplay. Pressing the **Stop** button ends the play session and takes you back to editing mode. Go ahead and try playing the game before we continue:

Adding objects to our Level

Now, we want to start adding our own objects to the Level. The central panel you see in Level Editor is known as the **3D Viewport**. A Viewport allows you to see the 3D content of the game, and it is important that you become familiar with navigating inside this panel. The Viewport can be navigated by moving the camera around using a combination of mouse movement and buttons. Holding down the left mouse button and dragging the mouse pointer inside the Viewport moves the camera view forward and backward and rotates it left and right. Holding down the right mouse button and moving the mouse allows you to look around by rotating the camera. Finally, holding down either the middle mouse button or a combination of both the left and right mouse buttons allows you to drag the camera up and down.

The simplest kind of object that can be dragged into the game world in Unreal Engine 4 is called an **Actor**. An Actor is a basic object with no inherent behavior other than the ability to be rotated, moved, and scaled, but it can be expanded to include more complex behavior by attaching Components. Our goal is to create a simple target Actor that changes color when shot with the included gun and projectile. We can create a simple Actor by following these steps:

1. Go to the **Modes** panel. Select the **Place** tab (which is the first tab on the left), click on the **Basic** tab, and then drag the object called **Cylinder** into the 3D Viewport. This creates a new Cylinder Actor and places it in our Level. You should see the Actor in the 3D Viewport as well as in the **World Outliner** panel, where it is named **Cylinder** by default.

2. Right-click the **Cylinder** object in the **World Outliner** panel, go to **Edit**, and then select **Rename**. Rename the **Cylinder** object to `CylinderTarget`, as shown here:

Exploring Materials

Earlier, we set ourselves the goal of changing the color of the Cylinder when it is hit by a projectile. To do so, we need to change the Actor's **Material**. A Material is an asset that can be added to an Actor's Mesh (which defines the physical shape of the Actor) in order to create its look. You can think of a Material as a coat of paint applied on top of an Actor's Mesh or shape. Since an Actor's Material determines its color, one method for changing the color of an Actor is to replace its Material with a Material of a different color. To do this, let's first create a Material of our own. It will make an Actor appear red.

Creating Materials

Follow these steps to create a Material:

1. Create a new folder inside the `FirstPersonBP` directory and name it `Materials`.
2. Navigate to the newly created folder and right-click in an empty space in the **Content Browser**. This generates a new asset creation popup.
3. Select **Material** to create a new Material asset. Name it `TargetRed`.

Material properties and Blueprint nodes

Double-click on TargetRed to open a new Editor tab for editing the Material, like this:

You are now looking at the Material Editor, which shares many features and conventions with Blueprints. The center of this screen is called the **grid**, and this is where we place all the objects that define the logic of our Materials. The initial object you see in the center of the grid screen, labeled with the name of the Material, is called a **node**. This node, as seen in the previous screenshot, has a series of input pins that other Material nodes can attach to in order to define this node's properties.

To give the Material a color, we need to create a node that provides information about the color to the input labeled **Base Color** on this node. To do so, right-click on an empty space near the node. A popup with a search box and a long list of expandable options appears. This shows all the available Material node options that we can add to this Material. The search box is context-sensitive, so if you start typing the first few letters of a valid node name, you will see the list below the search field shrink to include only those nodes that include those letters in their names. The node we are looking for is called **VectorParameter**, so we start typing this name in the search box and click on the **VectorParameter** result to add that node to our grid:

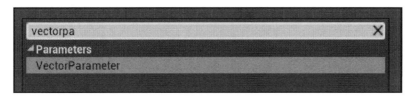

A vector parameter in the Material Editor allows us to define a color, which we can then attach to the **Base Color** input on the tall Material definition node. We first need to give the node a color selection. Double-click on the black square in the middle of the node to open **Color Picker**. We want to give our target a bright red color when it is hit, so either drag the center point in the color wheel to the red section of the wheel, or fill in the RGB or Hex values manually. When you have selected the shade of red you want to use, click on **OK**. You will notice that the black box in your vector parameter node has now turned red.

To help ourselves remember what parameter or property of the Material our vector parameter will be defined by, we should name it Color. You can do this by ensuring that you have the vector parameter node selected (indicated by a thin yellow highlight around the node), and then navigating to the **Details** panel in the Editor. Enter a value for **Parameter Name**, and the node label changes automatically:

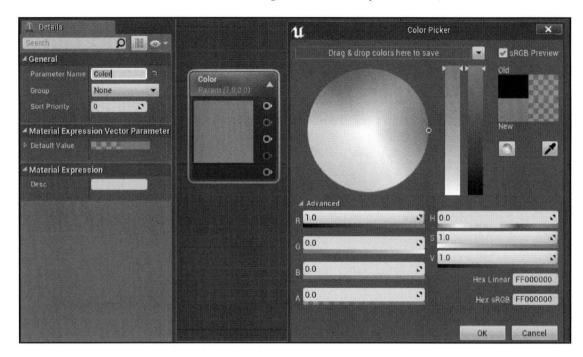

The final step is to link our color vector parameter node to the base Material node. In the same way as with Blueprints, you can connect two nodes by clicking and dragging from one node's output pin to another node's input pin. Input pins are located on the left-hand side of a node, while output pins are always located on the right-hand side. The thin line that connects two nodes that have been connected in this way is called a **wire**. For our Material, we need to click and drag a wire from the top output pin of the **Color** node to the **Base Color** input pin of the Material node, as shown in the following screenshot:

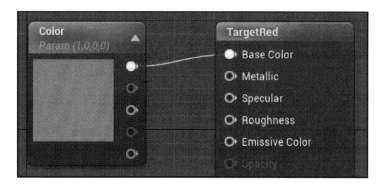

Adding substance to our Material

We can optionally add some polish to our Material by taking advantage of some of the other input pins on the Material definition node. 3D objects look unrealistic with flat single-color Materials applied, but we can add additional reflectiveness and depth by setting a value for the Materials' **Metallic** and **Roughness** inputs. To do so, follow these steps:

1. Right-click in an empty grid space and type `scalarpa` into the search box. The node we are looking for is called **ScalarParameter**:

2. Once you have a **ScalarParameter** node, select it and go to the **Details** panel. **ScalarParameter** takes a single float value (a number with decimal values). Set **Default Value** to `0.1`, as we want any additional effects on our Material to be subtle.

3. Change **Parameter Name** to **Metallic**, then click and drag the output pin from our **Metallic** node to the **Metallic** input pin of the Material definition node.

4. Let's make an additional connection to the **Roughness** parameter, so right-click on the **Metallic** node we just created and select **Duplicate**. This generates a copy of that node without the wire connection.

5. Select this duplicate **Metallic** node and then change the **Parameter Name** field in the **Details** panel to **Roughness**. Let's keep the same default value of 0.1 for this node.

6. Click and drag the output pin from the **Roughness** node to the **Roughness** input pin of the Material definition node.

The final result of our Material should look like this:

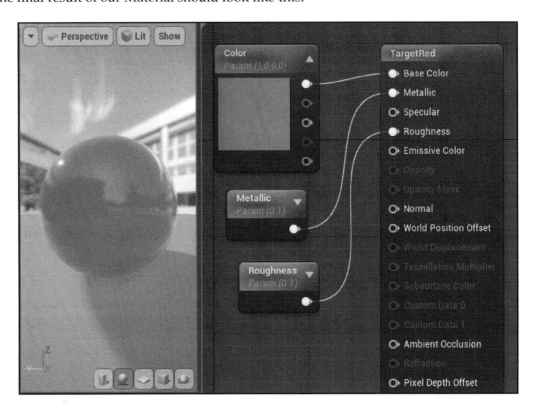

We have now made a shiny red Material that ensures our targets stand out when they are hit. Click on the **Save** button in the top-left corner of the Editor to save the asset, and click on the tab labeled FirstPersonExampleMap again to return to your Level.

Creating the target Blueprint

We now have a Cylinder in the world, as well as the Material we want to apply to the Cylinder when it is shot. The final piece of the interaction is the game logic that evaluates that the Cylinder has been hit, and then changes the Material on the Cylinder to our new red Material. In order to create this behavior and add it to our Cylinder, we have to create a Blueprint. There are multiple ways of creating a Blueprint, but to save a couple of steps, we can create the Blueprint and directly attach it to the Cylinder we created in a single click. To do so, make sure you have the `CylinderTarget` object selected in the **World Outliner** panel, and click on the blue **Blueprint/Add Script** button at the top of the **Details** panel. You will then see a **Select Path** window.

For this project, we are storing all our Blueprints in the `Blueprints` folder, which is inside the `FirstPersonBP` folder. Since this is the Blueprint for our `CylinderTarget` Actor, leaving the name of the Blueprint as the default `CylinderTarget_Blueprint` is appropriate:

The Blueprint Editor opens and `CylinderTarget_Blueprint` should now appear in **Content Browser**, inside the `Blueprints` folder. Now, let's look at the Viewport view of our Cylinder. From here, we can manipulate some of the default properties of our Actor or add more Components, each of which can contain their own logic to make the Actor more complex. We will explore Components more in `Chapter 6`, *Enhancing Player Abilities*; for now, we want to create a simple Blueprint that is attached to the Actor directly. To do so, click on the tab labeled **Event Graph**.

Exploring the Event Graph panel

By default, **Event Graph** opens with three unlinked Event nodes that are currently unused. An Event refers to an Action in the game that acts as a trigger for a Blueprint to do something. Most of the Blueprints you will create follow this structure: *Event (when)* | *Conditionals (if)* | *Actions (do)*. This can be worded as follows: when something happens, check whether *X*, *Y*, and *Z* are true. If so, do this sequence of Actions. A real-world example of this might be a Blueprint that determines whether or not the player can fire a gun. The flow is like this: *WHEN* the trigger is pulled, *IF* there is ammo left in the gun, *DO* fire the gun.

The three Event nodes that are present in our graph by default are three of the most commonly used Event triggers. **Event BeginPlay** triggers Actions when the player first begins playing the game. **Event ActorBeginOverlap** triggers Actions when another Actor begins touching or overlapping the space containing the existing Actor that is controlled by the Blueprint. **Event Tick** triggers the attached Actions every time a new frame of visual content is displayed on the screen during gameplay. The number of frames shown on the screen within a second vary depending on the power of the computer running the game, and this, in turn, affects how often **Event Tick** triggers the Actions:

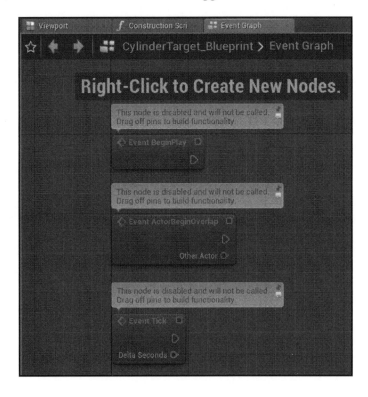

We want to trigger a change Material Action on our target every time a projectile hits it. While we could do this by utilizing the **Event ActorBeginOverlap** node to detect when a projectile object overlaps with the Cylinder Mesh of our target, let's simplify things by only detecting instances when another Actor hits our target Actor. Let's start with a clean slate, by clicking and dragging a selection box over all the default Events and hitting the *Delete* key on the keyboard to delete them.

Detecting a hit

To create our hit detection Event, right-click on empty graph space and type `hit` in the search box. The **Event Hit** node is what we are looking for, so select it when it appears in the search results. **Event Hit** triggers Actions every time another Actor hits the Actor controlled by this Blueprint:

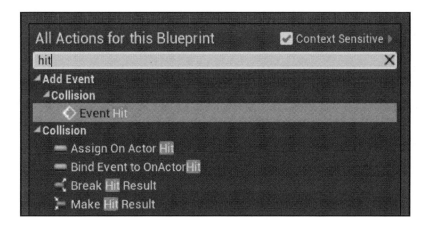

Once you have the **Event Hit** node on the graph, notice that **Event Hit** has a number of multicolored output pins originating from it. The first thing to notice is the white triangular pin that is in the top-right corner of the node. This is the execution pin, which determines the next Action to be taken in a sequence. Linking the execution pins of different nodes together is how we enables basic functionality in all Blueprints. Now that we have the trigger, we need to find an Action that will enable us to change the Material of an Actor. Click and drag a wire from the execution pin to an empty space on the right of the node.

Dropping a wire into empty space like this generates a search window, which allows you to create a node and attach it to the pin you are dragging from in a single operation. In the search window that appears, make sure that the **Context Sensitive** box is checked. This limits the results in the search window to only those nodes that can actually be attached to the pin you dragged to generate the search window. With **Context Sensitive** checked, type `set material` in the search box. The node we want to select is called **Set Material (StaticMeshComponent)**:

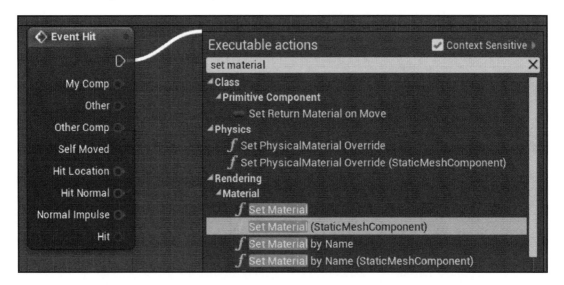

If you cannot find the node you are searching for in the **Context Sensitive** search, try unchecking **Context Sensitive** to find it from the complete list of node options. Even if the node is not found in the **Context Sensitive** search, there is still a possibility that the node can be used in conjunction with the node you are attempting to attach it to.

Swapping a Material

Once you have placed the **Set Material** node, notice that it is already connected via its input execution pin to the **Event Hit** node's output execution pin. This Blueprint now fires the **Set Material** Action whenever the Blueprint's Actor hits another Actor. However, we haven't yet set up the Material that will be called when the **Set Material** Action is called. Without setting the Material, the Action will fire but won't produce any observable effect on the Cylinder target.

To set the Material that will be called, click on the drop-down field labeled **Select Asset** underneath **Material**, which is inside the **Set Material** node. In the asset finder window that appears, type red in the search box to find the TargetRed Material we created earlier. Clicking on this asset attaches it to the **Material** field inside the **Set Material** node:

We have now done everything we need with this Blueprint in order to turn the target Cylinder red, but before the Blueprint can be saved, it must be compiled. Compiling is the process used to convert the developer-friendly Blueprint language into machine instructions that tell the computer what operations to perform. This is a hands-off process, so we don't need to concern ourselves with it, except to ensure that we always compile our Blueprint scripts after we assemble them. To do so, hit the **Compile** button in the top-left corner of the Editor toolbar, and then click on **Save**.

Now that we have set up a basic gameplay interaction, it is wise to test the game to ensure that everything is happening the way we want it to. Click on the **Play** button, and a game window will appear directly above the Blueprint Editor. Try both shooting and running into the `CylinderTarget` Actor you created:

Improving the Blueprint

When we run the game, we see that the Cylinder target changes colors upon being hit by a projectile fired from the player's gun. This is the beginning of a framework of gameplay that can be used to get enemies to respond to the player's Actions. However, you might also have noticed that the target Cylinder changes color, even when the player runs into it directly. Remember that we wanted the Cylinder target to turn red only when hit by a player projectile, and not due to any other object colliding with it. Unforeseen results like this are common whenever scripting is involved, and the best way to avoid them is to check your work by playing the game as often as possible as you are constructing it.

To fix our Blueprint so that the Cylinder target only changes color in response to a player projectile, return to the `CylinderTarget_Blueprint` tab and look at the **Event Hit** node again.

The remaining output pins on the **Event Hit** node are variables that store data about the Event that can be passed to other nodes. The color of the pins represents the kind of data variable they pass. Blue pins pass objects, such as Actors, whereas red pins contain a Boolean (true or false) variable.

The blue output pin, labeled **Other**, contains a reference to the other Actor that hit the Cylinder target. This is useful for us to ensure that the Cylinder target changes color only when hit by a projectile fired from the player, rather than changing color because of any other Actors that might bump into it.

To ensure that we are only triggering the Cylinder target in response to a player projectile hit, click and drag a wire from the **Other** output pin to an empty space. In this search window, type `projectile`. You should see some results that look similar to the following screenshot. The node we are looking for is called **Cast To FirstPersonProjectile**:

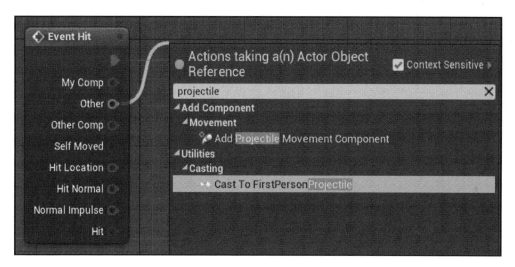

`FirstPersonProjectile` is a Blueprint included in Unreal Engine 4's **First Person** template, which controls the behavior of the projectiles that are fired from your gun. This node uses casting to ensure that the Action attached to the execution pin of this node occurs only if the Actor hitting the Cylinder target matches the object referenced by the casting node.

When the node appears, you should already see a blue wire between the **Other** output pin of the **Event Hit** node and the **Object** pin of the casting node. If not, you can generate it manually by clicking and dragging from one pin to the other. You should also remove the connections between the **Event Hit** and **Set Material** node execution pins so that the casting node can be linked between them. Removing a wire between two pins can be done by holding down the *Alt* key and clicking on a pin.

Once you have linked the three nodes, **Event Graph** should look like this:

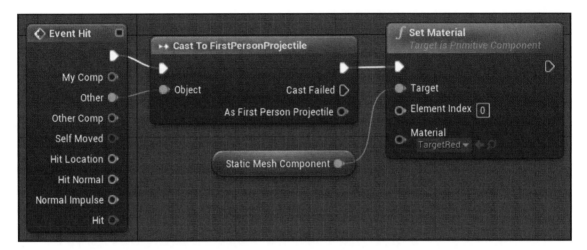

Now compile, save, and click on the **Play** button to test the game again. This time, you should notice that the Cylinder target retains its default color when you walk up and touch it, but if you move away and shoot it, it turns red.

Adding movement

Now that we have a target that responds to the player shooting, we can add some sort of challenge to start making our project feel like a game. A simple way to do this is to add some movement to our target. To accomplish this, we first have to declare that our target Actor is an object that is intended to move, and then we need to set up logic within the Blueprint that manages how it moves. Our goal is to make the target Cylinder move back and forth across our Level.

Changing the Actor's Mobility and Collision settings

To allow our target to move, we first have to change the Actor's **Mobility** setting to **Moveable**. This allows an object to be manipulated while playing the game. From the main Editor view, select `CylinderTarget_Blueprint`, and look at the **Details** panel. Underneath the **Transform** values, you can see a toggle for **Mobility**. Change this from **Static** to **Moveable**, as shown in the following screenshot:

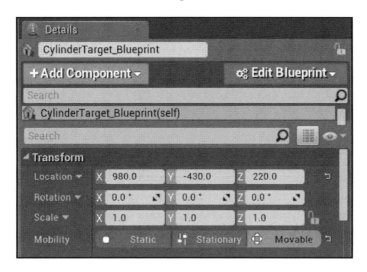

By default, basic Actors that are placed in the world are set to **Static**. Static means that the object cannot move or be manipulated during gameplay. Static objects are significantly less resource intensive to render, and this should be our default choice for non-interactive objects so that we can maximize frame rates.

It is important to note that the version of the target Cylinder that we changed in the Level is just one instance of the Blueprint template for the target Cylinder that we have created. An instance refers to an actual object that has been created, whereas our Blueprints are descriptions of the kinds of features that those instances will have once they are created.

Any changes we make to a target Cylinder that is already inside the Level is made for that particular target Cylinder only. To make changes to all future targets, we need to modify the Blueprint directly. To do so, open `CylinderTarget_Blueprint` again, either by navigating to the open tab in the Editor or by double-clicking on the `CylinderTarget_Blueprint` file in your `Blueprints` folder.

With the Blueprint open, we want to navigate to the **Viewport** tab that is located underneath the menu toolbar. Along the left side, you can see the **Components** panel, which lists all the Components that make up this Blueprint. Since we want to edit a property of the physical object, or Mesh, we click on **StaticMeshComponent**. We see a familiar-looking **Details** panel. It includes the same properties and categories that we saw when we edited the target Cylinder in the Level Editor. Here, we have to switch the same **Mobility** toggle, located underneath the **Transform** properties, from **Static** to **Movable**. This ensures that all future targets created from this Blueprint will already be set to be **Moveable**.

Because we want to target this object with our gun, we also need to ensure that the target is capable of being collided with so that our bullets don't pass through it. In the **Details** panel, find the category called **Collision** and look for **Collision Presets** in the drop-down menu. There are many other options in this drop-down, and by choosing the **Custom** option, you can even set the object's **Collision** interaction with different object types individually. For our purpose, we just need to ensure that this drop-down menu is set to **BlockAllDynamic**, which ensures that the Mesh registers collisions with any other object that also has a collider:

Breaking down our goal

Now that we have made our target moveable, we are ready to set up Blueprints that tell the Cylinder how to move. In order to move an object, we need three pieces of data:

- Where the Cylinder currently is
- What direction it is supposed to move in
- How fast it is supposed to move in that direction

To understand where the object currently is, we need to get some information about the world itself. Specifically, what are the coordinates of the Cylinder in the world? The speed and direction are the values we are providing to the Blueprint, but some calculations are necessary to turn those values into information that the Blueprint can use to move the object.

Storing data with variables

The first step is to create the two variables we need: `Direction` and `Speed`. Find the panel labeled **My Blueprint**. You should see an empty category marker called **Variables**, with a + sign to the right. Click on that + sign to create your first variable.

In the **Details** panel, you will see a series of fields for editing your new variable. The four fields that we have to edit are the **Variable Name**, **Variable Type**, **Instance Editable**, and **Default Value** fields. We want our first variable to contain information about the speed of movement, so name the variable `Speed`. For **Variable Type**, we want a variable that can hold a number that represents our desired speed, so select **Float** from the drop-down menu.

Check the box next to **Instance Editable** to enable the variable to be changed outside of this Blueprint. This is useful for quickly adjusting the value to our liking once we start testing the moving target in the game. The **Default Value** category is likely to not have a field, but to feature a message asking you to compile the Blueprint first. Do that, and a field for entering an initial value will appear. Change the default value to `200.0`.

Using the same process, create a second variable called `Direction`. Choose **Vector** for **Variable Type**. **Vector** contains information about the **X**, **Y**, and **Z** coordinates, and in this case, we need to indicate the direction of change we want for the object movement. Make the direction variable **Instance Editable** and set **Default Value** to -10.0 for the **Y** axis:

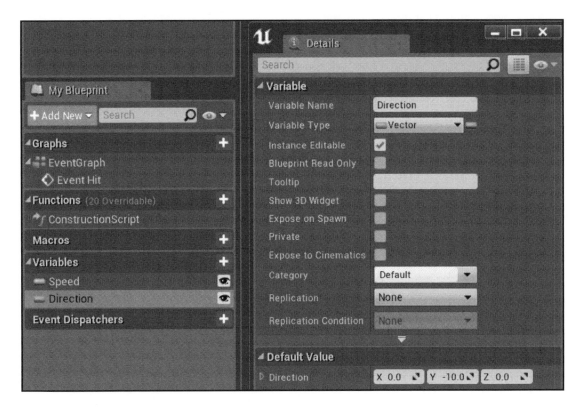

Readying direction for calculations

Now, let's explore the steps necessary to get the information we need to provide a movement instruction. It might look intimidating at first, but we will break down each section and see how each node fits into the larger goal.

The first calculation we need to perform is to take our vector value for direction and normalize it. Normalizing is a common procedure in vector math that ensures that the vector is converted to a length of one unit, which makes it compatible with the rest of our calculations. Fortunately, there is a Blueprint node that takes care of this for us.

Click on the **Direction** variable we created in the **My Blueprint** panel, and drag it to an empty space in **Event Graph**. A small popup appears, prompting you to select **GET** or **SET**. We want to retrieve the value we set for the direction, so let's choose **GET** to create a node containing the **Direction** variable's value. Click on the output pin of the **Direction** node, and drop it in empty graph space. Type normalize in the search field and select the **Normalize** node underneath the category-labeled vector. This connects your **Direction** variable to a node that automatically does the normalizing calculation for us:

 It is good practice to leave comments on the sets of Blueprints as you create them. Comments can help describe what a particular set of Blueprints is intended to accomplish, which can be helpful if you are returning to a Blueprint after some time and need to make sense of your prior work. To leave a comment on a Blueprint, click and drag a selection box around the nodes you want to create a comment around, in order to select them. Then, right-click on one of the selected nodes and select the bottom option, **Create Comment from Selection**.

Getting relative speed using delta time

To make our speed value relate to direction, we first need to multiply it by delta time. Delta time is based on the fact that the time taken between the frames of the gameplay can differ. By multiplying our speed value by delta seconds, we can ensure that the speed at which our object moves is the same, regardless of the game's frame rate.

To do this, drag the **Speed** variable onto **Event Graph** and choose **GET** to create the **Speed** node. Now, right-click on empty graph space and search for delta. Select the **Get World Delta Seconds** option to place the corresponding node on the **Event Graph**. Finally, drag the output pin from either the **Get World Delta Seconds** node or the **Speed** node, and drop it into an empty space. Type an asterisk in the search field (*Shift* + *8* on most computers) and select the **Float * Float** node.

Finally, drag and drop the other output pin onto the remaining input pin of the new multiplication node to multiply these two values, like this:

Translating the existing location

Now that we have a normalized vector direction and a speed value relative to time, we need to multiply these two values and then add them to the current location. First, find **StaticMeshComponent** from the **Components** panel and drag it onto **Event Graph**. This creates a node from which we can extract any data contained within **StaticMeshComponent** of the object.

Next, we want to get the Mesh Component's location. One of several ways to handle this is to look at the **Transform** properties of an object and extract the location from there. Click and drag the blue output pin into empty space, and then type Get World. Select the **GetWorldTransform** option to create the node. A Transform contains information about the rotation and scale of an object, in addition to its location. This is useful because we want to ensure that we preserve the rotation and scale of our target even as it is moving, and we need this data to create a Transform value from our new movement information.

Now, we want to break down the Transform into its Component parts so that we can use only the location in our calculations while preserving the rotation and scale. Drag the output pin from the **GetWorldTransform** node, and search for the **Break Transform** node to add to our graph. There is another way to access the Transform Components: you can right-click the output pin and select **Split Struct Pin**.

Now, we need to add the necessary nodes to add speed and direction to the location information we just extracted. Right-click on empty grid space, and then search for and select the **Make Transform** node. This marks the end of your calculations, so make sure that it is positioned to the right of all of your other nodes. The **Make Transform** node has three inputs: **Location**, **Rotation**, and **Scale**. The **Rotation** and **Scale** inputs should be connected to the **Rotation** and **Scale** output pins on the **Break Transform** node we created earlier.

Next, we need to multiply the **Direction** vector and the **Speed** float we calculated. Drag the output node of the **Normalize** node into empty space, and search using *. Select **Vector ***
Float and connect the green input pin to the output of the float multiplication node that we used with **Speed**.

Our final calculation step is to add **Speed** and **Direction** to the current location we calculated. Click on the yellow vector output pin of the new multiplication node, and then drag it into empty space. Search using + and select the **Vector + Vector** node. Ensure that one input pin of this addition node is connected to the previously mentioned vector multiplication node, and then connect the other input pin to the **Location** output pin of the **Break Transform** node. Finally, drag the output pin of our addition node onto the **Location** input pin of the **Make Transform** node. When you are finished, the result should look like this:

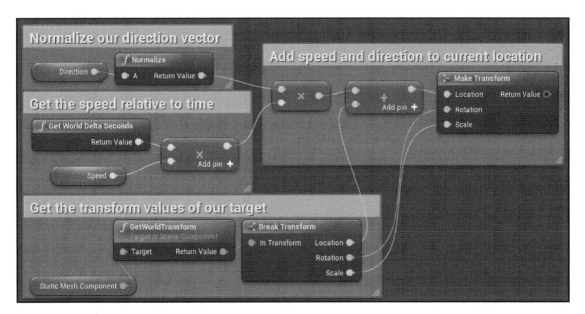

Updating location

Now that we have calculated the Transform, we can adjust the location of our target Actor by this value. We used delta time to make the Actor's speed and direction change consistent across frames, and as a consequence, we can simply use the **Event Tick** node to fire our move Action on every frame. Right-click on empty grid space, search for `Event Tick`, and place the node somewhere to the right of your **Make Transform** node.

To move the Actor, let's use the **SetActorTransform** node. Drag a wire from the execution pin of **Event Tick** to empty grid space, and search for `Set Actor Transform`. Place the node, and then connect the **Return Value** output pin on your **Make Transform** node to the **New Transform** input pin on the **SetActorTransform** node, as shown here:

Changing direction

If you were to compile the Blueprint, save, and play the game now, what would you expect to see? The target Cylinder would move according to our speed and direction as soon as the game began. However, since we don't have any instructions that cause the target to stop moving, it would proceed in the same direction for as long as the game runs, even moving through objects and out of the Level we created! To address this, we need logic that will change the target's direction periodically. This will result in a target that moves back and forth between two points regularly, much like a shooting gallery target.

To do this, we have to set up two nodes that will set the direction variable we created on two different values. Drag the direction variable into empty grid space and choose the **SET** option. This results in a node with *x*, *y*, and *z* axis fields. We can use them to change the value of the direction variable to be different from the initial default value that we gave it. We want two of these nodes, so once again, drag the direction variable into empty space, and then change the *y* axis values of the two nodes to 10.0 and −10.0 respectively.

Now, we need a way to switch between these two nodes so that the direction repeatedly shifts. The **FlipFlop** node was created for scenarios where we know we want to alternate between two sets of Actions that execute exactly once before switching each time. This fits our use case here, so right-click on empty grid space and search for FlipFlop. Select and place the node. Then, connect the **A** execution pin to one of the direction set node input pins, and the **B** execution pin to the other.

Finally, we need to ensure that there is some kind of delay between executing the direction shifts, otherwise, the direction will change for every frame and the object will go nowhere. To do so, drag the input execution pin of the **FlipFlop** node into empty space and search for the **Delay** node. This node allows us to set a delay duration in seconds that postpones the following execution commands by that length of time. Place this node before the **FlipFlop** node and give it a duration of 6 seconds. Placing this **Delay** node between our **Set Actor Transform** node and our **FlipFlop** node ensures that the direction switch enabled by **FlipFlop** only occurs every 6 seconds. The final product should look like what is shown in the following screenshot. Once you are done, remember to compile and save the Blueprint:

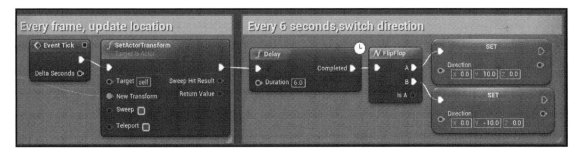

Testing moving targets

Now that we have updated our Blueprint, we can test to ensure that the `CylinderTarget` object moves as expected. First, we have to place the `CylinderTarget` object in a position that allows it to move along the *y* axis without bumping into other objects. The coordinates I used were 300 on the *x* axis, 500 on the *y* axis, and 220 on the *z* axis.

Note that these values only work relative to the default layout of the **First Person** template map. If you have made adjustments to your own Level, then you can adjust either the speed or the placement of the target in your Level, and test until you find a good patrol spot. Click on **Play**. If the Blueprint is functioning correctly, then you will see the Cylinder move back and forth between two points at a steady rate.

One of the advantages of using Blueprints is that they create a template of functionality that can be used across multiple objects in a scene. Find `CylinderTarget_Blueprint` in the `Blueprints` folder and drag it directly onto the 3D Viewport. You should see another Cylinder created, which inherits all of the functionality of our original Cylinder target. In this way, we can rapidly set up multiple moving targets using the single set of Blueprint logic we created.

Summary

In this chapter, we created a project and an initial Level using a first-person shooter template. We then set up a target object that reacts to the player's gunfire by changing its appearance. Finally, we set up a Blueprint that allows us to rapidly create moving targets. The skills we have learned about here will serve as a strong foundation for building more complex interactive behavior in later chapters, or even entire games of your own making.

You may wish to spend some additional time modifying your prototype to include a more appealing layout or feature faster moving targets. As we continue building our game experience, remember that you always have the opportunity to linger on a section and experiment with your own functionality or customization. One of the greatest benefits of Blueprint's visual scripting is the speed at which you can test new ideas, and each additional skill that you learn will unlock exponentially more possibilities for game experiences that you can explore and prototype.

In the next chapter, we will be looking more closely at the player controller that came with the **First Person** template. We will extend the existing Blueprint that governs player movement, and shoot with a gun that is tweaked to our liking and produces more interesting visual impacts and sound effects.

6
Enhancing Player Abilities

In this chapter, we will expand on the core shooting interaction that we created in Chapter 5, *Object Interaction with Blueprints*, by making modifications to the player character Blueprint. The player character Blueprint that comes with the **First Person** template initially looks complex, especially when compared to the relatively simple Cylinder target Blueprint that we have already created from scratch. We will be looking into this Blueprint and breaking it down to see how each of its sections contributes to the player's experience and allows them to control their character and shoot a gun.

It would be quick and easy to just use an existing asset that works, without spending time learning about how it accomplishes its functionality. However, we want to ensure that we can repair problems as they arise, as well as extend the functionality of the player controls to fit our needs better. For this reason, it is always advisable to take some time to investigate and learn about any external assets you might bring into a project that you are building.

By the end of this chapter, we want to succeed in modifying the player character, so that we can add the ability to sprint and destroy the objects we shoot with enjoyable explosions and sound effects. Along the way to achieving these goals, we will be covering the following topics:

- Player inputs and controls
- **Field of View (FOV)**
- Timelines and branching logic
- Adding sounds and particle effects to an object interaction

Adding the running functionality by extending a Blueprint

We'll begin our exploration of the `FirstPersonCharacter` Blueprint by adding simple functionality that will give our players more tactical options for moving around in the Level. At the moment, the player is limited to moving at a single speed. We can adjust this by using Blueprint nodes that listen for key presses and adjusting the movement speed attached to the **Character Movement** Component of the Blueprint.

Breaking down the Character Movement

Let's begin by opening the `FirstPersonCharacter` Blueprint, located in the same `Blueprints` folder as `CylinderTarget_Blueprint` from Chapter 5, *Object Interaction with Blueprints*. Find `FirstPersonCharacter` in **Content Browser** and double-click on the Blueprint. You will open **Event Graph** and see a large series of Blueprint nodes. The first group of nodes we will look at is bounded by the **Event Graph** comment labeled **Stick input**, as shown here:

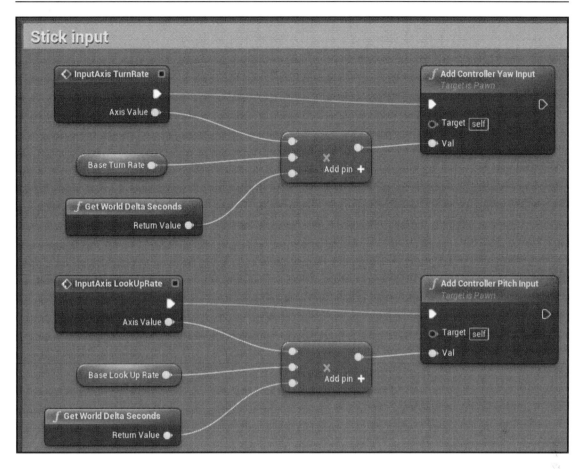

The red trigger nodes are triggered at every frame and pass the values of **TurnRate** and **LookUpRate** from a controller input. These values are most commonly mapped to the left/right and up/down axis triggers of an analog stick. Note that there are only two axis triggers. Detecting a look down or a turn left Event is covered by these very nodes and is represented as a negative number in **Axis Value** that is passed.

Then, the values from the two axis triggers are each multiplied by a variable, representing the base rate at which the player is intended to be able to turn around or look up or down. The values are also multiplied by the world delta seconds to normalize against varying frame rates, in spite of the triggers being called every frame. The value resulting from multiplying all the three inputs is then passed to the **Add Controller Pitch Input** and **Add Controller Yaw Input** Functions. These are the Functions that add translations between the controller input and the effect on the player camera.

Below the **Stick input** group of Blueprint nodes, there is another comment block, called **Mouse input**, and it looks quite similar to the **Stick input** group. **Mouse input** converts input from mouse movements (as opposed to controller axis sticks) into data, and then passes those values directly to the corresponding camera yaw and pitch input Functions, without needing the same kind of calculations that are necessary for analog input.

Now, let's look at the group of nodes that manage player movement, as shown in this screenshot:

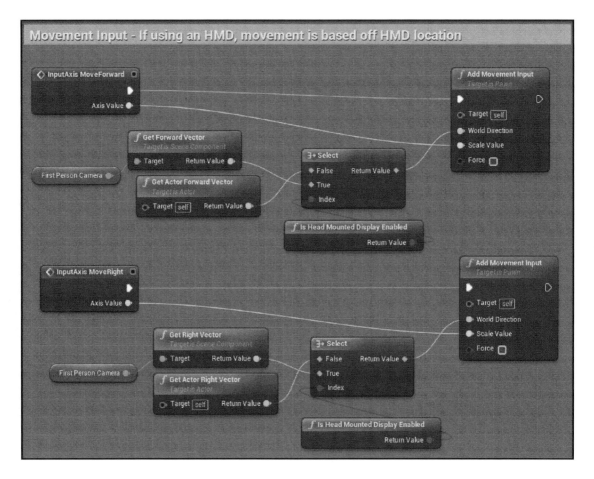

The **Select** nodes test whether the player is using a **virtual reality head-mounted display (VR HMD)**. If a VR HMD is enabled, then the vectors used are from **FirstPerson Camera**; if it isn't, then the vectors used are from the Actor root Component.

Functionally, the other nodes are set up similarly to the **Stick input** and **Mouse input** groups. The axis value is taken from the forward and right movement axis inputs on a controller or keyboard. Again, these nodes represent backward and left movements as well, in the form of negative values for the **Axis Value** outputs. The significant difference in movement translation is that we require the direction that the Actor is going to be moved in, so that the degree of movement can be applied in the correct direction. The direction is pulled from the **Get Actor Vector** nodes (both forward and right) and attached to the **World Direction** input of the **Add Movement Input** nodes.

The last movement-related group of nodes to look at is the node group contained within the comment block labeled **Jump**. This group is simply made up of a trigger node that detects the pressing and releasing of the key mapped to jumping and applies the Jump Function from when the button is pressed until it is released.

Customizing control inputs

We have seen how the **First Person** template has mapped certain player input Actions, such as moving forward or jumping, to Blueprint nodes in order to produce the behavior for the Actions. In order to create new kinds of behavior, we will have to map new physical control inputs to additional player Actions. To change the input settings for your game, click on the **Edit** button in the **Unreal Editor** menu, and select the **Project Settings** option. On the left side of the window that appears, look for the **Engine** category and select the **Input** option.

Inside the **Engine** category, in the **Input Settings** menu, you will see two sections under the **Bindings** category called **Action Mappings** and **Axis Mappings**. You may need to click the little triangle on the left of each section to show the existing mappings. **Action Mappings** is for keypress and mouse click Events that trigger player Actions. **Axis Mappings** is meant for mapping player movements and Events that have a range, such as the *W* key and *S* key both affecting the **Move Forward** Action, but on different ends of the range. Both our **Sprint** and **Zoom** Functions are simple Actions that are either active or inactive, so we will add them as **Action Mappings**.

Click on the + sign next to **Action Mappings** twice to add two new Action mappings. Name the first Action **Sprint**, and select the **Left Shift** key from the drop-down menu to map that key to your **Sprint** Event. Name the second Action **Zoom**, and map it to **Right Mouse Button**. The changes are saved when you close the window.

Your **Action Mappings** inputs should match what is shown in the following screenshot:

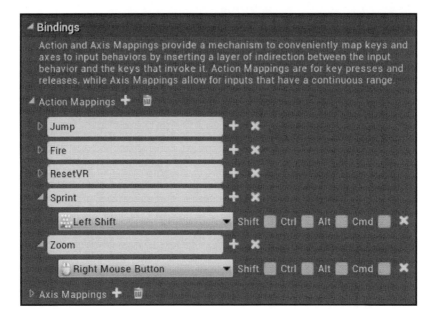

Adding a Sprint ability

Now that we have a basic understanding of how the movement input nodes take the controller input and apply it to our in-game character, we'll extend that functionality with a **Sprint** ability. We'll set up a new series of nodes within the `FirstPersonCharacter` Blueprint. They will look like this:

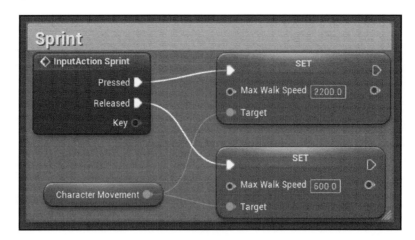

First, we will need to create a trigger that will activate our **Sprint** Action. Recall that we previously mapped the **Sprint** Action to the **Left Shift** key. To access that input trigger, right-click on the empty grid space to the left of the other movement Functions and search for Sprint. Select the **InputAction Sprint** Event to place the node.

Now, we want to modify the movement speed of the player. If you try adding a new node and searching for speed with context-sensitive search turned on, you will find only those nodes that are meant for retrieving the maximum speed and checking whether it is being exceeded. Neither of these will help you set the maximum speed of the player. To accomplish this, we need to retrieve a value from the **Character Movement** Component attached to the FirstPersonCharacter Actor. Look at the **Components** panel of the Editor and select **CharacterMovement (Inherited)**. The **Details** panel should change to show a long series of variables, as seen in the following screenshot:

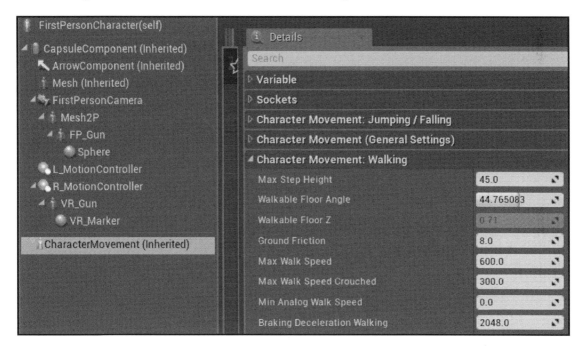

In this list of variables, you can find **Max Walk Speed** in the **Walking** category. This is the value that determines the maximum speed at which the player can move, and it should be the target of our **Sprint** Function. However, changing the value in the **Details** panel from the default of 600 would modify the player's movement speed consistently, regardless of whether **Left Shift** was being pressed or not. Instead, we want to pull this value out of the **Character Movement** Component and into our Blueprint's **Event Graph**. To do so, click on the Component in the **Components** panel and drag it onto **Event Graph**, near our **Left Shift** trigger. This will produce a **Character Movement** node, as seen in this screenshot:

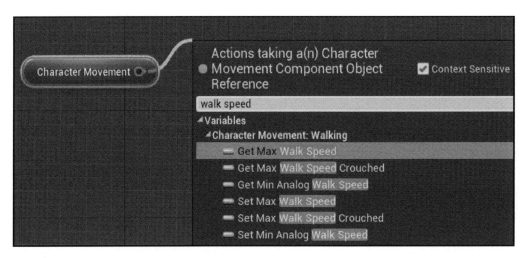

Click and drag the output pin from the **Character Movement** node to empty grid space, ensure that you have **Context Sensitive** checked, and type walk speed. This time, the **Set Max Walk Speed** Action will appear. Select it to connect the **Character Movement** node to the new node, setting the maximum walk speed value. Connect the **Pressed** output execution pin from the **InputAction Sprint** trigger to the input execution pin of the **Set Max Walk Speed** node, in order to enable you to press **Left Shift** to modify the maximum movement speed. Finally, change the **Max Walk Speed** value within the node from 0.0 to 2200, in order to provide a nice boost of speed over the default of 600.

We also need to ensure that the player slows down again once the *Shift* key is released. To do so, drag the output pin from the **Character Movement** node again, and then search for and select another **Set Max Walk Speed** node to place it on **Event Graph**. This time, connect the **Released** output execution pin of the **InputAction Sprint** node to the input execution pin of the new node. Then, change the **Max Walk Speed** value from 0.0 to the default of 600. To keep up with our good commenting practice, click and make a selection box around all four of our nodes, right-click on one of the selected nodes, and select **Create Comment from Selection** to label the group of nodes as **Sprint**.

Now, compile, save, and press **Play** to test your work. You should notice a significant boost in speed as long as you press down the **Left Shift** key.

Animating a zoomed view

A core element of modern first-person shooters is a variable FOV in the form of a player's ability to look down the scope of a gun to get a closer view of a target. This is a significant contributor to the feeling of accuracy and control that modern shooters provide. Let's add a simple form of this functionality to our prototype.

In an empty section of the grid next to your **Mouse input** nodes, right-click, search for zoom, and add an **InputAction Zoom** trigger node. We want to modify the FOV value that is contained within the **First Person Camera** Component, so we go to the **Components** panel and drag **First Person Camera** out onto **Event Graph**.

Drag the output pin into empty grid space, search for the **Set Field Of View** node, and place it. Lowering the FOV gives the effect of zooming into a narrower area in the center of the screen. Since the Default FOV value is set to 90, for our zoom, let's set the FOV in the set node to 45, like this:

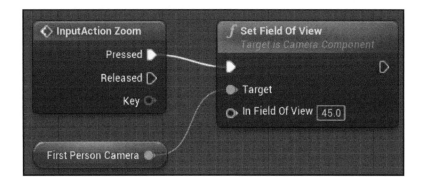

Click and drag the output execution pin from the right-click trigger node to the input execution pin of the set node. Compile, save, and click on **Play**. You will notice that when you are playing the game and press the right mouse button, the FOV will snap to a narrow, zoomed-in view. Any instance where the main camera snaps from one position to another can be jarring for a player, so we will have to modify this behavior further. Also, the FOV does not reverse when the key is released. We will solve both problems using a timeline.

Using a timeline to smooth transitions

To change the FOV smoothly, we will need to create an animation that shows a gradual change in the Actor over time. To do so, return to **Event Graph** of the FirstPersonCharacter Blueprint.

Press *Alt* and click on the **Pressed** output execution pin of the **InputAction Zoom** node to break the connection. Drag a new wire out from **Pressed** to empty grid space. Search for and select **Add Timeline** to add a timeline node. A timeline will allow us to change a value (such as the FOV on a camera) over a designated amount of time.

 There are different ways of accomplishing animations in Unreal Engine 4. Timelines are perfect for simple value changes, such as the rotation of a door. For more complex, character-based, or cinematic animations, you would want to look into **Sequencer**, which is the engine's built-in animation system. **Sequencer** and complex animations are out of the scope of this book, but there are many dedicated learning resources available for using **Sequencer**. I recommend starting with the Unreal documentation, which is available at https://docs.unrealengine.com/en-us/Engine/Sequencer.

To change the value within the timeline, double-click on the **Timeline_0** node. This will open up the **Timeline Editor**. You will see four buttons in the top-left corner of the **Editor**. Each of these will add a different kind of value that can be changed over the course of the timeline. Because FOV is represented by a numerical value, we will want to click on the button with the **f** label (**Add Float Track**). Doing so will add a track to the timeline and prompt you to name this track. Let's label this as **Field Of View**. We will now have to edit the values over different time intervals, as shown here:

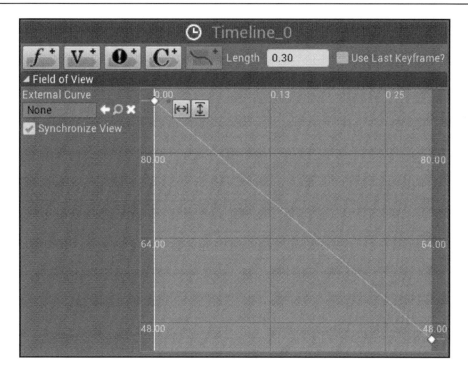

To accomplish this, hold down *Shift* and click on a point that is close to the **0.0** point on the graph. You will see the **Time** and **Value** fields appear in the top-left part of the graph. These allow precision tuning of our timeline. Ensure that the time is set to exactly 0.0 and set the value to 90, our default FOV. If the point disappears from the view, you can use the two small buttons in the top-left of the graph to zoom into the graph so that the point becomes visible.

We want the zoom animation to be quick, so at the top of the **Timeline Editor**, find the field next to **Length** and change to value to 0.3 to limit the range of the animation to 0.3 seconds. Now, press *Shift* and click at the end of the light gray area of the graph. Fine-tune the fields to 0.3 for **Time** and 45 for **Value**:

Notice how the line that represents the value gradually slopes down from 90 degrees to 45 degrees. This means that when this animation is called, the player's FOV will smoothly transition from being zoomed out to being zoomed in, rather than a jarring switch between the two values. This is the advantage of using timelines over changing the values directly with a set value Blueprint.

Now, return to **Event Graph**. We want to connect our timeline into our set FOV operation, just like what is shown in this screenshot:

Drag the new **Field Of View** output pin to the **Field Of View** field in the **Set** node, overriding your value of 45. Now, link the **Update** output execution pin from the **Timeline** node to the **Set** node. This sets up the Functions so that every time the FOV value is updated, it passes the new value to the **Set Field Of View** Function. Because of our timeline setup, many values between 90 and 45 will be passed to set, enabling a gradual transition between the two extremes over 0.3 seconds.

Finally, we want the zooming to end when the right mouse button is released. To do this, drag the **Released** pin from the **InputAction Zoom** node to the **Reverse** pin of the **Timeline** node. This will cause the timeline animation to play in reverse order when the right mouse button is released, ensuring that we have a smooth transition back to our normal camera view. Also, remember to apply a comment to the node group so that you remember what this functionality does if you revisit it later.

Now, compile, save, and play to test the transition in and out of your zoom view by holding down the right mouse button.

Increasing the projectile's speed

Now that we have given the player character a new gameplay option to navigate the world, our focus will be back to the shooting mechanics. Right now, the shots fired from the gun on the controller are spheres that slowly arc through the air. We want to better approximate the fast-moving bullets that we are used to in traditional shooters.

To change the properties of **Projectile**, we need to open the Blueprint called `FirstPersonProjectile`, which is located in the same `Blueprints` folder as `FirstPersonCharacter`. Once opened, look at the **Components** panel and click on **Projectile**. This is a projectile movement Component that has been added onto our sphere mesh and collider to define how the sphere will travel once it is created in the world.

In the **Details** panel, you will see that **Projectile** is made up of a long series of values that can be modified relative to movement. We are interested in only a couple of these at this time:

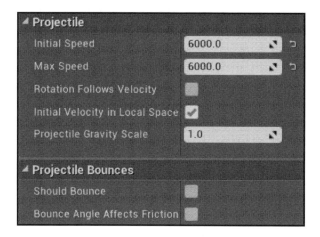

First, find the **Initial Speed** and **Max Speed** fields, which are currently set to 3000. **Initial Speed** determines how fast the projectile travels when it is first created at the tip of our gun, and **Max Speed** determines how fast it can reach if an additional force is applied to it after creation. If we had a rocket, we might wish to apply acceleration to the rocket after it is launched to signify the thruster engaging. However, since we are representing a bullet coming from a gun, it makes more sense to make its initial speed the fastest that the bullet will ever travel at. Adjust both **Initial Speed** and **Max Speed** to twice their original value: 6000.

Additionally, you might have noticed that the current projectile bounces off walls and objects as if it were a rubber ball. However, we want to mimic a harder and more forcefully impacting projectile. To remove the bouncing, look for the **Projectile Bounces** section in the **Details** panel and uncheck the box next to **Should Bounce**. The other values dictate the way in which the projectile bounces only if **Should Bounce** is checked, so there is no need to adjust them. One last change to make in **Event Graph** is to connect the **False** pin of the **Branch** node to the **DestroyActor** Function so that the projectile is always Destroyed when it collides with anything.

Now, compile, save, and click on **Play**. You will find that shooting the gun results in a much further-reaching projectile, which behaves more like a bullet, and that the projectile does not bounce off the walls anymore.

Adding sound and particle effects

Now that we have the player moving and shooting to our liking, let's turn our attention to the enemy targets. Shooting one of the target Cylinders currently results in it changing its color to red. However, there is nothing that the player can currently do to destroy a target outright.

We can add more dynamics to our enemy interaction by producing Blueprint logic that destroys the target if it is shot more than once, while also increasing the reward for the player by producing a satisfying sound and visual effect once the target is Destroyed.

Changing target states with branches

Since we want to generate effects that will be triggered by changes in the state applied to our target Cylinder, we have to ensure that this logic is contained within our CylinderTarget Blueprint. Open the Blueprint in your Blueprints folder, and take a look at the node group connected to the **Event Hit**. Right now, when our projectile hits the Cylinder object, these nodes tell it to swap to a red material. To add the ability to change how the Cylinder behaves when it is shot more than once, we will need to add a check to our Blueprints to count the number of times the Cylinder has been hit, and then trigger a different result, depending on its state.

Let's take a look at a setup that could help us handle this scenario:

To create conditional logic with multiple outcomes in Blueprints, we will take advantage of the **Branch** node. This node takes a Boolean variable as an input. Since Boolean values can only be either **True** or **False**, the **Branch** node can produce only two outcomes. These two outcomes can be executed by linking additional nodes to the two output execution pins, representing the **True** path and the **False** path.

The first step of creating **Branch** is to determine what will be represented by your Boolean, and what will cause the conditional value to change from **False** to **True**. In our case, we want to create a Primed state that shows that the target has been hit and that it could be Destroyed with a second hit. Let's go ahead and create a Primed Boolean variable.

Recall that variables are defined in the **My Blueprint** panel. You should already see our previously defined variables for Speed and Direction. Click on the + button to add a new variable. Set the **Variable Type** as Boolean. Give the name Primed to the new variable and check the box labeled **Instance Editable** to make this value easier to modify externally. Finally, compile and save the Blueprint. Because we do not want our targets to be in a Primed state before they have been hit for the first time, we will leave the default value of our variable as **False** (represented by an unchecked box).

Now that you have a Primed Boolean variable, drag it from the **My Blueprint** panel to **Event Graph**, and select the **Get** option that appears in the submenu on release. This will grab **True** or **False** state data from the variable and enable us to use it to **Branch** our Blueprints. Click and drag a red wire from the output pin of the new Primed node to empty grid space on **Event Graph**. Search for and add the **Branch** node.

Finally, we can add **Branch** to our **Event Hit** Blueprint group. Break the connection between the **Cast To FirstPersonProjectile** and **Set Material** nodes by holding down the *Alt* key and clicking on one of the execution pins. Drag the **Set Material** node out of the way for a moment, and then connect the output execution pin to the input execution pin of the **Branch** node. This Blueprint will now call the **Branch** evaluation every time the target Cylinder is hit by a projectile.

Now that we have our **Branch** node set up for activation, we need to provide the target Cylinder with instructions on what to do in each state. The targets we want to create can be described as being in one of these three states at any time: Default, Primed, or Destroyed. Since a destroyed Actor can't execute any behavior, there is no way to develop any behavior that happens after the target is Destroyed. As a consequence, we really have to concern ourselves with only the primed and the pre-primed Default states.

Let's handle the Default state first. Since this **Branch** dictates what happens to the Cylinder in each state after it has been hit, we want to execute the **Material** change that we previously attached to the Event. If the target has not yet been hit, and it has now been hit for the first time, we have to change **Material** to **TargetRed**. Additionally, we will also have to set our Primed Boolean variable to **True**. This way, when the target is hit again, the **Branch** node will route the behavior to the other execution sequence. The **False** execution sequence of nodes will look like this:

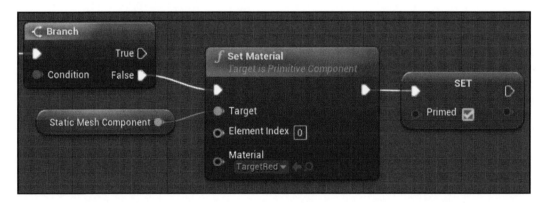

Drag the **Set Material** node you moved aside before to the right of the **Branch** node, and then connect the **False** output execution pin of the **Branch** node to the **Set Material** node's input execution pin. Now, drag the Primed variable from the **My Blueprint** panel to **Event Graph**, and select the **SET** option. Connect this node to the **Set Material** node's output execution pin, and click on the checkbox next to Primed within the **SET** node. This will ensure that the next time **Target** is hit, **Branch** evaluates to **True**.

Triggering sound effects, explosions, and destruction

The next step is to define the sequence of actions that will be triggered from the **True** path of the **Branch** node. Earlier, we identified three things we wanted to accomplish when destroying a target. These were hearing an explosion, seeing an explosion, and actually removing the target object from the game world. We'll start with the often undervalued, but always critical, element of satisfying game experiences: sound.

The most basic interaction we can design with sound is to play a `.wav` sound file at a location in the game world once, and this will work perfectly for our purpose. Drag a wire from the **True** execution node of the **Branch** node to empty grid space, and search for the **Play Sound at Location** node:

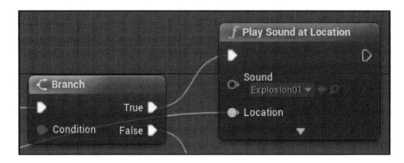

Play Sound at Location is a simple node that takes a **Sound** file input and a **Location** input, and then—as you might have guessed—plays the sound at that location. There are several sound files included in the default assets we brought into this project, and you can see the list of these by clicking on the drop-down menu underneath the **Sound** input. Find and select **Explosion01** to set an explosion **Sound** effect.

Now that we have set **Sound**, we need to determine where the sound will play. We can use a process similar to the one we used to set the FOV by taking the Static Mesh Component of the Cylinder target, extracting its location value, and then linking that location vector directly to our **Sound** node. However, the **Event Hit** trigger will make this process easier on us.

One of the many output pins on the **Event Hit** node is called **Hit Location**. This pin contains the location in the space where the two objects evaluated by **Event Hit** collide with one another. The location of our projectile hitting the target is a perfectly reasonable place to generate the explosion effect, so go ahead and drag a wire from **Hit Location** on the **Event Hit** node to the **Location** input pin on **Play Sound at Location**.

Compile, save, and play to test the Blueprint. Shooting one of the moving targets once will cause it to turn red. Every hit after that should produce an explosion sound effect.

Now that we have set up the sound of our explosion, let's add the visual effect and destroy the Cylinder, using the following setup:

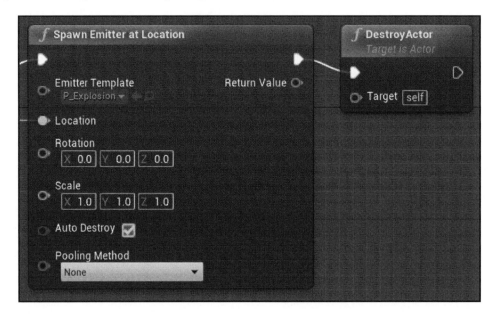

Drag a wire from the output execution node of **Play Sound at Location** to empty grid space. Search for and select the **Spawn Emitter at Location** node.

 An emitter is an object that will produce particle effects in a particular location. Particle effects are collections of small objects that combine to create the visual effect of objects that are fluid, gaseous, or otherwise intangible, such as waterfall impacts, explosions, or light beams.

The **Spawn Emitter at Location** node looks similar to the **Sound** node we are attaching it to, but with more input parameters and the **Auto Destroy** toggle. In the drop-down menu beneath **Emitter Template**, find and select the **P_Explosion** effect. This is another asset that came packed with the standard assets we pulled into our project and will produce a satisfying-looking explosion wherever its emitter is attached.

Since we want the explosion to be generated in the same location as the sound of the explosion, we will click and drag the same **Hit Location** pin of the **Event Hit** node over into the **Location** pin of **Spawn Emitter at Location**. The explosion is a 3D effect that looks the same from all angles, so we can leave the **Rotation** input alone. The toggle for **Auto Destroy** determines whether or not the emitter can be triggered more than once. We will destroy the Actor that contains this emitter once this particle effect is created, so we can leave the toggle box checked.

Finally, we want to remove the target Cylinder from the game world after the sound and visual explosion effects are played. Drag the output execution pin from the **Spawn Emitter at Location** node and drop it into empty grid space. Search for and add the **DestroyActor** node. This node takes only a single target input, which defaults to **self**. Since this Blueprint contains the Cylinder objects we want to destroy and **self** is exactly what we want to destroy, we can leave this node as is.

Extend the comment box around the entire **Event Hit** sequence of nodes, and update the text to describe what the new sequence accomplishes. I chose When hit, turn red and set to primed. If already primed, destroy self. The final result of this chain of Blueprints should look similar to the following screenshot:

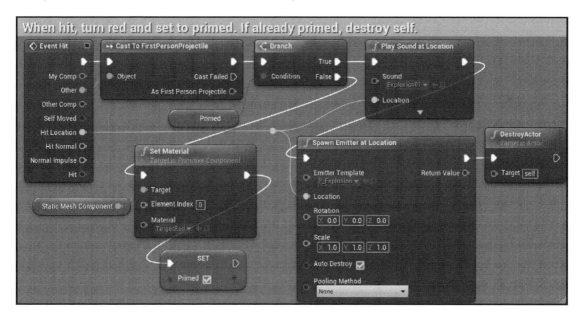

Once you have left a useful comment around the Blueprint nodes, compile, save, and click on **Play** to test the new interactions. You should see and hear the Cylinders explode once they have been shot twice by the player's gun.

Summary

We've now started going down the path of making our game feel satisfying to the player. We have added sound and visual effects, a player character that has most of the capabilities we would expect from a modern shooter, and targets that react to the player's interactions. The skills we have covered in the first chapters have been combined to start creating increasingly complex and interesting behavior.

In this chapter, we created some customized player controls to allow sprinting and zooming in with our gun. In the process, we explored how the movement controller translates information from a player's inputs into the game experience. We also opened the door to creating simple animations using timelines. Then, we added more feedback to the player's interaction with the environment by attaching an explosion effect and sound to the enemy targets, as well as adding another requirement for them to be hit by two projectiles.

In the next chapter, we will explore adding a UI to our game that provides the player with feedback on their state relative to the world.

Creating Screen UI Elements 7

At the core of any gaming experience is the method the game designers use to communicate the goals and rules of the game to the player. One method of doing this, which is common across all forms of games, is through the use of a **Graphical User Interface (GUI)** to display and broadcast important information to the player. In this chapter, we will set up a GUI that will track the player's health, stamina, and ammo, and we will set up a counter that will display the objectives to the player. You will learn about how to set up a basic **User Interface (UI)** using Unreal's GUI Editor and how to use Blueprints to tie that interface to gameplay values. We will create UI elements using the **Unreal Motion Graphics UI Designer (UMG)**.

In the process, we will cover the following topics:

- Creating simple UI meters with UMG
- Connecting UI values to player variables
- Tracking the ammo and eliminated targets

Creating simple UI meters with UMG

The creation of UI elements is done in the UMG, which is a visual UI authoring tool. We can use the UMG to create a menu and game **Heads-Up Display (HUD)**. A HUD is a kind of transparent display that provides information without requiring the user to look away. We want to show meters on the HUD with the amounts of health, stamina, and ammo the player currently possesses. These meters that appear on the HUD are known as **UI meters**.

To create a HUD that will display the UI meters for health, stamina, and ammo, we will first need to create variables within the player character that can track these values. Before doing so, ensure that the box labeled **Instance Editable** is checked so that other Blueprints and objects can manipulate the variables. When a variable is made editable, it will be shown with a yellow open eye symbol next to its name in the **Variables** section of the **My Blueprint** panel. Now, to create simple UI meters, follow these steps:

1. Open the `FirstPersonCharacter` Blueprint from the `Blueprints` folder of your project. Within the Blueprint, we are going to define variables that will represent additional states that the player and game will care about.
2. Find the **Variables** category of the **My Blueprint** panel in the Blueprint Editor. Click on the **+** sign to add another variable, and call it `PlayerHealth`.
3. With `PlayerHealth` selected, find the **Details** panel and change **Variable Type** to **Float**.
4. Follow the same steps again to create a second **Float** variable called `PlayerStamina`.
5. Next, create a third variable, but this time, select the **Integer** variable as **Variable Type** and call it `PlayerCurrentAmmo`.
6. Finally, create a second **Integer** variable called `TargetKillCount` and compile the Blueprint. The result of the player variables should look like this:

Now, we need to set the default values of our four new variables. We can do so by clicking on each of these variables and changing the field under **Default Value** in the **Details** panel. I set `PlayerCurrentAmmo` to `30` and `TargetKillCount` to `0`, but you can tweak the default values to whatever you think is appropriate for your desired game experience at any time. `PlayerHealth` and `PlayerStamina` should both be set to `1.0`, as we will represent those with UI meters that will display the degree of fullness between `0` and `1`. Once you have set the defaults, compile and save your Blueprint.

Now, we will learn about how to draw shapes that represent UI meters.

Drawing shapes with Widget Blueprints

The UMG Editor uses a specialized type of Blueprint called a **Widget Blueprint**. Since the **First Person** template has no UI elements by default, we should create a new folder to store our GUI work. Follow these steps to create a folder and a Widget Blueprint:

1. Return to the `FirstPersonExampleMap` tab and navigate to the **Content Browser** panel.
2. Open the `FirstPersonBP` folder, right-click in empty grid space next to the list of folders, and select the **New Folder** option. Let's keep things simple and call this folder `UI`.
3. Open the `UI` folder you just made, and then right-click in empty folder space. Go to **User Interface | Widget Blueprint** and name the resulting Blueprint `HUD`.
4. Double-click on this Blueprint to open the UMG Editor. We will use this tool to define how our UI is going to look on the screen.
5. In the UMG Editor, find the panel labeled **Palette**. Inside it, open the category named **Panel**. You will see a series of containers listed that can organize the UI information.
6. Select and drag **Horizontal Box** out of the **Palette** panel onto the **Hierarchy** panel, releasing it on top of the `Canvas Panel` object.

7. You should now see a **Horizontal Box** object nested underneath the Canvas Panel object in **Hierarchy**. Our immediate goal is to create two labeled Player Stats Bars using a combination of vertical boxes, text, and progress bars. The final setup will look like this:

8. Two vertical boxes will contain the text and progress bars of our Player Stats UI. Look again at the **Panel** category within the **Palette** panel, and then drag the **Vertical Box** object onto the **Horizontal Box** object you created in **Hierarchy**. Do this a second time so that the two vertical boxes are aligned underneath **Horizontal Box**.

9. To keep things organized, let's apply labels to our objects. Click on **Horizontal Box** and look at the **Details** panel on the right side of the Editor. Change the top field, which shows the label of **Horizontal Box**, to Player Stats:

10. Using the same method, change the labels of the two vertical boxes underneath `Player Stats` to `Player Stats Text` and `Player Stats Bars`.

11. Now, look under the **Common** category of the **Palette** panel to find the textboxes and progress bars we need to create the UI. Drag two **Text** objects onto your `Player Stats Text` object, and two `Progress Bar` objects onto `Player Stats Bars`.

We already have the UI elements that will be used to display `Player Stats` in our HUD. The next step is to adjust their appearance and their positions on the screen.

Customizing the meter's appearance

Now, we want to adjust the UI elements and place them on the screen. Select the `Player Stats` object from **Hierarchy** and look at the central graph panel. You will see some size controls that allow you to manipulate the size of the selected objects. Resize the elements so that you can see two sets of the words **Text Block** and two tiny gray progress bars stacked on top of each other.

The large rectangular outline in the **Graph** view represents the boundaries of the screen that the player will see, which is called the **canvas**. This is the `Canvas Panel` object that is at the top level of **Hierarchy**. Elements positioned toward the top-left corner of the canvas will appear in the top-left corner of the in-game screen. Since we want our health and stamina bars to appear in the top-left corner, make sure that the `Player Stats` object is still selected and move the entire group close to, but not touching, the top-left corner of the canvas.

Next, take a look at the **Hierarchy** panel again. Select the top progress bar underneath `Player Stats Bars`. In the **Details** panel, change the top label field to `Health bar`. Then, find the **Size** toggle under the **Slot** category, and click on the **Fill** button to adjust the vertical height of the bar. Finally, find **Fill Color and Opacity** under **Appearance**, and set the color to a shade of red.

Now, let's repeat this operation for the player's stamina. Click on the second progress bar. In the **Details** panel, click on the **Fill** button and set the progress bar's label to `Stamina Bar`. Find **Fill Color and Opacity** and adjust the color to something similar to green. Finally, click on the `Player Stats Bars` vertical box, and then on the **Fill** button, to scale the horizontal size of both the bars.

We have our meters looking as we want them to, so now, let's adjust the text labels. Click on the first text bar underneath Player Stats Text in the **Hierarchy** panel. In the **Details** panel, change the **Text** field under the **Content** category to Health, and click on the **Align Right** button next to **Horizontal Align** to position the text against the bar. If you wish to change the font size or style, then you can adjust it from the **Font** drop-down menus and fields underneath the **Appearance** category. After you have adjusted Health, click on the second textbox object. Change the **Text** field of this one to Stamina, click on the **Align Right** button, and adjust the font size and style to your liking.

The final bit of adjustment to make is to anchor the meters to a side of the screen. Since screen sizes and ratios can vary, we want to ensure that our UI elements remain in the same relative position on the screen. **Anchors** are used to define a Widget's desired position on a canvas, regardless of the screen size. To establish an anchor for our meters, select the Player Stats top-level object and then click on the **Anchors** drop-down on the **Details** panel. Select the first option that appears, which shows a gray rectangle in the top-left corner of the screen, as shown in the following screenshot:

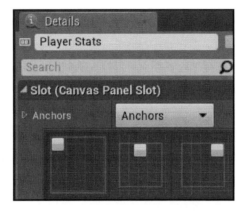

This will anchor our meters to that corner, ensuring that they will always appear in the top-left corner, regardless of the resolution or ratio. If you want to add more nuances to the anchors, then you can click on the expansion arrow to the left of **Anchors** to expose the precision transform controls. By using this, you will have the ability to anchor an object to any point on the canvas. You can also accomplish the same effect by dragging the eight-leaved white flower shape that appears when you set an anchor at the location where you would like the anchor to be on the canvas.

You can now adjust the size and position of the Player Stats group of objects within the **Canvas** panel to mimic how you want them to appear in your game. The final product should look something like this:

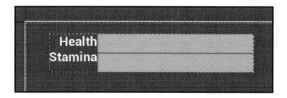

We conclude the customization of the player stats UI elements. Now, we need some UI elements to display the ammo and enemy counters.

Creating ammo and enemy counters

Now that we have a display for Player Stats, let's work on our ammo counter and gameplay goal displays. Both of these will work in a similar way to our player statistics meters, except that we want to represent their values through text rather than a continuous meter.

To begin the setup, drag two additional **Horizontal Box** objects down from **Palette** to the Canvas Panel object in the **Hierarchy** panel. Rename these horizontal boxes to Weapon Stats and Goal Tracker by clicking on the **Horizontal Box** in the **Hierarchy** panel and changing the top field in the **Details** panel that appears.

Now, drag two **Text** objects onto Weapon Stats. Select the first text object, and change both its name and the **Text** value under **Content** to be Ammo : (including the space and colon). In order to ensure that the size of this display matches the meter text, set the font **Size** to 24. You can leave all other values untouched for now.

Next, select the second text object and change its name to Ammo Left. This value is going to change as ammo is used, but we should give it some default. Since we have set the default of our ammo variable on the player Blueprint to be 30, go ahead and change the **Text** value of Ammo Left to 30 as well.

Finally, let's adjust the position of our ammo tracker. Click on the **Weapon Stats** object, and then drag the box on the **Graph** panel toward the top-right corner of the canvas. You will need to resize the box until Ammo :30 can be fully seen inside the containing box. The last step will be to set the anchors on the Weapon Stats object in the top-right corner, which is the third option provided in the **Anchors** drop-down menu in the **Details** panel:

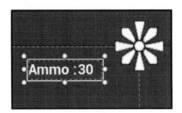

We can now replicate this procedure for the goal tracker. Drag two additional **Text** objects onto the Goal Tracker object in **Hierarchy**. Change the first text object's name and **Text** value to be Targets Eliminated :. Label the second text object Target Count and set its text value to a default of 0.

Knowing what goal the player is working against is one of the most important pieces of information that a game can convey. We can reflect this by giving our Goal Tracker a larger font size than the rest of the UI. Set the font size of both text objects to 32 to give the goal tracker more prominence on the screen.

Finally, adjust the size and position of the Goal Tracker object so that all the text can be seen and is positioned in the top-center of the Canvas panel. Leave a little additional space to the right side of 0 so that the Goal Tracker container has room to display multi-digit numbers. Then, set the anchor point of Goal Tracker to be in the top center by selecting the second option from the **Anchors** drop-down menu:

With the UI elements aligned the way we want them, we now need to ensure that the game will actually know how to display the HUD. To do this, we need to revisit the character Blueprint.

Displaying the HUD

To display the HUD, follow these steps:

1. Return to the `FirstPersonExampleMap` tab and **Content Browser**. Find and open the `FirstPersonCharacter` **Blueprint** in the `Blueprints` folder.

2. In **Event Graph**, right-click on any empty grid space to open **Context Menu**, and then search for **Event BeginPlay** and click on it. The Editor will move to the position in **Event Graph** where **Event BeginPlay** is already placed.

3. Press the *Alt* key and click on the white pin of **Event BeginPlay** to disconnect it. Move the **Event BeginPlay** node to the left.

> In most cases, **Event BeginPlay** will call the subsequent Actions as soon as the game is started. If the Actor the Blueprint is attached to isn't present when the game starts, then instead, it will trigger as soon as the Actor is spawned. Since the `FirstPersonCharacter` player object is present as soon as the game begins, attaching our Blueprint logic to this trigger will spawn the HUD immediately.

4. Drag a wire from the output execution pin of **Event BeginPlay**, and add a **CreateWidget** node. Within the node, you will see a drop-down menu labeled **Class**. This is our opportunity to use the Widget Blueprint we created. Recall that we named our Widget Blueprint as `HUD`. If you open the drop-down menu, then you will see the **HUD** option. Select it to have the player character Blueprint generate the UI elements you created. The following screenshot shows the **Create HUD Widget** node associated with our HUD Widget Blueprint:

5. Although we now have a Widget generated when the game starts, there is a final step required to get the Widget containing our UI elements to actually appear on the screen. Drag the **Return Value** output pin into empty grid space, and add an **Add to Viewport** node.

6. This will link the Widget information to the display the player sees when interacting with the game. The output execution pin should automatically connect with the new node, completing our Blueprint chain.

7. Delete the previous nodes that were connected to **Event BeginPlay** because they deal with the case of playing the game in VR and we will not use VR in this example game.

8. Create a comment for yourself around the three nodes. Label the comment as Draw HUD on Screen. The final product should appear as follows:

9. Now, compile, save, and click on **Play** to test the game. You should see the two meters representing the player's health and stamina, as well as numerical counters for ammo and eliminated targets. But as you shoot from your gun, you may notice one very important problem: none of the UI values change! We will address this missing Component in the next section.

Connecting UI values to player variables

To allow our UI elements to pull data from our player variables, we need to revisit the HUD Widget Blueprint. Navigate to the FirstPersonExampleMap tab, go to the **Content Browser** panel, and open the HUD Widget Blueprint in the UI folder.

In order to get our UI to update with Player Stats, we will create a **binding**. Bindings give us the ability to tie Functions or properties of a Blueprint to a Widget. Whenever the property or Function is updated, that change is reflected in the Widget automatically. So, instead of manually updating both the player's health stats and our Widget every time the player takes damage (so that the health meter display changes), we can tie the meter to a player value: health. Then, only one value will need to be updated.

Creating bindings for health and stamina

To create the binding of the health variable with the Health bar UI, follow these steps:

1. In the HUD Blueprint Editor, find the **Hierarchy** panel and click on the Health bar object nested underneath the Player Stats Bars object.

2. With Health bar now selected, locate the **Percent** field in the **Progress** category of the **Details** panel. Click on the **Bind** button next to **Percent** and select **Create Binding**, as shown in this screenshot:

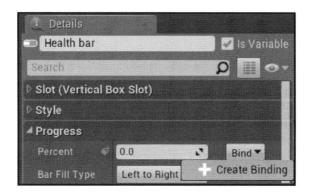

3. The HUD Editor will switch from the **Designer** view to the **Graph** view. A new Function has been created, allowing us to script a connection between the meter and the player's health variable. Right-click on any empty graph space, and add a **Get Player Character** node.

4. Drag a wire from the **Return Value** output pin of the new node to empty space, and add the **Cast To FirstPersonCharacter** node.

5. Break the execution pin connection between the **Get Healthbar Percent** 0 and **Return Node** nodes, and instead, connect **Get Healthbar Percent** to our casting node, as shown here:

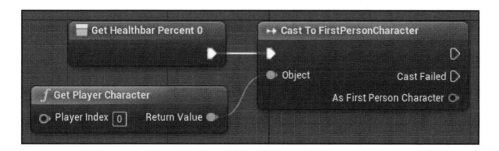

This combination of nodes retrieves the player character object for use within the HUD Blueprint. However, any custom Functions or variables we created for the player character in the `FirstPersonCharacter` Blueprint will remain off limits until we cast the player character object to the `FirstPersonCharacter` Blueprint. Remember that casting works to check and ensure that the input object is the specific object you are casting to. So, the preceding combination of nodes is essentially saying that *if the player character is a FirstPersonCharacter, then allow me to access the FirstPersonCharacter functions and variables tied to that player character.*

6. Next, drag a wire from the **As First Person Character** output pin to empty grid space, and add a **Get Player Health** node. Finally, connect the **Cast To FirstPersonCharacter** node execution pin to **Return Node**, as shown in the following screenshot:

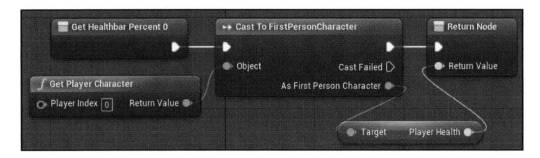

7. That's all we need to do to connect **Player Health** to the `Health bar` UI. We need to follow the same operation for the player's stamina. Click on the large button in the top-right of the screen labeled **Designer** to return to the **Canvas** view, and then select **Stamina Bar** in the **Hierarchy** panel. By following the steps outlined previously for `Health bar`, create a binding that connects the `FirstPersonCharacter` variable of **Player Stamina** to the meter:

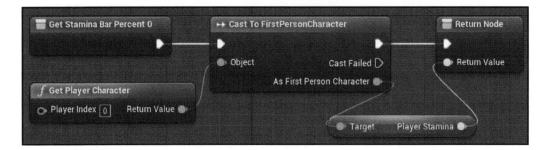

8. Compile and save your work. If you click on **Play**, then you will now notice that the health and stamina meters are filled in with red and green bars, respectively. The next step is to hook up our bindings for the ammo and goal counters.

Making text bindings for the ammo and goal counters

The ammo and goal counters will be represented by texts on the HUD. Follow these steps in order to bind the ammo counter:

1. Click on the **Designer** button to return to the canvas interface once more. This time, we want to select the Ammo Left text object in **Hierarchy**, which can be found under Weapon Stats.

2. In the **Details** panel, find the **Bind** button next to the **Text** field and create a new binding, as shown here:

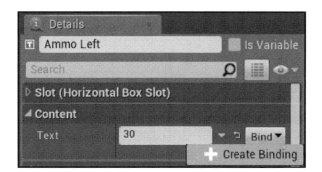

3. We will follow the same pattern for this binding as we did for health and stamina. In the **Get Ammo Left Text 0** graph view that appears, create a **Get Player Character** node, cast it to the **Cast To FirstPersonCharacter** node, and then link the **As First Person Character** pin to get **Player Current Ammo**.

4. Finally, attach both the cast node and the **Player Current Ammo** node to **Return Node**. You will notice that when you attach the **Player Current Ammo** output pin to the **Return Value** input pin, a new **ToText (integer)** node will be created and linked automatically. This is because Unreal Engine knows that for you to display a numerical value as text on the screen, it first needs to convert the number into a text format that the Widget knows how to display. The conversion node will be hooked up already, so there is no need to make further modifications. The next screenshot shows the nodes that are used in the binding:

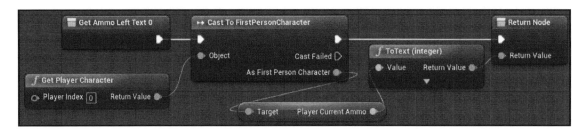

5. The final binding to create is for our `Goal Tracker` target count. Return to the **Designer** view and select the `Target Count` object in **Hierarchy**, under `Goal Tracker`. Click on the **Bind** button next to the **Text** field in the **Display** panel. By following the preceding steps, create a Blueprint chain that grabs the player character, casts it to the **Cast To FirstPersonCharacter** node, and connects the **Target Kill Count** variable to the casting and return nodes. As with the ammo count, the conversion to a text node will be automatically generated and connected for you. The final result should look like this:

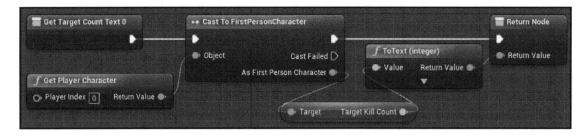

6. We've now successfully bound all our UI elements to player variables. Now is a good time to compile and save our work. Because of our bindings, the UI will now do its job of responding to Events that occur within our game. However, we still need to create the Events that will trigger changes in the variables we have connected. In the next section, we will modify the player variables based on Actions that the player takes while playing.

Tracking the ammo and eliminated targets

To get our UI to respond to the player interacting with the environment, we need to modify the Blueprint scripting that controls the player and targets. To begin, let's get the ammo counter to decrease when the player fires a shot from their gun.

Reducing the ammo counter

We need to modify the player fire logic so that the ammo counter is decreased when the player fires their gun. The Blueprint nodes managing the firing of the player's gun are contained within the `FirstPersonCharacter` Blueprint. Find this Blueprint within the `Blueprints` folder of **Content Browser** and open it. Now, find the large series of Blueprint nodes contained within the **Spawn projectile** comment block. We want to ensure that the counter tracking the player's current ammo count reduces by one each time the player fires a shot. The Blueprint scripting required to do so looks like this:

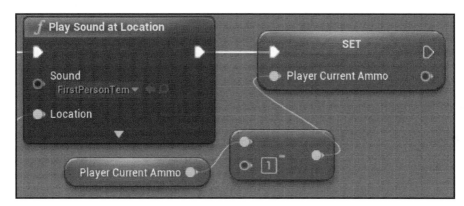

Find the final node in the chain, **Play Sound at Location**. Drag a wire from the output execution pin of this node to empty grid space and add a **SET Player Current Ammo** node. Then, drag a wire from the **Player Current Ammo** input pin to empty space and create an **integer – integer** node. Next, drag a wire from the top input pin of this node out and add a **GET Player Current Ammo** node. Finally, in the bottom field of the **integer – integer** node, add 1. This sequence translates to the following: *after firing a sound, set the player's current ammo count to the existing ammo count minus one.* Compile, save, and press **Play** to see your ammo counter decrease every time you fire a shot from your gun.

The **SET Player Current Ammo** node and the subtract node of the previous screenshot can be replaced by the **DecrementInt** node, which subtracts 1 from the input variable and sets the new value in the input variable. There is also the **IncrementInt** node, which adds 1 to the input variable.

Increasing the targets eliminated counter

Now, we want to increase our targets eliminated counter by 1 every time a target Cylinder is destroyed. Recall that the Blueprint scripting that controlled the destruction of the Cylinder targets was attached to the `CylinderTarget_Blueprint` Blueprint. Open this Blueprint, which is contained inside the `Blueprints` folder of **Content Browser**.

There is only one chain of Blueprint nodes inside this Blueprint, which are all triggered by **Event Hit**. We will have to add our new nodes close to the end of this chain, after all nodes except **DestroyActor**. There must not be other nodes after a **DestroyActor** node whose **Target** is **self** because this node removes the current instance from the Level. Break the link between the **Spawn Emitter at Location** and **DestroyActor** nodes, and then move **DestroyActor** to the right to give plenty of room for our new Blueprint scripting. The goal is to create a series of nodes that will extract the current **Target Kill Count** from the player character and increase it by one before going on to destroy the Actor. The end result will look like this:

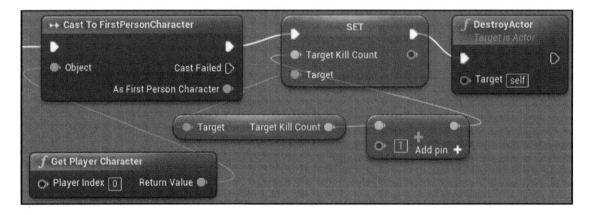

Target Kill Count is a variable of the `FirstPersonCharacter` Blueprint, so just as we did when we created our bindings earlier in the chapter, we need to get the player character object and cast it to the **Cast To FirstPersonCharacter** node. Add a **Get Player Character** node, and then connect its **Return Value** pin to a **Cast To FirstPersonCharacter** node.

Now, drag a wire from the **As First Person Character** pin to empty grid space, and then add a **GET Target Kill Count** node. From that node's output pin, create an **integer + integer** node, changing the bottom field to 1. Next, drag this new node's output pin into empty space and create a **SET Target Kill Count** node. Additionally, you have to drag a wire from the casting node's **As First Person Character** output pin to the **Target** input pin of the **SET Target Kill Count** node. Finally, connect the execution pins of the **Cast To FirstPersonCharacter**, **SET Target Kill Count**, and **DestroyActor** nodes, ensuring that **DestroyActor** is the final node in the chain. Compile, save, and **Play** the game to see the targets eliminated counter on the screen increase every time you destroy a target Cylinder:

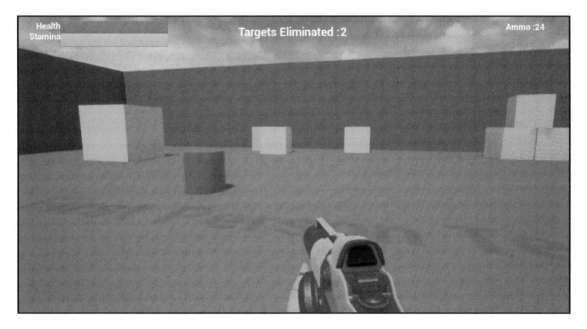

Now, the ammo and goal counters are being modified by Events that occur within our game and the updated values are displayed immediately in the HUD.

Summary

In this chapter, we enhanced player experience by adding a HUD that tracks the player's interaction with the environment. In doing so, we developed another conduit through which we can communicate information to the player of our game. By now, we have the skeletal structure of a First Person Shooter, including guns that shoot, targets that explode, and a UI that exposes the state of the world to the player. We have already come a long way from the initial test scene, which featured minimal player interaction.

In the next chapter, we will begin transitioning from building the foundation of our game structure to constructing the design of our game. The core of any game is made up of the rules that the player must follow in order to create a fun experience. While the game, in its current form, features some basic rules that define how the targets react on being shot, the overall experience lacks a goal for the player to achieve. We will rectify this by establishing a win condition for the player, as well as providing additional constraints that make the experience holistic and consistent.

8
Creating Constraints and Gameplay Objectives

In this chapter, we'll define a rule set for our game, which will guide the player through the gameplay experience. We want to give the player the ability to start the game and immediately identify what they have to do in order to win the game. In its most basic form, a game could be defined by the win condition and the steps the player can take to reach that win condition. Ideally, we want to ensure that each step the player takes toward that goal is fun.

We'll begin by applying some constraints to the player in order to increase the level of difficulty. A game without a challenge quickly becomes boring, and we want to ensure that every mechanic in our game provides the player with an interesting choice or challenge. We'll then set up a goal for the player to achieve, along with the necessary adjustments to our enemy targets to make that goal challenging to reach.

In this process, we'll work to accomplish the following:

- Reducing stamina while the player is sprinting as well as regenerating it while the player is not sprinting
- Preventing the player's gun from firing if they run out of ammo
- Creating ammo pickups that allow the player to regain ammo
- Defining a win condition based on the number of targets eliminated
- Creating a menu that allows the player to replay or quit the game upon winning

Constraining player Actions

One important consideration to make when adding enhanced capabilities to the player is the impact that the ability has on both the challenge and feel of the game experience. Recall that we added the ability for the player to sprint in Chapter 6, *Enhancing Player Abilities*, by holding down the *Shift* key. As it currently stands, holding down the *Shift* key while moving provides a significant increase in the speed at which the player can move. Without constraints applied to this ability, such as an enforced waiting period between uses, there would be nothing discouraging the player from holding down the *Shift* key at all times as they move.

This goes against the goal we set out to accomplish by adding a sprint functionality, which was to provide more options to the player. If an option is so attractive that the player feels compelled to utilize it at all times, then it doesn't actually increase the number of interesting choices available to the player. From the player's perspective, the result would be the same if we just increased the base speed of the player to the sprint speed.

We can rectify this and other issues currently faced by our game prototype by adding constraints that limit a player's abilities to increase decision making.

Draining stamina while sprinting

To add a constraint to the sprinting ability of the player, we'll need to return to the Blueprint where we originally defined the ability. Open the FirstPersonCharacter Blueprint located in the Blueprints folder of **Content Browser**.

First, we need to create a couple of variables that will keep track of whether or not the player is sprinting and how much stamina sprinting should cost. Find the **Variables** category of the **My Blueprint** panel and click the + button twice to add two new variables. Rename the first variable to **Sprint Cost** and assign it the **Float** type. Make sure to click the checkbox next to **Instance Editable** as **True** and set the variable's default value to 0.1. Rename the second variable IsSprinting. Set the variable type to **Boolean** and make the variable editable. After compiling the Blueprint, find some empty graph space near the block of Blueprint nodes you created for the sprint Function, which should have a comment block labeled **Sprint** around it.

We are going to create a custom Event to drain the player's stamina at a consistent rate while they are sprinting. A custom Event allows us to trigger the Blueprint nodes that are attached to the Event whenever another Blueprint node calls that Event. In this way, groups of Blueprint nodes within the same Blueprint can communicate with one another, even when they are not connected directly:

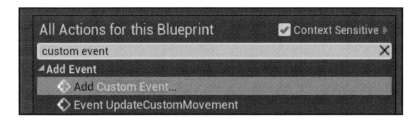

Search for a `custom event` node and add it, putting it a moderate distance away from your other sprint nodes. When you click on the **Add Custom Event...** node, look at the **Details** panel and find the **Name** field. This allows you to create the name of your custom Function. The name you give to the custom Event is important as you are establishing the name by which the Function will be referenced by the Function calls that trigger it. In this case, let's call the Function `Sprint Drain`. Type `Sprint Drain` into the **Name** field and press the *Enter* key to establish the Event. The Blueprint structure we'll follow for this sequence looks like this:

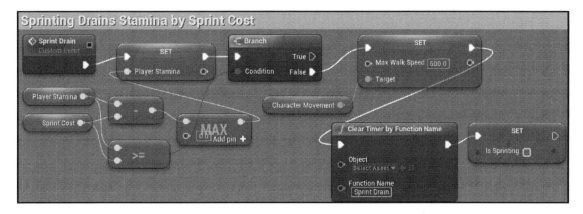

First, drag a wire from the **Sprint Drain** Event onto empty grid space and add a **SET Player Stamina** node. Next, attach the **Player Stamina** input pin to a **MAX (Float)** node. This node will output the highest of the float numbers given as inputs. We want to ensure that **Player Stamina** never dips below zero, so leave the bottom pin at 0.0 and drag a wire from the top input pin of this node and attach it to a **Float – Float** node. Attach a **GET Player Stamina** node to the top input pin of the **Float – Float** node. In the bottom pin, we'll establish the amount of stamina that is drained while sprinting.

We could enter a number into the field next to the bottom input pin of this node. However, if we ever wished to change the amount of stamina drained by sprinting, then we would need to open this Blueprint, find this node, and adjust the value within this small textbox each time. A better habit to get into is to use a custom, public variable that we attach to this pin, which will allow us to tweak the amount of stamina drain incurred by sprinting continually, without even entering the Blueprint Editor interface. Because we already created variables for both sprint cost and checking whether the player is sprinting, we'll use the **Sprint Cost** variable here. Either drag the **Sprint Cost** variable onto the bottom input pin of **Float - Float**, or drag a wire from the bottom pin out and search for **GET Sprint Cost**.

Next, we want to stop both the sprint and the stamina drain effect when the player runs out of stamina. Drag a wire from the output execution pin of the **SET Player Stamina** node and attach it to a **Branch** node. Now, drag a wire from the **Condition** input pin of this node and attach it to a **Float >= Float** node. Drag a second wire from the **GET Player Stamina** node onto the top input pin of the **Float >= Float** node and drag a second wire from the **GET Sprint Cost** node to the bottom input pin. This will determine whether or not the player has enough stamina to continue sprinting.

When the player does not have enough stamina to take another tick of stamina-draining sprinting, we need to force the player back to walking speed and clear the timer that will be calling this custom Function. Do so by dragging the **Character Movement** Component down from the **Components** panel and drop it near the **Branch** node. Drag a wire from this node and attach it to a **SET Max Walk Speed** node. Set the **Max Walk Speed** field to 600 to match the default walk speed we established. Now, connect the input execution pin of this node to the **False** output execution pin of the **Branch** node.

Next, drag a wire from the **SET Max Walk Speed** node's output execution pin and attach it to a **Clear Timer by Function Name** node. Type in Sprint Drain precisely into the **Function Name** input field to link it to the custom Event. The **Object** input indicates the object that implements the timer. You do not need to change it because its default value is **self**, which means it is the current Blueprint. Finally, attach a **SET Is Sprinting** node to the output execution pin of **Clear Timer by Function Name**, ensuring that the checkbox is left unchecked.

Now, select all five nodes and create a comment around them explaining their utility for draining the player's stamina. I chose **Sprinting Drains Stamina by Sprint Cost**. The next step will be to call our new custom Event from inside the Blueprint nodes that manage our sprint. Remember to compile and save the Blueprint.

Using looping timers to repeat Actions

Now, we want to customize our sprint Blueprint nodes to fire the custom Event that we just created so that the player's stamina drains as they sprint, as seen in the following screenshot:

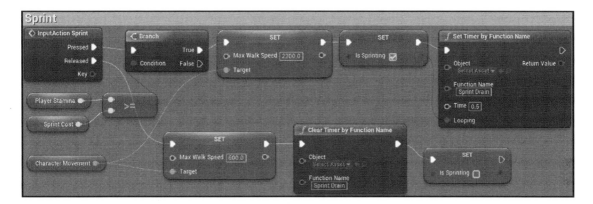

From the output execution pin of the node setting walk speed to 2200.0, drag a wire onto empty space and add a **SET Is Sprinting** node. Check the checkbox inside this node to set the **Boolean** value to **True** when the player is sprinting. Next, we want to make sure that stamina is continually drained as long as the left *Shift* key is held down. To do so, we can utilize a timer, as shown in the following screenshot:

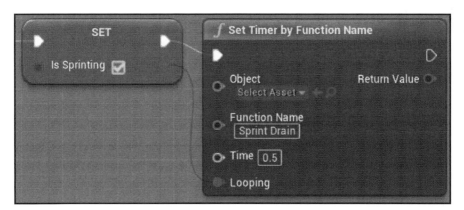

Timers allow us to perform an Action after a designated amount of time has expired or even fire an Action repeatedly on a set-time interval. This second functionality is going to serve the purpose of looping our Sprint Drain Function repeatedly.

Drag a wire from the execution output pin of the **SET Is Sprinting** node onto empty graph space and add a **SET Timer by Function Name** node. Inside this node, click on the field underneath the **Function Name** label, and type in `Sprint Drain` to connect the timer to our custom Event.

The second input we want to adjust in the timer node is labeled **Time**, which will determine the interval in seconds at which our sprint draining Event is triggered. Put `0.5` into the **Time** field to give the draining effect a notable and steady default rate. If you expect that you might want to tweak this value repeatedly, then you could also choose to create a custom float variable and attach that to this input instead, in a way similar to how we handled **Sprint Cost**. Finally, drag a wire from the red output pin of the **SET Is Sprinting** node and attach it to the **Looping** input pin to ensure that **Sprint Drain** is called repeatedly at each time interval as long as the **Is Sprinting** Boolean is set to **True**.

With this completed, this Function will now ensure that the value we designated for the **Sprint Cost** variable will be drained from the player stamina meter every `0.5` seconds, starting when the left *Shift* key is pressed as long as the player is sprinting. However, we want the drain effect to stop when the player stops sprinting by letting go of the key. To accomplish this, we need to stop the timer using **Clear Timer by Function Name**, just as we did inside the **Sprint Drain** Function:

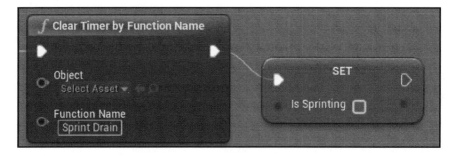

Attach a **Clear Timer by Function Name** node to the output execution node of the **SET Max Walk Speed** node, which is attached to the **Left Shift** node's **Released** output pin. This node will abort out of the timer attached to the Function name given. Type `Sprint Drain` into the **Function Name** field of this node to link the node to the timer node we just made. End this sequence by attaching a **SET Is Sprinting** node to the output execution pin of **Clear Timer by Function Name** and leave the checkbox unchecked.

As an alternative to **Clear Timer by Function Name**, you could use the **Pause Timer by Function Name** node. Pausing the timer works almost identically, except that the remaining time on the timer countdown before it was paused would persist when the timer is activated again. So, if you paused a 10-second timer that had 5 seconds left until the next activation, then the attached Function would trigger after 5 seconds instead of 10 at the next activation.

Compile, save, and test the game. As you sprint around the Level, you should see your stamina meter deplete in regular increments while the left *Shift* key is held down. The next step to constrain sprinting is to ensure that the player cannot initiate a sprint if they are drained of stamina.

Blocking Actions with branches

Preventing the player from sprinting when they don't have sufficient stamina can be accomplished by adding a **Branch** node right after the sprint Function trigger. Find the **InputAction Sprint** node and break its **Pressed** execution pin connection with the **SET Max Walk Speed** node. Add and connect a **Branch** node to the **Pressed** execution pin. Its output execution pin should then be connected to the **SET Max Walk Speed** node to, again, establish a complete chain. Now that the **Branch** node is set up, we need to establish the condition that will allow the left *Shift* trigger to continue activating the speed change through the **True** branch.

There is a faster way to add a node between two connected nodes. In the previous example, you could drag from the **Pressed** execution pin of the **InputAction Sprint** and select the **Branch** node from the menu. The **True** execution pin of the **Branch** node is automatically connected to the **SET Max Walk Speed** node.

Drag the **Condition** input pin of the **Branch** node onto empty grid space and add a **Float >= Float** node. Drag the **Player Stamina** and **Sprint Cost** variables onto the grid, selecting the **GET** node for both. Attach **GET Player Stamina** to the top input pin of the **Float >= Float** node and attach **GET Sprint Cost** to the bottom input. The final result should look like this:

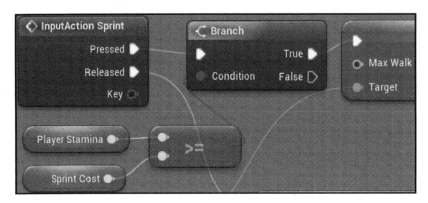

Regenerating stamina

The final element of stamina and sprinting we'll create is background stamina regeneration, so that the player has a way of recovering from running out of stamina. To accomplish this, we'll be taking advantage of the **Event Tick** trigger to increment the player's stamina gradually:

To create the Event shown in the preceding screenshot, start by finding some empty grid space and add an **Event Tick** node. Attach a **Branch** node to the **Event Tick** node's output execution pin. Drag the **Is Sprinting** variable onto the **Condition** pin to create a **GET Is Sprinting** node that is attached to the **Branch** node.

As **Event Tick** fires each frame, we want to force this Function to wait until a regular amount of time in seconds has passed. To do this, we use a **Delay** node. Drag a wire from the **False** output execution pin of the **Branch** node and attach it to a **Delay** node. Set the **Duration** field to 1.0 to ensure that the stamina recharge only happens once per second.

> The **Event Tick** node should not have complex operations because it can slow down the performance of the game since it is executed every frame. An alternative to the **Event Tick** node is the use of timers.

Next, drag out the **Player Stamina** variable, create a **SET** node, and attach it to the **Completed** output execution pin of the **Delay** node. Drag a wire from the input pin of this node to empty grid space and add a **Min (Float)** node. This node will output the lowest value float that is linked among its inputs. As our stamina meter has a scale from zero to one, and we want to ensure it never goes over one, type 1 into the bottom input field.

Now, drag a wire from the top input pin and attach it to a **Float + Float** node. Attach a **GET Player Stamina** node to the top input pin of this addition node. For the bottom pin, we want to determine a recharge rate. Create a new variable inside the **My Blueprint** panel and call it **StaminaRechargeRate**. Set its type to **Float**, check the checkbox labeled **Instance Editable**, and set its default value to 0.05. Finally, drag that variable out and attach a **GET Stamina Recharge Rate** node to the bottom input pin of the **Float + Float** node.

Compile, save, and press **Play** to test our work. You'll now see that running out of stamina will block subsequent uses of sprint until additional stamina has been restored through the recharging effect.

Preventing firing Actions when out of ammo

For the next constraint that we'll place on player abilities, we need to restrict the player from firing their gun when they reach an ammo count of 0. To do so, find the group of nodes that manages the firing of the gun, which is grouped by the comment block labeled **Spawn projectile**. We will add a **Branch** statement right after the **InputAction Fire** trigger that starts this chain of nodes:

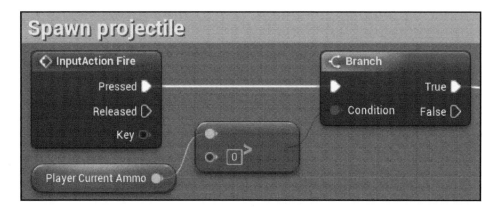

Start by breaking the connection between **InputAction Fire** and **Montage Play** nodes, and then add and connect a **Branch** node between them. Now, find the **Player Current Ammo** variable from the **My Blueprint** panel and drag it near the **Branch** node, selecting the **GET** option in the submenu to place the **GET Player Current Ammo** node. Drag a wire from the output pin of this node and add an **Integer > Integer** node. Leave the bottom input field at its default value of 0. Connect the output pin of the node to the input **Condition** pin of the **Branch** node.

Now, compile, save, and test your game. You should find that the gun no longer fires when the ammo counter reaches 0.

Creating collectible objects

Restricting the player from firing their gun when they run out of ammo forces the player to be considerate of the accuracy of the shots they attempt within the game. However, limiting ammo would be unduly punishing without a way of acquiring more. We don't want ammo to naturally recharge like our stamina meter. Instead, we'll create a collectible item to allow the player to regain ammo by exploring and traversing the Level.

Setting up collection logic

To create a collectible item, we first want to start a new Blueprint that will determine the properties of each instance of that object that appears in the world. To do so, navigate to the **Content Browser** and open the `Blueprints` folder. Add a new Blueprint class, choose the **Actor** class type, and name it `AmmoPickup`. Once the Blueprint is made, double-click on `AmmoPickup` to open the Blueprint Editor.

In the **Viewport** window that appears, we will see a simple white sphere. This is the default appearance given to empty Actor objects before a Mesh has been applied. To give the object a visible shape in the game, we first need to add a **Static Mesh** Component to the Blueprint. Find the **Components** panel, click **Add Component**, and choose the **Static Mesh** option.

In the **Details** panel that appears, find the **Static Mesh** category with the field that currently hosts the word **None** as no **Static Mesh** has been attached yet. In addition to attaching the **Static Mesh** Component to the Blueprint, which allows a Mesh to be associated with this Blueprint, we also need to designate which Mesh will be displayed for that **Static Mesh** Component.

Click on the drop-down menu for **Static Mesh**, and then click on the bottom-right button labeled **View Options**. In the pop-up menu that appears, ensure that you have checked the checkboxes next to both **Show Plugin Content** and **Show Engine Content**. This ensures that the assets included from plugins you installed in the engine, and the default assets Epic included in the engine, are seen in the asset search results:

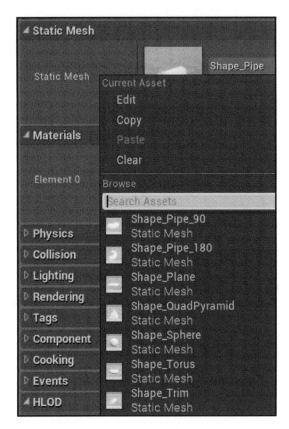

With the drop-down menu now properly searching for engine assets, search for **Shape_Pipe** and choose it. This Mesh was not made for ammo pickups explicitly, but this item will be small enough that we can make it serve our purpose. Right below the **Static Mesh** category, find the **Materials** field and attach the Material called **M_Door**. Finally, edit the **Transform** category's **Scale** values to be half their default size, 0.5, across the *x*, *y*, and *z* axes. You can click the lock icon on the right of the **Scale** fields so that all axes scale proportionally when you change the value of one of the fields.

While design prototyping a game, it is most often useful to take advantage of readily available assets rather than taking the time to create each asset from scratch. This allows you to focus your time and effort on determining what mechanics will result in the best play experience rather than spending time creating art assets that might later be discarded if the mechanic is removed from the design.

After adding the Mesh, we need to add a collider of some kind so that other objects, such as the player character, can physically interact with our pickup. In the **Components** panel, with the **Static Mesh** Component already selected, click on **Add Component** and add a **Capsule Collision** Component. A thin orange line will appear in the **Viewport** panel, representing the boundaries of the capsule shape collision. Minor adjustments to the position, rotation, and scale of the collision will be necessary in order to ensure that the entire Mesh is contained inside of the collision that should surround it. This can be done using the transform controls at the top of the **Viewport** panel or by using the following shortcut keys: *W* (for moving), *E* (for rotating), and *R* (for scaling):

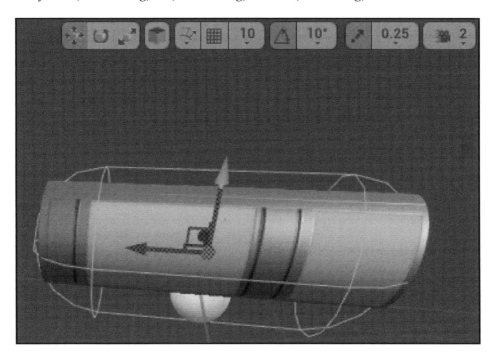

With the Mesh and collider added, click on the **Event Graph** tab to begin adding Blueprint logic to our collectible. In the **Event Graph** tab, start by adding the **Event ActorBeginOverlap** trigger. This trigger will activate subsequent Blueprint nodes when the object attached to this Blueprint collides with any other object. In this case, we want our ammo collectible to be picked up when the player walks into the object:

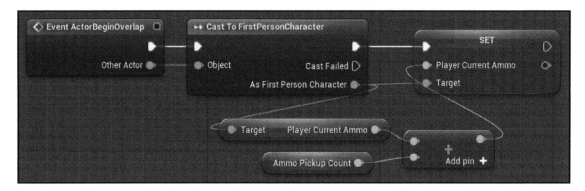

To ensure that the ammo collectible only activates when the player walks over it and that collecting an ammo pickup can impact the player's ammo counter, we first need to ensure that we are casting as the player. Attach a **Cast To FirstPersonCharacter** node to the **Event ActorBeginOverlap** trigger. Finally, connect the **Other Actor** output pin to the input **Object** pin of the casting node.

Now, we have a triggered Event that happens when the player character moves over our collectible object. When this happens, we want to add ammo to the player's ammo count. To do so, drag out a wire from the **As First Person Character** output pin and attach it to a new **SET Player Current Ammo** node. Next, drag a second wire from the **As First Person Character** output pin and attach it to a **GET Player Current Ammo** node. Drag the output pin from this new node and attach it to an **Integer + Integer** node. Next, drag the output pin from the **Integer + Integer** node back to the **Player Current Ammo** input pin of the **SET Player Current Ammo** node.

The final step is to determine how much ammo to add when ammo collectibles are picked up. To allow this number to be flexible, let's create a new editable variable called **Ammo Pickup Count**. Add this variable from the **My Blueprint** panel and set it to an **Integer** type variable. Ensure that the **Instance Editable** checkbox is checked, compile the Blueprint, and then set the variable's default value to 15. Finally, drag a **GET Ammo Pickup Count** node and attach it to the bottom input pin of the **Integer + Integer** node.

Next, let's trigger a sound and destroy the object when the collectible is picked up, as shown in the following diagram:

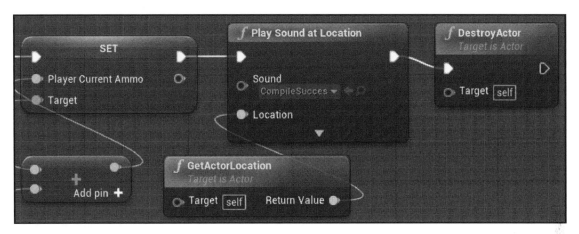

Drag a **Play Sound at Location** node and connect it to the output pin of the **SET Player Current Ammo** node. Using only the sounds provided in the engine, I found the **CompileSuccess** sound wave to work for our needs, so ensure that **View Engine Content** is checked under **View Options**, and then select that file from the **Sound** drop-down menu.

We want to trigger that sound at the location of the ammo pickup, so attach a **GetActorLocation** node to the **Location** pin of the **Sound** node. Finally, add a **DestroyActor** node at the end of the chain to ensure that each collectible can only be grabbed once. Compile and save the Blueprint.

Now, return to the Level and drag the `AmmoPickup` Blueprint into the Level. Do this two or three times in different locations around the Level in order to seed the area with ammo pickups. When you are satisfied, save and click **Play** to test the game. You should see your ammo counter increase every time you step onto one of the ammo pickups.

Setting a gameplay win condition

One of the final steps we need in order to establish a full game loop is to create a condition for the player to win. To do so, we will modify our **HUD** Blueprint and controller Blueprints to account for a target goal that the player must strive to hit.

Displaying a target goal in the HUD

First, we need to create a variable that will establish how many targets we are asking the player to destroy in order to achieve a win. Open up the `FirstPersonCharacter` Blueprint and create a new variable called `Target Goal`. Make it an **Integer** variable type, ensure **Instance Editable** is checked, and then set its default value to 2 for now.

Now that we have created a `Target Goal` variable, we should display this information to the player. Open the **HUD** Blueprint widget we created under our `UI` folder. From the **Designer** view, find the **Hierarchy** panel. Drag two more **Text** objects from the **Palette** panel onto the **Goal Tracker** object in the **Hierarchy** panel. For the first text object, change the **Text** field to `/`, (including the spaces before and after the slash). For the second text object, change the name to `Target Goal`, find the **Text** field, and enter 0. You might have to adjust the size of the **Goal Tracker** object and click the button next to it to create a new binding.

Now, looking at the **Graph** view, select the new **Get Target Goal Text 0** Function. Similar to the other HUD bindings we created in `Chapter 7`, *Creating Screen UI Elements*, we'll need to take the `Target Goal` variable from the `FirstPersonCharacter` Blueprint and return that value in this Function, as shown in the following screenshot:

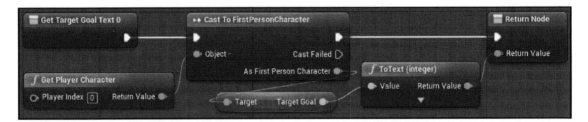

Create a **Get Player Character** node and drag its output pin onto a **Cast To FirstPersonCharacter** node. Drag a wire from the casting node's **As First Person Character** output pin, and attach it to a **Get Target Goal** node. Next, drag the `Target Goal` output pin onto the **Return Value** input pin of **Return Node**. Finally, connect the casting node to **Get Target Goal Text 0** on the input execution pin, and to **Return Node** on the output.

Compile, save, and press **Play** the game. You should see that the target counter increments upward as targets are destroyed. The displayed goal number shown on the right of the target counter does not change. Now, we need to ensure that the player gets feedback when they reach their `Target Goal`.

Creating a WinMenu screen

To give the player feedback once they have won our game, we are going to create a
WinMenu screen that will appear upon destroying the required number of targets. To create
a menu, we are going to need another Blueprint widget, like what we developed for the
HUD. Navigate to the **UI** folder we created and add a new **Blueprint Widget**, which is
found under **User Interface** in the add menu. Name this Blueprint WinMenu.

We are going to set up three elements for this menu screen. The first will be a simple text
object that broadcasts **You Win!** to the player. The other two elements will be buttons that
allow the player to restart the game or quit it. To start with, drag two **Button** objects and
one **Text** object onto **CanvasPanel**. Next, select the **Text** object and change its **Text** field to
say **You Win!**. Change the font size to 72 and the font color to light green, and then resize
and reposition the text object on the canvas so that it appears in the top-middle of the
screen, but a little lower than where you placed your HUD objects in the previous chapter.
Finally, anchor the object to the top-middle of the screen by selecting the second option
from the **Anchors** selector.

Now, drag an additional **Text** object and place it on top of both **Button** objects. Rename the
two **Button** objects as the **Restart** and **Quit** buttons. Change the size of the buttons so that
they are roughly the same size as our **You Win!** textbox and stack them below the text
display. Anchor both buttons to the center of the screen.

Next, select the **Text** object under the **Restart** button and change its **Text** field to **Restart**.
Then, change the font size to 60. Change the font color to black to ensure it shows up on
our gray buttons. Finally, click on the second button of both the **Horizontal Alignment** and
Vertical Alignment settings. Do the same operations on the **Text** object attached to the **Quit**
button, except that the **Text** field should display the text **Quit**:

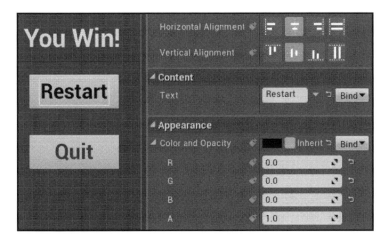

Now, we need to add Actions that will fire when the buttons are pressed. Click on the **Restart** button object, scroll down to the bottom of the **Details** panel, and click on the **+** button next to the **On Clicked** Event. This will add an Event that triggers when the button is clicked.

You will be taken to the graph view, where an **On Clicked (Restart)** button node will appear. Attach an **Open Level** node to this. Type in the name of your Level into the **Level Name** field, ensuring the accuracy of spelling. If you've been following along and have not changed the name of Level from the template, then this will be FirstPersonExampleMap. Doing this will reopen the Level when the player clicks on the button, resetting all aspects of the Level, including targets, ammo collectibles, and the player.

After the **Open Level** node, attach a **Remove from Parent** node. This node tells our WinMenu objects to stop displaying. We want the menu to go away once the Level is reset.

Now, return to the designer view and click on the **Quit** button object. Click on the **+** button next to the **On Clicked (Restart)** Event here as well. You'll be taken back to the graph view, but this time, with a new **On Clicked (Quit)** button node. Attach a **Quit Game** node to this Event so that the player can shut down the game by clicking the **Quit** button, as shown here:

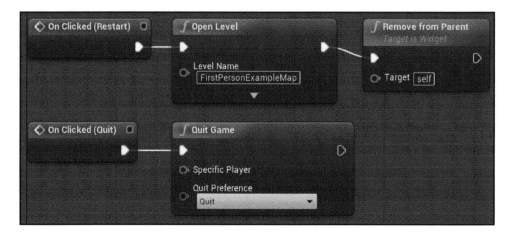

Displaying the menu

Now that our menu has been created, we need to tell the game when to show it to the player. As we called our HUD objects from within the FirstPersonCharacter Blueprint, let's go ahead and call this menu from the same location. Open FirstPersonCharacter in the Blueprints folder.

We are going to need to trigger an Event that will signal the end of the game. Before we even determine what that signal will be, we can create a custom Event node to represent it. Add a custom Event node to some empty graph space and rename it **End Game**.

When the victory condition is met, we want to stop the player from continuing to move around the game world. To do so, attach a **Set Game Paused** node to our Event and check the **Paused** checkbox. Next, add a **Get Player Controller** node below the **End Game** Event node. Drag out its **Return Value** output pin and attach it to a **SET Show Mouse Cursor** node. Check the checkbox next to **Show Mouse Cursor** and attach this node to the output execution pin of **Set Game Paused**. This will enable the player to regain control over the mouse cursor after the game is paused, as shown here:

Now that we have stopped the game from playing, we want to actually display the menu. Attach a **Create Widget** node to the end of the chain and select `WinMenu` from the **Class** dropdown. To conclude this Blueprint chain, drag a wire from the **Return Value** output pin and attach it to an **Add to Viewport** node:

Triggering a win

The final step for us is to determine the conditions that will result in the **End Game** custom Event being triggered. We want the Event to happen once the player has killed a sufficient number of target Cylinders to meet the target goal. We can evaluate this each time a target is destroyed. To do so, open `CylinderTarget_Blueprint` in the `Blueprints` folder and navigate to the end of the Blueprint chain in **Event Graph**.

We want to create a **Branch** node that will allow us to check if the last destroyed target was the last one needed to reach the goal. Attach a **Branch** node to the **SET Target Kill Count** node near the end of the chain. You can reattach the **DestroyActor** node to the **False** output of the **Branch** node.

Now we need to establish the condition that the branch will check. We are going to want to compare the **Target Kill Count** variable to see if it has reached or exceeded the `Target Goal` variable. To do so, create an **integer >= integer** node and drag its output pin to the **Condition** pin of the **Branch** node.

Next, find the **GET Target Kill Count** node that already exists and drag a second wire from its output pin to the top input pin of the **integer >= integer** node. Then, find the **Cast To FirstPersonCharacter** node and drag out a wire from its **As First Person Character** output pin onto a new **GET Target Goal** node. Drag the output pin of this new node to the bottom input pin of the **integer >= integer** node.

Now, drag the third wire from the **Cast To FirstPersonCharacter** node's output pin and attach it to a new **End Game** node, which will call our custom Event. Connect this node to the **True** output of the **Branch** node, and then make a second connection to the **DestroyActor** node after it. This should complete your branching logic and produce a result that looks like this:

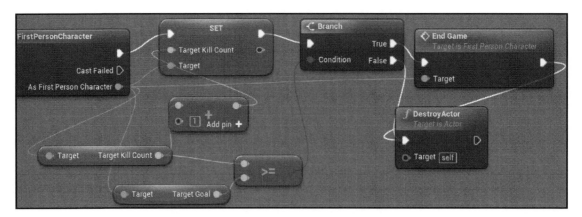

Compile, save, and press **Play** to test the game. If all the Blueprints are set up correctly, then you should see the game pause and a victory menu appear as soon as you destroy a second target. Clicking on the **Restart** button will reload the Level from the start, and clicking **Quit** will close the play session.

Summary

In this chapter, we have enhanced the play experience by providing productive constraints on the player's abilities and established a goal for the player to accomplish. In the process, you have learned about how to use timers to repeat Actions, how to create collectible objects in the game world, and how to create a menu system.

This chapter concludes section 2. The elements that make up the foundation of a video game experience are all present in the game that we've built. If you desire, you could spend some time customizing the Level layout to create a properly challenging game experience that is uniquely yours.

In section 3, we'll begin tackling a more advanced subject of Blueprint scripting and game development: **artificial intelligence (AI)**. We will also add new features to the game and see how to build and publish the game.

In the next chapter, we will replace our target Cylinders with smart enemies that can patrol between points and pursue the player around the Level.

Section 3: Enhancing the Game 3

In this section, you will learn the basic **Artificial Intelligence (AI)** techniques required to create a smart enemy using Behavior Trees and Navigation Meshes. Additionally, new features will be added to the game in order to make it more interesting. We will also demonstrate how to build and publish a game.

This section includes the following chapters:

- Chapter 9, *Building Smart Enemies with Artificial Intelligence*
- Chapter 10, *Upgrading the AI Enemies*
- Chapter 11, *Game States and Applying the Finishing Touches*
- Chapter 12, *Building and Publishing*

9
Building Smart Enemies with Artificial Intelligence

In this chapter, we'll add an additional challenge to our gameplay by making enemies that pose a threat to the player. To do so, we'll leave behind our target Cylinders in favor of enemies that have AI behavior. We want to set up enemies that have the potential to pose a threat to the player and are capable of analyzing the world around them in order to make decisions. To accomplish this, we are going to learn about Unreal Engine 4's built-in tools for handling AI behavior and how those tools interact with our Blueprint scripting. In the process, we will cover these topics:

- Setting up the enemy Actor to navigate
- Creating navigation behavior
- Making the AI chase the player

Setting up the enemy Actor to navigate

Until now, our targets have been represented by basic Cylinder geometry. This worked well for prototyping a non-responsive target that is only present as an aiming challenge for the player. However, an enemy that will move around and present a threat to the player will need a recognizable appearance that will at least indicate its direction of travel to the player. Fortunately for us, Epic has created a freely available asset package with Unreal Engine 4, which we can use to add a humanoid model to our game—one that is perfect for our new enemy type.

Importing from the Marketplace

For this step, we'll step out of the Unreal Engine Editor and will focus on Epic Games Launcher. Open Epic Games Launcher and navigate to the **Unreal Engine** section along the left-hand side of the window, and then to the **Marketplace** tab on the top. Search for `animation starter pack` and click on the image of the pack with the **Free** label to open the asset page:

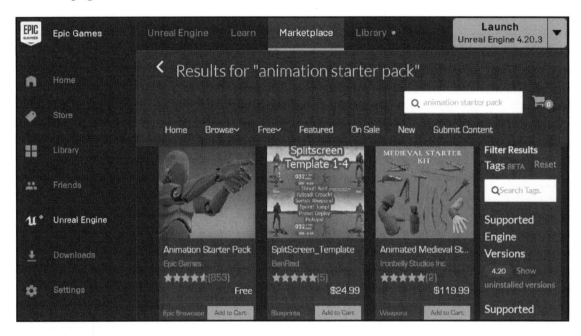

Next, click on the yellow **Free** button. After a moment, the button should turn into a yellow **Add to project** button. Click on this button and select the project you have been using to build your game. A folder called `AnimStarterPack` will be added to the `Content` folder of your project.

Expanding the play area

In order to provide an interesting environment for our intelligent enemies to chase the player, we might need to make some changes to the default first-person example map layout. The existing layout, while being serviceable for shooting targets, is likely to be too cramped for a player to be able to successfully avoid an enemy that is chasing them.

Level design does not directly intersect with Blueprint scripting, so we won't go through a step-by-step process of how you should modify your Level. Instead, we'll take this chance to customize the experience for the kind of game experience you would like to provide. At a minimum, you'll want to modify the layout of the map so that there is additional space to move around. You might also create some areas for the player to be able to take cover or areas that would make for interesting patrol points for enemies. Basic manipulation of the Level can be accomplished by moving existing objects around in the 3D Viewport. You can expand the size of the play space by moving the walls that make up the boundaries. You can also add additional basic objects, such as cubes and spheres, to your Level to serve as additional obstacles or cover.

To quickly add a little bit of additional variety to the gameplay, I chose to create an elevated area that is accessible by a ramp to both the player and enemies. I also expanded the play area to be twice as wide as it was earlier. The following screenshot is an image of the quick layout modifications I made:

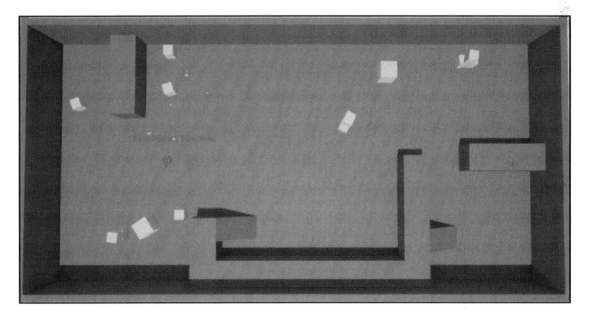

As you change the position of static objects in the Level, you will see a prompt that **lighting needs to be rebuilt**. This is because lighting information is attached (or in engine terms, it's *baked*) to static objects ahead of time to increase the performance once the game is being played. After you are done with your changes to the Level, click on the **Build** button to rebuild the lighting information with your new object layout. Also, note that when changing the physical dimensions and placement of the walls that surround the template map, you will also want to increase the size of `LightmassImportanceVolume`. This will ensure that your entire playable area gets the same high-quality lighting treatment.

Making the Level traversable with a NavMesh

In order to create AI behavior that allows our enemies to traverse the Level, we need to create a map of the environment that the AI will know how to read and navigate with. This map is created with an object known as a **NavMesh**. To create a NavMesh, find the **Modes** panel. With the **Place** tab selected, click on **Volumes** and then drag the **Nav Mesh Bounds Volume** object out onto the Level.

Now, you will want to move and scale up the **Nav Mesh Bounds Volume** object until the entire walkable space of your Level is contained within it. When you think you have your walking areas contained within the volume, press the *P* key on your keyboard to see whether the NavMesh is placed correctly. If so, you'll see a green Mesh on top of your floors, as seen in the following screenshot:

You can press *P* at any time to toggle the green NavMesh visibility on and off.

Setting the stage for intelligence with AI assets

With our Level and NavMesh now set up, we can return our focus to creating the enemy. First, we need to establish a Blueprint that will contain the enemy character. From your project directory in **Content Browser**, create a new folder called `Enemy`. Open this folder, then right-click on some empty space and select **Blueprint Class**. Open the **All Classes** group at the bottom of the popup and type `ASP` into the search bar. Select the `Ue4ASP_Character` object to create a new character Blueprint. We'll name this Blueprint `EnemyCharacter`.

Now that we have a Blueprint to contain our enemy character, we need to create three additional objects that will work together to manage the behavior of our enemy. The first of these is called **Behavior Tree**. A Behavior Tree is the source of the decision-making logic that will instruct our enemy on what conditions should cause it to perform which Actions. To create a Behavior Tree, right-click on the `Enemy` folder and then on the **Artificial Intelligence** category. Then, select **Behavior Tree**, and name it `EnemyBehavior`.

The second object we need to create is an **AI Controller**. The AI Controller will serve as a connection between the character and the Behavior Tree. It routes the information and Actions that are generated within the Behavior Tree to the character, which will enact those Actions. To create an AI Controller, right-click on the `Enemy` folder and click on **Blueprint Class**. Then, search for and select **AIController**, and name it `EnemyController`.

The final object we'll create to control the behavior is called a **Blackboard**. A Blackboard is a container for all of the data that an AI controller needs in order to be governed by its Behavior Tree. To create a Blackboard, right-click on the `Enemy` folder and click on the **Artificial Intelligence** category. Then, select **Blackboard**. Predictably, we'll name this Blackboard `EnemyBlackboard`.

Next, we should make some modifications to `EnemyCharacter`. Because we created `EnemyCharacter` as an `Ue4ASP_Character` object type, it inherited information about the desired mesh, texture, and animations from the character created for the `animation` pack we imported. Some of this information, such as the mesh and support for the animations, is information we will want to keep. However, we need to ensure that `EnemyCharacter` knows how to be controlled by the right AI Controller. To change this, open the `EnemyCharacter` Blueprint now.

With `EnemyCharacter` open, look at the **Components** panel. Click on **EnemyCharacter(self)**, which will be the top item in the **Components** list. Now, look at the **Details** panel and find the **Pawn** category. The last element of this category will be a drop-down list for **AI Controller Class**. Change the selection of this drop-down list to our new `EnemyController`.

While we're editing `EnemyCharacter`, we should change the color of the enemy as well. Currently, the **Static Mesh** shows a white humanoid that appears to be of the same style as that of the player's arms and gun. To better indicate to the player that the character is an enemy, we can change **Static Mesh** to use the same **TargetRed** Material we used for the Cylinders in the previous chapters. To do so, click on **Mesh (Inherited)** and find the **Materials** category in the **Details** panel. Change **Element 0** of the Material to the **TargetRed** Material we created. You should see the humanoid character in **Viewport** change to a red color. Select **CapsuleComponent (Inherited)**, check the **Hidden in Game** property in the **Rendering** category, and change **Collision Presets** to **BlockAllDynamic**. Compile and save it and return to the Level Editor. Drag the `EnemyCharacter` Blueprint onto the Level to create an instance of an enemy in our map. Rename the instance of `EnemyCharacter` in **World Outliner** to `Enemy1`.

Creating navigation behavior

The first goal for our enemy will be to get it to navigate between points that we create on the map. To accomplish this, we'll need to create points on the map that the enemy will navigate to, and then we need to set up the behavior that will cause the enemy to move to each of the points in a cycle.

Setting up patrol points

Let's start by creating the path we want the AI to patrol. While you're still in the Level Editor, look at the **Modes** panel. With the **Place** tab selected, click on **All Classes** and drag a **Target Point** object onto the area of the map that you would like for the enemy to start the patrol from. Now, look at the **World Outliner** panel and click on the folder icon with a plus symbol that sits to the right of the search bar. Click on this to create a new folder called `PatrolPoints`. This folder will contain all of the points we create so that we can keep the main list tidy. Drag the **Target Point** object in the outliner into this new folder and rename the object as `PatrolPoint1`.

Now, go to the **Details** panel of `PatrolPoint1` and click on the green **Add Component** button. Add **Sphere Collision** to the patrol point. Adding a collider will allow us to check whenever the enemy Actor overlaps with the patrol point.

Duplicate the `PatrolPoint1` object in **World Outliner** by right-clicking on it, clicking on **Edit**, and then on **Duplicate**. The new object will automatically be named as `PatrolPoint2`. Drag the second patrol point somewhere else in the Level; far away enough from the first so that movement between the two points would be noticeable:

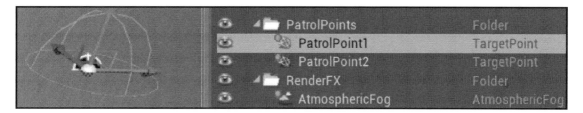

The **Target Point** icon is a small crosshair icon that will only appear in edit mode for the Level but is invisible to the player while the game is running. This allows us to visualize the route we are creating for the enemy without having a visual artifact in play mode that looks distracting or gives information away.

Enabling communication between assets

With our patrol points established, we can transition to building the intelligence of our enemy. To begin, we are going to give our Blackboard the ability to store information about the location of a patrol point. Open `EnemyBlackboard` from the **Content Browser**. Click on **New Key** and select **Object** as the **Key Type**. Click on the expansion arrow next to **Key Type** and change the **Base Class** to **Actor** with the dropdown. Name this new object key `PatrolPoint`, as shown in the following screenshot:

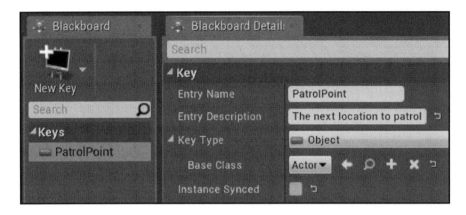

Now that we have a `PatrolPoint` key set up within **Blackboard**, we need to set the value of that key within **Blackboard** to the actual `Patrolpoint` object in the world. We can do this from the `EnemyCharacter` Blueprint, so open the character Blueprint now.

 When you open a Blueprint that does not have any scripts or variables, a simple Editor is displayed only to edit the default values. You need to click on the **Open Full Blueprint Editor** link at the top to see the usual layout.

We want to create a sequence that starts when the enemy character is created and then grabs `EnemyBlackboard`. The **Set Value as Object** node will then set the key value, called `PatrolPoint`, inside **Blackboard** to the value contained within a variable we will create for the character Blueprint representing the enemy's **Current Patrol Point** target, as shown in the following screenshot:

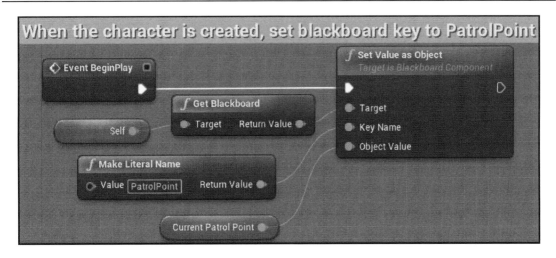

First, we want to create variables that will store our two patrol point objects. Add a new variable from the **My Blueprint** panel and call it `PatrolPoint1`. Set **Variable Type** to **Actor** and check the **Instance Editable** attribute. Now, right-click on the variable and duplicate it. Name this duplicate `PatrolPoint2`. Finally, duplicate the **Actor** variable a third time and name this variable `CurrentPatrolPoint`. We will change the patrol point stored in this variable each time we want to move the enemy to a new location.

With the three variables created, we want to use the **Event BeginPlay** node, which is already in Event Graph. Add a **Get Blackboard** node, drag a wire from the **Target** input pin, and search for and select **GET Reference to Self** to attach a **Self** node to the pin. Now, drag a wire from the **Return Value** pin and attach it to a **Set Value as Object** node. Connect this node's input execution pin to the **Event Begin Play** node.

Returning to the **Set Value as Object** node, drag a wire from the **Key Name** input and attach it to a **Make Literal Name** node. Set the **Value** field within this node to a patrol point so that it references the key we created inside **Blackboard**. Finally, drag the **Current Patrol Point** variable to Event Graph and select **GET**. Connect the **GET Current Patrol Point** node to the **Object Value** input pin of **Set Value as Object**. Select all these nodes and create a comment for yourself that describes the functionality.

Next, we want to create a series of nodes that will swap the patrol point the enemy is moving toward each time they successfully reach one of their two patrol points. To do this, we will create two branches that will trigger off the detection of a collider overlap, as shown in the following screenshot:

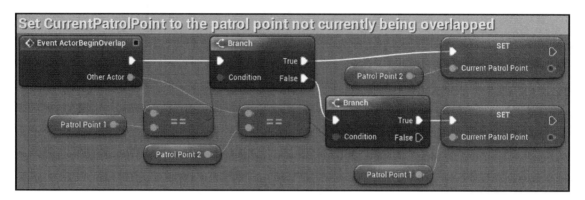

Begin by creating an **Event ActorBeginOverlap** node. Attach this node to a **Branch** node. Drag a wire from the **Condition** input of the **Branch** node onto an **Equal (Object)** node. This node evaluates whether the two objects attached to the two inputs of the node are identical to one another. In our case, we want to evaluate whether the object being overlapped by the enemy is the same object that is attached to the **Patrol Point 1** variable.

Drag a wire from the **Other Actor** output pin of the **Event ActorBeginOverlap** node and attach it to the top input pin of the **Equal (Object)** node. Now, drag the **Patrol Point 1** variable onto the graph and attach a **GET Patrol Point 1** node to the bottom input pin of the **Equal (Object)** node. If these two objects are equal, then we will change the **Current Patrol Point** variable to **Patrol Point 2**. From the **True** output pin of the **Branch** node, attach a wire to a **SET Current Patrol Point** node and attach a **GET Patrol Point 2** node to its input pin.

Next, we need to create a second branch series to test against the other patrol point. Drag a wire from the **False** output pin of the **Branch** node and attach it to a second **Branch** node. Attach the **Condition** input pin of this new **Branch** node to a new **Equal (Object)** node. Connect the top input pin of the **Equal (Object)** node to the **Other Actor** output pin of the **Event ActorBeginOverlap** node.

Drag the second patrol point variable onto the graph and attach a **GET Patrol Point 2** node to the bottom input pin of **Equal (Object)**. Now, attach the **True** output pin of the second **Branch** node to a new **SET Current Patrol Point** node. Then, attach a **GET Patrol Point 1** node to the input pin of **SET Current Patrol Point**.

Finally, attach the output execution pins of both **SET Current Patrol Point** nodes to the input execution pin of the **Set Value as Object** node, which is in the other block of Blueprint nodes we used to set **Blackboard Key**. This final step is important to ensure that the updated **Current Patrol Point** value gets sent to the Blackboard every time the value of the variable changes.

This finishes the work we have inside `EnemyCharacter`. Next, we need to go to the AI Controller and instruct it to run the Behavior Tree that we'll set up. Return to **Content Browser** and open `EnemyController`.

In the Event Graph of `EnemyController` Blueprint, add an **Event BeginPlay** node. Connect this node to a **Run Behavior Tree** node. Finally, set the **BTAsset** input parameter inside this node to `EnemyBehavior`. That's all there is to do with the controller, as shown in the following screenshot:

Teaching our AI to walk with the Behavior Tree

We can now move on to the heart of the AI: the Behavior Tree. Return to **Content Browser** and open `EnemyBehavior`. On the right, change **Blackboard Asset** to `EnemyBlackboard`. You should now see our `PatrolPoint` Blackboard Key appear in the **Blackboard** panel on the bottom left.

Now, look at the **Behavior Tree** panel, which will look similar to the Event Graphs we are used to seeing inside of Blueprints. This is where we'll create the branching logic that will determine which Actions to perform, based on the conditions the enemy is currently experiencing. The top Level of the logic tree will always be the **ROOT** node, which simply serves to indicate where the logic flow will start from.

The darker line at the bottom of the Behavior Tree nodes is the connection point between nodes. You can click and drag a wire from the dark area at the bottom of the **ROOT** node and drop it onto empty grid space to get a new selection menu popup that will allow you to add additional nodes to the Behavior Tree. Do so now and select the **Selector** option, as shown in the following screenshot:

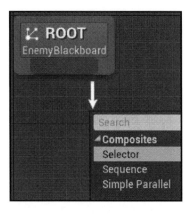

 The two primary branching node types you'll utilize are **Selector** and **Sequence**. A **Selector** node runs each of the nodes connected underneath it—called its **children**—from left to right, but succeeds and stops running as soon as one child successfully runs. Thus, if a **Selector** node has three children, then the only way the third child node will be run is if the first two children failed to execute because the conditions attached to them were false. A **Sequence** node is just the opposite. It also runs all the children in a sequence from left to right, but the **Sequence** node only succeeds if all of the children succeed. The first child to fail causes the whole sequence to fail, ending the execution and aborting the sequence.

Underneath the **Selector** node, attach two **Sequence** nodes next to one another. Select the **Sequence** node on the left and change **Node Name**, in the **Description** panel, to `Move to Patrol`. Next, select the other **Sequence** node and change its name to `Idle`.

 Notice the faint grey circles with numbers inside of them that are positioned to the upper-right corner of the two **Sequence** nodes. These indicate the execution order of the nodes, which are ordered according to their left-to-right positions. The first node to be evaluated will be labeled with a **0** badge.

Now, we need to add Actions that will be triggered by the nodes. Drag a wire down from the **Move to Patrol** node and attach a **Move To** node. This node will be purple in color, visually distinguished as a node that results in Actions. These nodes are called **task nodes** and will always be the bottommost nodes in a Behavior Tree. As a consequence, you will notice there is no attachment point for additional nodes at the bottom of a task node, as shown in the following screenshot:

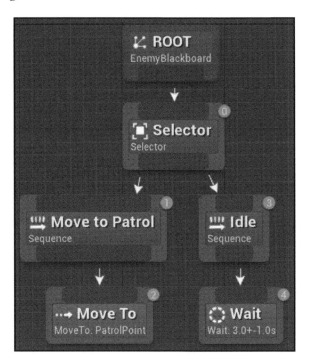

Looking at the **Details** panel of our newly added **Move To** task node, you will notice a few new options that will allow us to tweak the movement of our enemy character. The first of these is a field called **Acceptable Radius**. This field indicates the acceptable distance that the enemy can be away from the target to complete the task. We don't want the enemy to move sideways or strafe toward the target, so we can leave **Allow Strafe** unchecked. **Blackboard Key** determines the location that the Actor will be moved to. As we only have one **Blackboard Key**, this field should be automatically set to our intended target, which is `PatrolPoint`.

Next, drag a wire down from the node that we called **Idle** and attach it to a **Wait** task node. The **Wait** node contains only two configuration fields. The value of the **Wait Time** field determines how long the enemy will wait between movements to the next `PatrolPoint`. Set this value to `3.0` to add a 3-second pause between patrols. The field below, named **Random Deviation**, allows us to add randomness to the amount of time that passes while the enemy waits. Enter `1.0` into this field to add a 1-second variation to our 3-second wait time. This will result in a pause of random length between 2 and 4 seconds between patrols.

Save the Behavior Tree and then return to the `FirstPersonExampleMap` tab. Find the enemy we placed, called **Enemy1**, and select it in **World Outliner**. In the **Details** panel, navigate down to the **Default** category and set **Patrol Point 1** to the `PatrolPoint1` object, set **Patrol Point 2** to the `PatrolPoint2` object, and set **Current Patrol Point** to the patrol point object furthest away from the enemy's starting position. We want to set these patrol points on the enemy instance in the world, rather than as defaults on the variables within the enemy Blueprint, because we want each enemy that we create in the future to have its own set of patrol points. This is shown in the following screenshot:

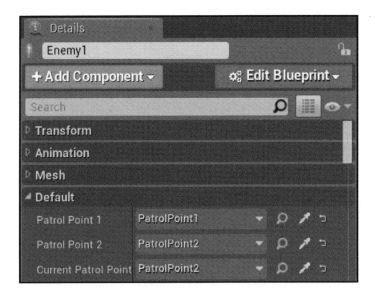

Save and click **Play** to test. You should see the red enemy character start navigating to the first of the two patrol points. When it reaches the first point, it will briefly pause and then start walking to the second patrol point. This pattern will continue back and forth as long as the game is running.

Making the AI chase the player

Now that we have a patrol behavior established, we should make the enemy pose some threat to the player. To do so, we will give the enemy the ability to see the player and pursue them.

Giving the enemy sight with Pawn Sensing

To grant the enemy the ability to detect the player, we need to add a `PawnSensing` Component to `EnemyController`. To do this, open the `EnemyController` Blueprint and click on the **Add Component** button in the **Components** panel. Search for and add the **PawnSensing** Component. This Component gives us the ability to add a few additional event triggers to the `EnemyController` Event Graph. The one we are interested in now is called **On See Pawn (PawnSensing)**, as shown here:

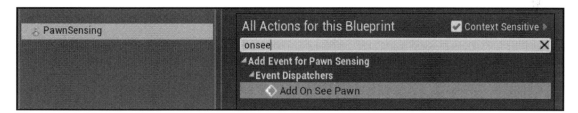

There is a second system that can be used for AI behavior development and environment sensing, called the **Environment Query System** (EQS). As of Unreal Engine version 4.20.3, this feature is still in the experimental development phase. However, the EQS features are expected to take over as the primary system for developing AI that can sense the environment around them. The PawnSensing behavior we cover in this book will remain usable alongside the EQS system, and many of these concepts will transfer over.

Ensure you have the new **PawnSensing** Component selected in the **Components** panel, and then, with **Context Sensitive** searching checked, search for and add the **On See Pawn (PawnSensing)** node to the Event Graph. This Event fires when the enemy is able to see the player along a line of sight. To transmit this information to our Behavior Tree, we will first need to create a new **Blackboard Key** store and pass this information to it. You can see how this is accomplished in the following screenshot:

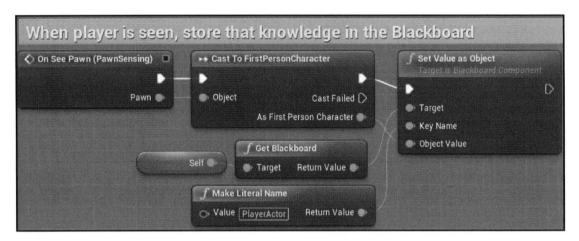

Drag a wire from the **Pawn** output pin of the **On See Pawn (PawnSensing)** node we just created and attach it to a **Cast To FirstPersonCharacter** node. This will ensure that the enemy only reacts to the player being seen, as we do not want to trigger a chase behavior when it sees other enemies.

Next, we need to get a reference to the Blackboard. Add a **GET Blackboard** node to **Event Graph**. Drag a wire from the **Target** input pin of this node and attach a **Self** node to it. Now, drag a wire from the **Return Value** output pin and attach it to a **Set Value as Object** node. Then, connect the **As First Person Character** output pin of the casting node to the **Object Value** input pin of the **Set Value as Object** node. Also, connect the execution pins of the **Cast To FirstPersonCharacter** and **Set Value as Object** nodes.

The final step to pass the information about the player being spotted to the Blackboard is to establish the key that will store the data. Drag a wire from the **Key Name** input pin of **Set Value as Object** and attach it to a **Make Literal Name** node. We don't yet have a key created on the Blackboard for this purpose, but that will be our next step. For now, Enter **PlayerActor** into the **Value** field of this node. As always, create a comment around the block of nodes to remind yourself of its functionality, then compile and save your work.

Adding conditions to the Behavior Tree

Now, we need to create our **Blackboard Key** and create the Behavior Tree branch that will instruct the enemy to chase the player. Open `EnemyBehavior` from **Content Browser** and then click on the **Blackboard** tab. Click on the **New Key** button and create a new key of the **Object** type called **PlayerActor**. With the **PlayerActor** key selected, look at the **Blackboard Details** panel. Click on the expansion arrow next to **Key Type** and change the **Base Class** to **Actor** with the dropdown. For reference, fill in the **Entry Description** field to indicate that this key will store **The Player Character** and leave **Instance Synced** unchecked, as shown in the following screenshot:

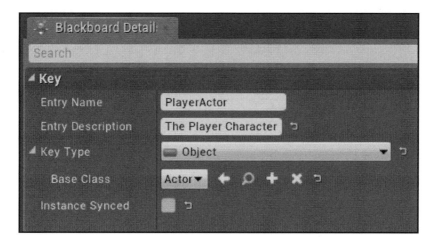

Now, save and click on the **Behavior Tree** tab. We will need another **Sequence** node that will connect to tasks to get the enemy to chase the player. Drag a wire down from the **Selector** node and create a **Sequence** node to the left of our **Move to Patrol** sequence node. Because we want the enemy seeing and chasing the player to take higher priority over their patrol and idle behaviors, we want to ensure this sequence is the left-most branch underneath the selector. Change this new node's name to **Attack Player**.

Next, we want to ensure that the tasks attached to **Attack Player** only trigger when the enemy actually sees the player. To do this, we'll add a **Decorator** node. A **Decorator** node attaches to the top of sequences and provides conditions that must be met before that sequence can be triggered. Right-click on the **Attack Player** node, hover over **Add Decorator** to expand the menu, and select **Blackboard** to add a new decorator that triggers off **Blackboard Key**. You will see a new blue box appear directly above the **Attack Player** sequence. Click on this and look at the **Details** panel, as shown in the following screenshot:

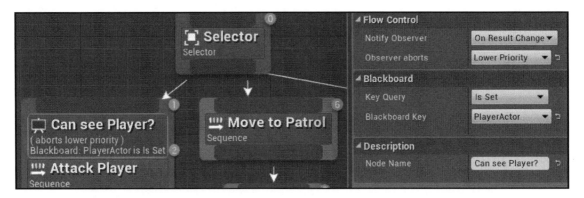

In the **Details** panel, find the **Observer aborts** dropdown and select the **Lower Priority** option. Combined with the **On Result Change** option that is selected by default for **Notify Observer**, this will indicate that when this condition changes to **True**, all the other sequences that are of lower priority should be aborted. This will be visually indicated with a blue highlight around all the lower-priority sequence nodes in the Behavior Tree view when you have this decorator selected.

Next, ensure that **Key Query** is set to **Is Set** and change **Blackboard Key** to **PlayerActor**. This will check to ensure that the **PlayerActor** Blackboard Key has a value set before it allows **Attack Player** to run. Recall that **PlayerActor** is only set when the enemy has established a line of sight with the player through its pawn-sensing Component. Finally, change the name of this node to **Can see Player?** to reflect its functionality.

Creating a chasing behavior

Now, we need to create a series of task nodes underneath the **Attack Player** sequence that will make up the enemy's chasing behavior. Because we already have **Blackboard Key** that stores the player Actor, including its location data, moving the enemy character to the player is easy. Drag a wire from the **Attack Player** sequence node and attach it to a **Move To task** node. Click on this node, and in the **Details** panel, change **Blackboard Key** to **PlayerActor**.

That's all that is necessary to get the enemy chasing the player! You can compile, save, and press **Play** to test-run this behavior. When you run in front of the enemy on its patrol path, it will break out of its path and begin pursuing you around the Level. However, you will notice that no matter what you do, the enemy will never relent in its pursuit. As our end goal is to have the enemy reach the player and then return to its patrol, we'll need to create some way for the enemy to break out of the chase behavior.

To create a pause to allow an attack to happen, first, create a **Wait** node and place it to the right of the **Move To** node. Change the **Wait Time** on this node to 2 seconds, which is roughly the time we might expect an attack to take. Combined with the **Move To** node, this will cause the enemy to chase the player until they are in range, and then wait 2 seconds before taking another Action.

Now, we need to create a way for the **PlayerActor** key to be reset so that the **Can see Player?** decorator can fail after the pause happens, thus ending the chase behavior. There is no built-in task to cover this functionality, so we'll need to create a custom task to handle this. Click on the **New Task** button, which is along the top menu of the Behavior Tree, and select the **BTTask_BlueprintBase** option if the dropdown appears. This creates a new task using the basic Blueprint class as its base class.

You'll be instantly taken to a new tab where you can begin editing the behavior of this task, but first, let's return to **Content Browser** to rename this task to something useful. Find the new task object called **BTTask_BlueprintBase_New** in the `Enemy` folder and rename the object to `ResetValueTask`. Double-click on `ResetValueTask` to return to the task's tab. If the Blueprint opens as a data-only Blueprint, then click on **Open Full Blueprint Editor** at the top.

Before adding any nodes, change the **Node Name** field in the **Details** panel to Reset Value. Now, go to the **My Blueprint** panel and add two variables. Rename the first variable Key, and change its type to **BlackboardKeySelector**. Rename the second variable Actor, and change its type to **Actor**. Finally, ensure that both of the variables have the **Instance Editable** checkbox checked, as shown in the following screenshot:

With our variables created and our nodes named, we can start creating the behavior of our task. Add an **Event Receive Execute** trigger node to the Event Graph. This node simply triggers the attached behaviors when the task is activated within the Behavior Tree. Next, drag a wire from the execution pin and attach a **Set Blackboard Value as Object** node. Drag the **Key** variable onto the **Key** input pin. Then, drag the **Actor** variable to the **Value** input pin. Finally, drag a wire from the output execution pin of the **Set Blackboard Value as Object** node and attach it to the **Finish Execute** node. Check the checkbox next to the **Success** input of this node. After giving the block of nodes a descriptive comment container, the final result should look like this:

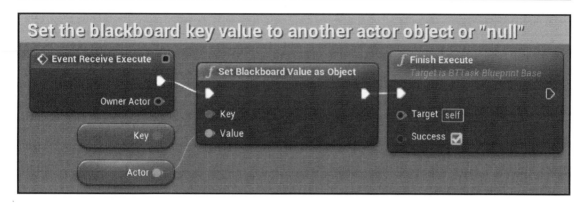

This task will allow us to designate **Blackboard Key** from the **Details** panel of the task in the Behavior Tree and set that key to an Actor of our choosing. We could have replaced the generic public variables we created with the specific values we want to set with this node, namely changing the **PlayerActor** key to null or empty. However, when making new tasks, it is good practice to make them generically useful with reusable behavior that changes depending on the inputs given in the Behavior Tree. With the task made to fit our needs, compile the Blueprint, save, and return to the EnemyBehavior Behavior Tree.

Back in the Behavior Tree, drag a wire down from **Attack Player** and add our new ResetValueTask task node to the right of both the **Move To** and **Wait** nodes. In the **Details** panel, change the **Key** to **PlayerActor** and leave the **Actor** dropdown with a **None** value. Finally, change **Node Name** to **Reset Player Seen**:

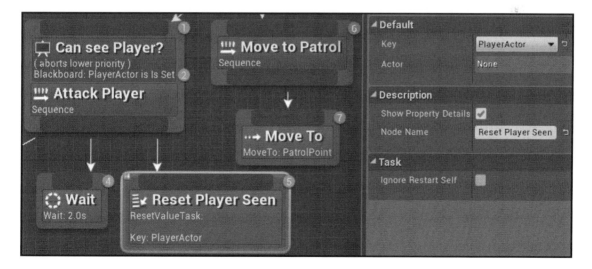

This completes our work in the Behavior Tree to establish a chasing behavior. Save and press **Play** to test the behavior. As you navigate the player character in front of the patrolling enemy, the enemy will stop its patrol and chase the player. When the enemy reaches the player, it'll stop for 2 seconds before returning to its patrol path. If it re-establishes the line of sight with the player, then it will interrupt its patrol and begin chasing the player again.

Summary

In this chapter, we began the process of changing our simple, moving targets into fleshed-out game enemies that can challenge the player. In the process, you learned about the fundamentals of how AI Controllers, Behavior Trees, and Blackboards can be leveraged together to create an enemy with the ability to sense the world around them and make decisions based on that information.

As we continue the process of developing our AI to pose a serious challenge to the player, you can use the skills you have learned to consider other kinds of behaviors you might be able to provide to an enemy. Continued exploration of AI mechanics will see you continually coming back to the core loop of sensing, decision-making, and acting that we began implementing here.

In the next chapter, we'll extend our AI behavior to create an enemy that can truly challenge the player. We will add the ability for the enemy to listen for the player and investigate a sound, as well as give the enemy an attack ability to damage the player when they get too close. To balance the game around this new threat, we'll also give the player the ability to fight back against the enemies.

10
Upgrading the AI Enemies

In this chapter, we will add more functionality to our AI enemies in order to introduce the potential for the player to fail, and to create greater gameplay diversity. At this point, we are going to begin settling on the kind of challenge we want to offer the player. We are going to create zombie-like enemies that will relentlessly pursue the player, creating an action-focused experience, where the player must try to survive against hordes of enemies. We will start by giving more capability to the AI, including the ability to deal damage and use wandering patterns, in order to increase the difficulty of player survival. We will then turn our attention to the player, giving them the ability to fight back against these dangerous enemies. Finally, we will complete the balancing of our increased difficulty by creating a system to spawn new enemies in the game world over time. In the process, we will cover the following topics:

- Introducing an enemy melee attack that will damage the player's health
- Giving the AI the ability to hear the player's footsteps and shots
- Having the enemy investigate the last known location of the player based on sound
- Allowing the player to destroy the enemies with their gun
- Spawning new enemies in the world
- Setting AI enemies to wander the Level randomly

Creating an enemy attack

If the enemies we create are going to pose a genuine obstacle in the way of the player achieving the goals we create for them, then we will first need to give the enemies the ability to damage the player. In Chapter 9, *Building Smart Enemies with Artificial Intelligence*, we set up the basic structure of an enemy attack pattern. It is triggered when the player enters the enemy's line of sight. We are now going to introduce a damage Component to this attack, ensuring that there is some consequence of the enemy reaching the melee range of the player.

Making an attack task

To create an attack task that does damage, we will extend the **Attack Player** sequence we created in the enemy Behavior Tree. Open EnemyBehavior from **Content Browser**. From the **Behavior Tree** view, click on the **New Task** button and select the BTTask_BlueprintBase option from the drop-down menu that appears. As we did with the custom task to reset key values in Chapter 9, *Building Smart Enemies with Artificial Intelligence*, we will navigate to the Enemy folder in **Content Browser** and rename the newly created **BTTask_BlueprintBase_New** object to DoAttackTask. Double-click on DoAttackTask to return to **Event Graph** for the new task.

We will need to create two variables within the task, one to store the target of the damage, and one to store the amount of damage to be applied. From the **My Blueprint** panel, use the + sign button next to **Variables** to create two variables. Call the first variable TargetActor, set its type to **Blackboard Key Selector**, and check the box next to **Instance Editable** in the **Details** panel. Now, rename the second variable as Damage, set its type to **Float**, and ensure that it is set to be editable. Finally, set the Damage variable's default value to 0.3:

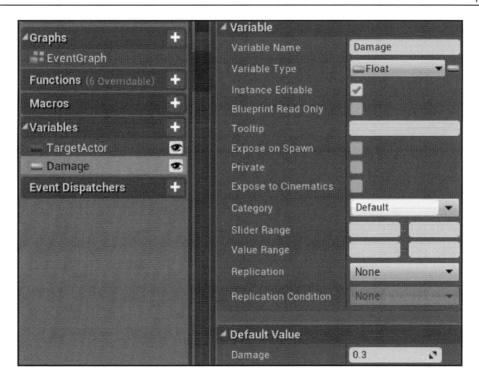

With the variables created, look at **EventGraph** of the task. We first want to grab the **Target Actor** variable, where we will later store a reference to the player. To begin, place an **Event Receive Execute** node in an empty grid space. Now, drag a wire from the output execution pin of the Event node to the graph and, in the search box, search for `IsValid` under the **Utilities** category. Attach the **IsValid** node to the Event node.

Add a **Get Blackboard Value as Actor** node to the graph. Drag the **Target Actor** variable to the **Key** input pin of **Get Blackboard Value as Actor**. Then, connect the **Return Value** output pin to the **Input Object** input pin of the **IsValid** node. Attach an **Apply Damage** node to the **Is Valid** output execution pin of the **IsValid** node. Next, establish how much damage is done on each attack by dragging the `Damage` variable onto the **Base Damage** input pin of the **Apply Damage** node. Connect the **Return Value** output pin to the **Damaged Actor** input pin of **Apply Damage** to establish the target of the damage.

Finally, conclude the task by attaching a **Finish Execute** node to the **Apply Damage** node and checking the box next to the **Success** input. After applying a descriptive comment around this group of nodes, your final result should look like this:

With the custom attack task created, return to **Behavior Tree**. Because we are creating this attack as a melee attack, we want the enemy to only perform the attack after reaching the player. Find the **Attack Player** sequence node in **Behavior Tree**, drag a wire down from the bottom of the node, and add a new **DoAttackTask** task node between the **Move To** and **Wait** task nodes, which already exist, as shown here:

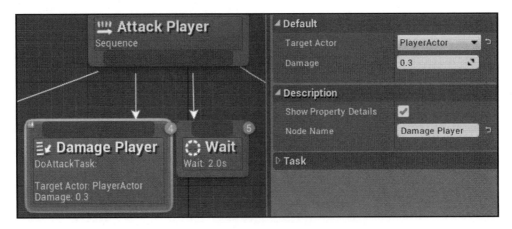

Click on the **DoAttackTask** node and change the **Target Actor** selection in the **Details** panel to `PlayerActor`. You can also change **Node Name** to `Damage Player` to add some descriptive details to your use of the task. With our Behavior Tree set up to use our custom task that applies damage, we should be in a good position to test our work. However, if you compile, save, and test, you will find that the health meter does not appear to be affected when the enemy closes in on you, despite the damage being applied. To fix this, we must add an Event to change the health meter when damage is dealt. Go to **Content Browser**, navigate to the `Blueprints` folder, and open `FirstPersonCharacter`.

Updating the health meter

You will recall that in previous chapters, we linked the meters that are displayed on our **Heads-Up Display (HUD)** to variables contained within `FirstPersonCharacter`. In order to show the health meter decreasing in response to taking damage, we must decrease the player health variable each time damage is received. We also want to ensure that the player's health can never go below 0 to avoid potential bugs that an unexpected negative health value might cause. The end result will look like this:

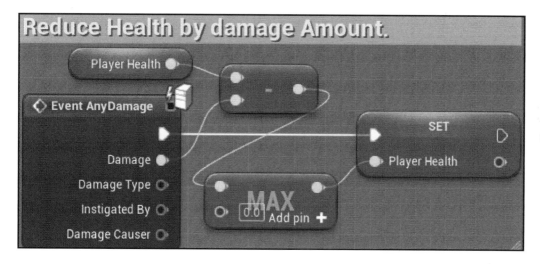

Begin by adding the **Event AnyDamage** Event node to empty graph space. Drag the **Player Health** variable onto the graph and use it to create a **GET Player Health** node. Attach this variable node to a **float - float** node. Now, drag a wire from the **Damage** output pin of the Event node and attach it to the bottom input pin of the **float - float** node.

To ensure that the health value never goes below 0, drag a wire from the output pin of the **float - float** node and attach it to a **MAX (float)** node. Leave the bottom input field at its default value of 0.0. This node will return the higher of the two values given as inputs. This way, if the calculated health ever goes below the lowermost value of 0.0, then it will return 0.0 rather than the player's health value calculated after the damage is subtracted. Finally, connect the output pin of the **MAX (float)** node to a **SET Player Health** node to adjust the variable value, and thus the health meter display.

Select all these nodes and create a comment that describes the functionality. Then, compile, save, and press **Play** to test this. You should now notice the player's health meter depleting when an enemy gets within range of the player and stops to attack.

Making enemies hear and investigate sounds

Now that our enemy is attacking the player, we want to give some additional attention to the means by which the enemy can detect the player. Enemies that can only pursue players who walk directly in front of them can easily be avoided. To address this, we will take advantage of our **PawnSensing** Component to have the enemy detect nearby sounds that the player makes. If the player makes a sound within the detection range of an enemy, then the enemy will walk to the location of that sound to investigate. If they catch the player in their sight, they will make an attempt to attack, otherwise, they will wait at the location of the sound for a moment before returning to their patrol.

Adding hearing to the Behavior Tree

The first step to introducing any additional functionality to the AI is figuring out where that logic will fit within the Behavior Tree. Go to **Content Browser**, open the `Enemy` folder, and open `EnemyBehavior`. We are contemplating adding a sequence of Events that occur when the enemy hears a sound. We want the enemy to continue attacking the player once they see them, so investigating a sound should constitute a lower priority on the Behavior Tree. Move the **Attack Player** sequence and all of its task nodes further to the left in the **Behavior Tree**, leaving room between **Attack Player** and **Move to Patrol**. This is where we will add our hearing sequence. Drag a wire down from the **Selector** node and attach it to a new **Sequence** node. Rename this node as `Investigate Sound`.

To have an enemy investigate the point where it heard a sound, we will need to keep track of two bits of information. The first is whether or not a sound has been heard. The second is the location that the sound came from, and hence the location that the enemy AI should investigate. We will create two keys within the Blackboard to store this information. Click on the **Blackboard** tab of `EnemyBehavior`.

Next, click on the **New Key** button and choose to make a key of the **Vector** type. Call this key `LocationOfSound`. Click on **New Key** a second time, this time making it a **Bool** type, and call it `HasHeardSound`. With the keys created, click on the **Behavior Tree** tab to return to the Behavior Tree view.

Before we begin creating tasks, we can set up the condition that will determine when the investigation of a sound should take place. To do this, right-click on the **Investigate Sound** sequence node, hover over **Add Decorator**, and click on the **Blackboard** option. Now, click on the blue decorator and look at the **Details** panel. Under **Flow Control**, change the **Observer aborts** value to **Lower Priority**. This will ensure that the investigation can begin as soon as a sound is heard, even if the enemy is midway through a patrol task, by aborting the lower priority tasks. Now, look at the **Blackboard** category and change **Blackboard Key** to **HasHeardSound**. Combined with **Key Query** being **Is Set**, this will allow the **Investigate Sound** sequence tasks to fire only when a sound has actually been heard. Finally, name the node something representative of its Function. I suggest Heard Sound?:

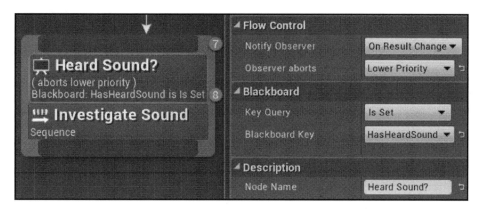

Setting up the investigating tasks

With the decorator set, we can move on to creating some of the tasks we will use to cause the enemy to investigate the location of the sound. The first Action of our investigation sequence will be to move the enemy to the location of the sound. We have already done something very similar in the attack sequence. Drag a wire down from the **Investigate Sound** sequence and attach it to a **Move To** task node.

In the **Details** panel of the **Move To** node, change **Blackboard Key** to **LocationOfSound**. Now, drag a second wire down and attach it to a **Wait** node. Change **Wait Time** to 4 seconds and **Random Deviation** to 1 second. This will cause the enemy to move to the location of the sound that it heard and wait at that location for 3 to 5 seconds, looking for the player.

Once the enemy is finished waiting at the investigation location, we want to reset the **Boolean** key that contains the information that a sound was heard. We do this so that when a new sound is heard, the key can be set to true one more time, causing another investigation to occur. We have already created a custom task called **ResetValueTask**. We need another task that does a similar job but is capable of resetting a Boolean value.

Click on the **New Task** button at the top of the Behavior Tree, and then select the **BTTask_BlueprintBase** option from the drop-down menu that appears. Return to **Content Browser** and find the new task object, called **BTTask_BlueprintBase_New**, in the **Enemy** folder. Rename this object as `ResetBoolTask`. Double-click on **ResetBoolTask** to return to the task's tab. We will assemble sets of Blueprint logic to handle cases where we need to reset the variable telling the AI that a sound was heard. The Blueprint nodes that we will construct can be seen in the following screenshot:

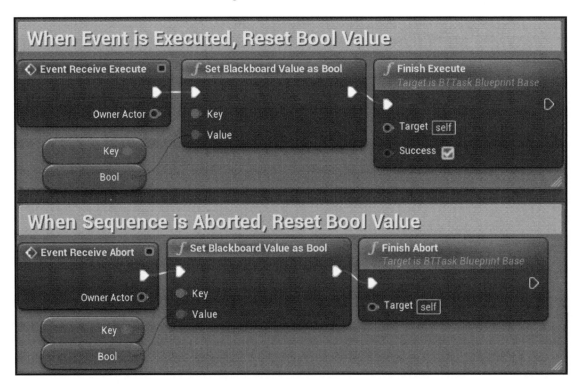

Look at the **My Blueprint** panel and add two variables. Call the first variable `Key` and change its type to **BlackboardKeySelector**. Rename the second variable as `Bool` and change its type to **Boolean**. Finally, ensure that both of these variables have the **Instance Editable** box checked.

Now, let's add the behavior for the task. Add an **Event Receive Execute** trigger node to the Event Graph. Drag a wire out from the execution pin and attach a **Set Blackboard Value as Bool** node. Next, drag the **Key** variable onto the **Key** input pin. Then, drag the **Bool** variable onto the **Value** input pin. Finally, drag a wire from the output execution pin of the **Set Blackboard Value as Bool** node and attach it to a **Finish Execute** node. Check the box next to the **Success** input of this node.

In addition to handling the execution Event, we will also have to address what happens when the hearing sequence in the Behavior Tree is aborted by the higher priority execution of the attack sequence. Even if the hearing sequence is aborted while in progress, we still need to ensure that the **HasHeardSound** variable is reset. We can do this using **Event Receive Abort**.

Add an **Event Receive Abort** trigger node to the graph, and then attach it to another **Set Blackboard Value as Bool** node. As before, drag the **Key** variable onto the **Key** input pin and the **Bool** variable to the **Value** input pin. Finally, drag a wire from the output execution pin of the **Set Blackboard Value as Bool** node, and then attach it to a **Finish Abort** node. Save the task and return to **EnemyBehavior**.

Drag a wire down and place a **ResetBoolTask** task node to the right of the **Wait** node. Change the **Key** selection to **HasHeardSound** inside the **Details** panel of **ResetBoolTask**. You should also change **Node Name** to Reset Player Heard in order to be more specific about its functionality. The final sequence of tasks should look like this:

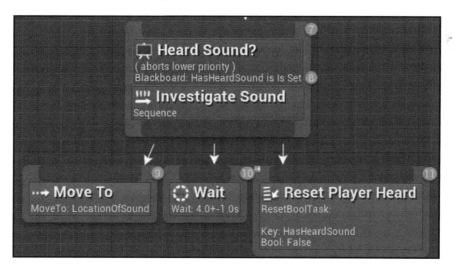

Interpreting and storing the noise Event data

The **PawnSensing** Component we added to **EnemyController** gives us the foundation to build both visual and auditory sensing in our enemy AI. Thus, we want to return to **EnemyController** and add some Blueprints that will instruct our AI how to react to the sounds in the world around them. Go to **Content Browser**, open the Enemy folder, and then open **EnemyController**.

In the **Components** panel, click on the **PawnSensing** object, and then use either the **search** Function or the **Events** section of the **Details** panel to add an **On Hear Noise (PawnSensing)** node. This node will activate any time the **PawnSensing** Component attached to **EnemyController** detects a special kind of sound broadcast by a pawn noise emitter. We will have to set up the Blueprint so that the enemies only detect noises that are made a short distance away, otherwise, it would feel unfair for the player to shoot their gun from the opposite corner of the map and let every enemy instantly know their location.

Attach a **Branch** node to the **On Hear Noise (PawnSensing)** node. Before continuing with the nodes that will store the data about the noise Event, we will first check whether the noise has occurred close enough to the enemy to trigger our investigate Action. To evaluate this, we have to compare the location of the noise Event detected and the location of the enemy. We will accomplish this by setting up a vector comparison, as shown in the following screenshot:

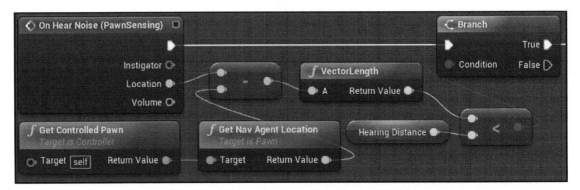

To figure out the location of the enemy doing the listening, create a **Get Controlled Pawn** node. Then, drag a wire out from the **Return Value** output pin and attach it to a **Get Nav Agent Location** node. These two nodes will output the location of the pawn object that is controlled by the AI controller we are currently editing.

We want to subtract the vector location of the enemy from the vector location of the noise to get our distance, so let's drag a wire from the **Location** output pin of **On Hear Noise (PawnSensing)**, and then attach it to a **Vector - Vector** node. Next, connect the bottom input pin of the **Vector - Vector** node to the **Return Value** output pin of **Get Nav Agent Location**. Drag a wire from the output pin of the **Vector - Vector** node, and then attach it to a **Vector Length** node. This will translate the vector length to a float number.

We can now evaluate whether the float number calculated is less than the threshold distance we want to define for the enemy's hearing range. Drag a wire from **Return Value** of the **Vector Length** node, and then attach it to a **Float < Float** node. Remember that, as with any arbitrary value that defines a property, you can create a variable here to replace the number field and make it easier to adjust your threshold at a later time. To do so, create a new variable of the float type and give it a default value that matches the number you want. I called this variable HearingDistance and gave it a value of 1600, which worked well for the layout of my Level. You may need to adjust this value to be appropriate for your map and intended gameplay. Attach your variable to the bottom input pin of the **Float < Float** node, or just type in the value.

To complete the condition, attach the output pin of **Float < Float** to the **Condition** input pin of the **Branch** node. This completes the steps we need in order to ensure that the sound being heard is within the range to act upon. Now, we need to store the data about that sound in our Blackboard so that the Behavior Tree can access it. The Blueprint nodes needed to accomplish this can be seen in the following screenshot:

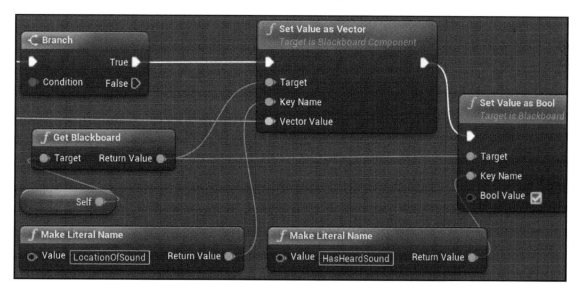

Start by dragging a wire from the **True** output execution pin of the **Branch** node, and then attach it to a **Set Value as Vector** node. You must uncheck **Context Sensitive** in the menu in order to see the **Set Value as Vector** node. We need to fill in the three inputs for this node to store data about our sound location. First, drag a wire from the **Target** input pin, and then attach it to a **Get Blackboard** node. Then, drag a wire from the **Target** input of **Get Blackboard** and attach it to a **Self** node. Next, drag a wire from the **Key Name** input of **Set Value as Vector** and attach it to a **Make Literal Name** node. Type LocationOfSound in the **Value** input as we want to store the vector location in the corresponding key in the Blackboard. Finally, drag a wire all the way from the **Location** output pin of the **On Hear Noise (Pawn Sensing)** Event node to the **Vector Value** input pin of the **Set Value as Vector** node.

The last thing we need to do is store the information that a sound has been heard in the Blackboard. Drag the output execution pin of **Set Value as Vector** out and attach it to a **Set Value as Bool** node. Drag a second wire from the **Return Value** output pin of the **Get Blackboard** node you used earlier to the **Target** input pin of **Set Value as Bool**. Now, drag a wire from the **Key Name** input pin out and attach it to a new **Make Literal Name** node. Inside this **Value** input, type HasHeardSound. Finally, ensure that the **Bool Value** checkbox input of **Set Value as Bool** is checked in order to designate that a sound has been heard. Wrap this entire series of nodes in a useful comment container, then compile and save your work.

Adding noise to the player's Actions

Now that we have modified our enemy AI to be able to detect sounds that are broadcast to the listener, we need to create the Blueprint nodes that will trigger the hearing response and attach them to player Actions. This will give us the opportunity to introduce additional risk-versus-reward choices. If firing the gun to take out an enemy has the potential of alerting all nearby enemies of the player's presence and location, then the player might think twice about choosing to open fire on the enemy until they are sure that they have the advantage.

The **PawnSensing** Component of **EnemyController** is only able to detect noise if it is created from **PawnNoiseEmitter**. The existing sound effect that we play when the player fires their gun will not trigger the enemy's **PawnSensing** Component. It is important to know that the nodes that produce noise for pawn sensing have no direct relationship with the sound a player hears. The noise exists only in terms of producing an Event that the AI can hear and respond to.

Open `FirstPersonCharacter` from the `Blueprints` folder under **Content Browser**. Click on the **Add Component** button and add **PawnNoiseEmitter**. This Component must be added to an Actor in order for the noises it broadcasts to be detected by a pawn sensor. We will now change two player abilities, namely sprinting and shooting, to produce detectable noise by utilizing this Component.

We will begin by adding noise to sprinting. We could have attached our noise-producing node at the end of the block of nodes that triggers a sprint. However, that would produce noise only one time per button push. Sprinting should logically produce noise with every footfall, as a repeated Event, for as long as the player is actively sprinting. Since we are actively draining the stamina of the player while they are holding down the sprint button, we also have the opportunity to repurpose this drain Function to produce noise repeatedly.

Start by finding the block of nodes that begins with the **Sprint Drain** custom Event. Drag a wire from the execution output pin of the **Set Player Stamina** node, and then attach it to a **Make Noise (PawnNoiseEmitter)** node. It is important that you choose the version of **Make Noise** that is produced from the **PawnNoiseEmitter** Component, which is indicated by `PawnNoiseEmitter`, displayed in parentheses next to the node name in the **Executable actions** search window. Only this version of the node will produce noise that is detectable by the **PawnSensing** Component of **Enemy Controller**:

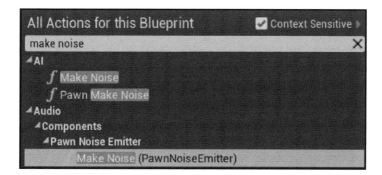

With **Make Noise (PawnNoiseEmitter)** connected, drag a wire out from the **Noise Location** input pin and attach it to a **GetActorLocation** node. Then, drag a wire from the **Noise Maker** input pin of **Make Noise (PawnNoiseEmitter)** and attach it to a **Self** node.

Finally, change the **Loudness** input field to 1. After editing the comments around these nodes to reflect the new functionality, the final result should look like this:

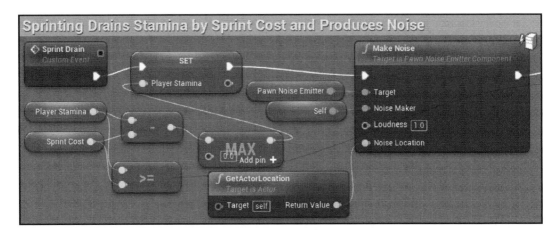

Next, we want to find the block of nodes that spawns the projectile when the player fires the gun. In Chapter 7, *Creating Screen UI Elements*, we added a few nodes to the end of this sequence. They reduced the ammo count every time a shot was fired. Find the **SET Player Current Ammo** node, and then drag a wire from its output execution pin to a **Make Noise (PawnNoiseEmitter)** node. Mimicking the steps followed for the sprint noise, attach a **Self** node to the **Noise Maker** input pin, attach a **GetActorLocation** node to the **Noise Location** input pin, and set the **Loudness** input to 1.0. You have the option to use a second wire from the **Return Value** output pin of the existing **GetActorLocation** node, which is attached to **Play Sound at Location**, rather than create a redundant node. This is shown in the following screenshot:

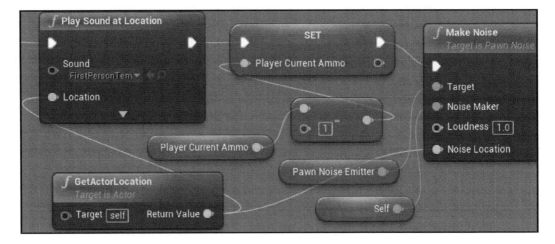

Compile, save, and then click on **Play** to test your work. While behind an enemy, or otherwise outside their line of sight, sprinting or firing your gun should result in the enemy approaching the position you were at when you made the noise. If they establish a line of sight with you during their investigation, then they will begin heading directly toward you.

Making the enemies destructible

With detection possible with both sight and sound, you might now find it difficult to avoid being spotted by enemies. We will now turn our attention to the other side of gameplay balancing, and equip the player with the means of combating the enemies.

Saving time by reusing existing Blueprint content

Recall that in earlier chapters, we created enemy targets that the player could destroy after a couple of hits with a projectile. We want to give the player a similar ability to mitigate the threat provided by our new enemies. To do so, we can repurpose the Blueprint nodes we already created to handle damage-taking and destruction.

Navigate to **Content Browser**, go inside the `Content/FirstPersonBP/Blueprints` folder, and open `CylinderTarget_Blueprint`. In **Event Graph**, find the sequence of nodes that are triggered by the **Event Hit** node. Click and drag a selection box around every node in this sequence, ensuring that you don't miss any connected nodes. With all the nodes in this sequence selected, right-click on any one of them and select the **Copy** option, as shown here:

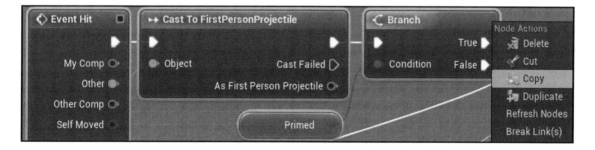

With the nodes copied, return to **Content Browser** and open EnemyCharacter inside the Enemy folder. Navigate sufficiently far away from other nodes to give yourself plenty of room, and then click on the *Ctrl + V* (PC) or *Command + V* (macOS) to paste the previously copied Blueprint nodes in this Event Graph. If you try compiling now, then you will see a few errors and warnings appear on some of the nodes, as seen in the following screenshot:

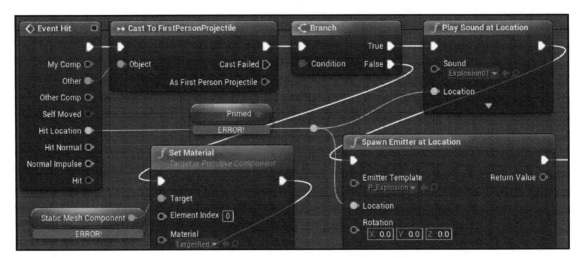

The errors you see are present on nodes that relied on Components and properties of the target cylinder Blueprint, but to which we no longer have access inside the **EnemyCharacter** Blueprint, most notably the **Primed** variable. The concept of priming an enemy before defeating them doesn't translate well in humanoid enemies anyway, so delete the **Get Primed** and **Set Primed** nodes, as well as the **Set Material** node attached to the **False** output execution pin of the **Branch** node. We will replace the primed concept with a more traditional health-tracking system.

We will need a variable to track the enemies' health as damage is applied. From the **My Blueprint** panel, create a new variable called **Enemy Health**. Change its type to **Integer**, and check the **Instance Editable** box. Finally, change its default value to the number of hits you would like each enemy to take before being killed. In my example, I chose to set this value to 3. Next, we will use this variable to check whether a hit would destroy the enemy or simply reduce its health by one. The nodes used to handle this **Branch** logic are shown in this screenshot:

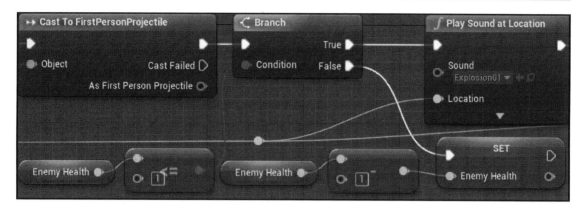

First, we need to determine the conditional node that will **Branch** whether or not an enemy is destroyed by a hit. Because we want the enemy to be destroyed when they reach zero health, we can make a comparison between the existing **Enemy Health** and the integer of 1. Moreover, because this evaluation happens before health is reduced, and each hit is going to reduce health by one, we know that receiving a hit with 1 health or less remaining will result in the enemy's health being 0.

Put this reasoning into practice by finding the **Branch** node that is led to by the **Cast To FirstPersonProjectile** node. Drag a wire from the **Condition** input of this node, and then attach it to an **integer <= integer** node. Drag the **Enemy Health** variable onto the top input pin of this node, and type 1 in the bottom input field.

Next, we need to decrease **Enemy Health** by 1 each time the enemy is hit with a shot but is not destroyed. Drag a wire from the **False** output execution pin of the **Branch** node, and then attach it to a **SET Enemy Health** node. Now, connect the **Enemy Health** input pin to an **integer <= integer** node. Finally, drag the **Enemy Health** variable onto the top input pin of **integer <= integer** and type 1 in the bottom input field.

From now on, when the player shoots an enemy a number of times equal to the value given to **Enemy Health**, they will explode and be destroyed in a similar fashion to how the cylinder targets behaved in previous chapters. Compile, save, and then press **Play** to see this in Action.

Spawning more enemies during gameplay

Now that we are able to destroy enemies, we need to ramp up the difficulty for the player again. To do so, we are going to spawn new enemies in the Level as the player is playing the game. In this way, the game can continue if the player destroys the first few enemies, and if they are too slow to defeat enemies, then the difficulty will gradually increase.

Choosing a spawn point where enemies will appear

First, we must decide where in the Level our enemies will spawn from. We will spawn enemies in random spots within a circular distance from an object placed in the Level. Return to the Level Editor by clicking on the `FirstPersonExampleMap` tab. Find the **PatrolPoint1** object in the **World Outliner** panel. Duplicate the object by right-clicking on it, selecting **Edit**, and then selecting **Duplicate**. Rename the new object as `SpawnPoint`. Move the **SpawnPoint** object close to the center of your Level, ensuring that it is located a bit off the ground in a player- and enemy-accessible area.

We will place the Blueprint nodes that will create new enemies inside **Level Blueprint**. A Level Blueprint is a special Blueprint that is tied to the entire level, serving as a global Event Graph. Level Blueprints are especially well suited for setting up Level-specific items, such as enemy placements and door behavior. To edit the Level Blueprint, click on the **Blueprints** button in the Level Editor toolbar and select the **Open Level Blueprint** option.

Managing spawn rates and limits with variables

Rather than relying on the placement of enemies in a Level on a set patrol, we are going to gradually spawn those enemies in the Level to present an increasingly aggressive threat to the player. As a consequence, we will set up our spawning logic to trigger repeatedly in a loop, with the time between spawns determined by a variable. In the **My Blueprint** panel, add a new variable called `SpawnTime`. Set its type to **Float**, make it editable, and set the default value to `10.0` for a 10-second spawn rate.

In addition to setting the spawn rate, we will also want some form of limiter on the spawning of enemies. Without this, an enemy would spawn every 10 seconds until the game ends, potentially filling the map with dozens of enemies. To prevent this, we will create an additional variable to set a cap on the number of enemies. Create another variable and call it MaxEnemies. Set the variable type to **Integer** and make it editable. I set the default value of **MaxEnemies** to 5, but you can set the number as high or as low as you think is the appropriate maximum number of enemies that your Level can support:

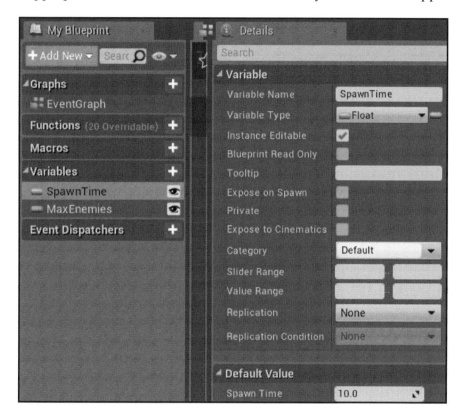

In order for **MaxEnemies** to Function as a cap on the number of enemies present in the level, we need a way of keeping track of the current number of enemies. To do this, we will temporarily leave the Level Blueprint, and instead, open the FirstPersonCharacter Blueprint, which is found in the Blueprints folder of **Content Browser**. Inside FirstPersonCharacter, create a new variable called CurrentEnemyCount. Set its type to **Integer** and ensure that **Instance Editable** is checked.

Level Blueprints can receive information from other Blueprints through casting, but there is no easy way to get information stored in a Level Blueprint and use it in other Blueprints. As a consequence, any variable you make that is likely to be affected by Actions in other Blueprints, such as the **CurrentEnemyCount** variable, is better placed outside of the Level Blueprint. In this case, we are storing it with the rest of our game data information on the player object.

Now that we have a variable to track the current enemy count, we need to decrease this value whenever an enemy is destroyed. Recall that the Blueprint nodes managing enemy destruction are located in the `EnemyCharacter` Blueprint. Open the `Enemy` folder in **Content Browser**, and then open the `EnemyCharacter` Blueprint:

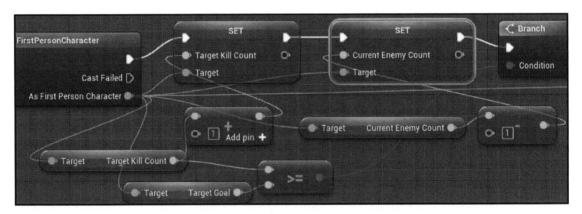

In the `EnemyCharacter` Blueprint, locate the series of nodes that are triggered by the **Event Hit** node. Near the end of this node sequence, find the **Cast To FirstPersonCharacter** node. Create some additional space between the **Set Target Kill Count** node and the **Branch** node, and then break the connection between their input and output execution nodes. Drag a wire out from the **As First Person Character** output pin of **Cast To FirstPersonCharacter**, and attach it to a **Set Current Enemy Count** node. Drag a wire from this node's **Current Enemy Count** input pin to an **integer - integer** node.

Now, drag another wire from the **As First Person Character** output pin of **Cast To FirstPersonCharacter**, and then attach it to a **GET Current Enemy Count** node. Attach this node to the top input pin of the **integer - integer** node, and then fill in the bottom input field with 1. Next, connect the **SET Target Kill Count** node to the input execution pin of **SET Current Enemy Count**. Finally, connect the output execution pin of this node to the **Branch** node.

Now that we have established variables to determine the spawn rate and cap the number of enemies in a level, we should return to the Level Blueprint. Click on the tab with a Blueprint icon that is labeled `FirstPersonExampleMap`.

Spawning new enemies in the Level Blueprint

In the Level Blueprint, turn your attention to the Event Graph. We want to initiate the spawning logic as soon as the game is played, and do so in a loop after every few seconds at a rate determined by the **Spawn Time** variable. Add an **Event BeginPlay** node to the Event Graph, and attach it to a **Set Timer by Function Name** node. Drag the **SpawnTime** variable onto the **Time** input pin, and check the box next to the **Looping** input pin. Finally, type `Spawn` inside the **Function Name** input field. We will create a custom **Spawn** Function that will be called on each pass through this loop. Remember to create a comment around these nodes as a reminder of the Function of this loop:

Now, add a **Custom Event** node to empty grid space by searching for and selecting **Add Custom Event...**, and then rename the node as `Spawn`. Drag a wire from the **Spawn** node and attach it to a **Cast To FirstPersonCharacter** node. Now, attach the output execution pin of this node to a **Branch** node.

Drag a wire out from the **Object** input node of **Cast To FirstPersonCharacter**, and then attach it to a **Get Player Character** node. Then, drag a wire from the **As First Person Character** output pin and attach it to a **Get Current Enemy Count** node. Drag out the **Current Enemy Count** output pin of this node and attach it to an **integer < integer** node. Next, drag the **Max Enemies** variable onto the bottom input pin of this node. Finally, drag a wire out from the **Condition** input pin of the **Branch** node and attach it to the **integer < integer** node's output pin. Your nodes should now match the following screenshot:

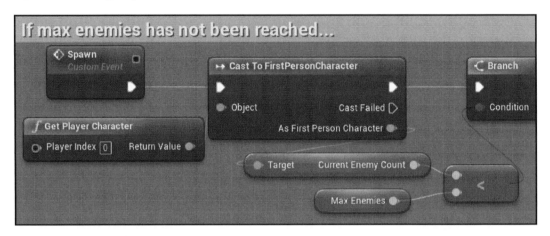

The next step is to actually spawn an enemy. To do this, drag a wire out from the **True** output execution pin of the **Branch** node, and then attach it to a **Spawn AI From Class** node. This node is custom-built to spawn new AI objects and requires you to designate a pawn and a Behavior Tree. Select **Enemy Character** from the drop-down menu on the **Pawn Class** input pin, and then select EnemyBehavior for the **Behavior Tree** input. Now, we need to get random locations and rotations for the remaining inputs of this node. The Blueprint nodes used to accomplish this can be seen in this screenshot:

Start by switching tabs back to the Level Editor. Inside the **World Outliner** panel of FirstPersonExampleMap, click on the **SpawnPoint** object so that it is highlighted. With **SpawnPoint** selected, return to the **Level Blueprint** tab. Go to the far-left of the other nodes, right-click in empty grid space, ensure that **Context Sensitive** is checked, and select the **Create a Reference to SpawnPoint** option. Attach the node that appears to a **Get Actor Location** node. Then, attach the **Return Value** output pin of this node to a **Get Random Point in Navigable Radius** node.

Get Random Point in Navigable Radius takes a location as an input and returns a random location within a designated distance away as an output. Set the **Radius** input of this node to a high number. I found 1000.0 to be an appropriate number to make most of my Level available for spawning. Attach the **Return Value** output pin to the **Location** input of the **Spawn AI From Class** node.

Next, drag a wire from the **Rotation** input pin of **Spawn AI From Class**, and then attach it to a **Make Rotator** node. This node converts three **Float** inputs into a rotation value. We only want to choose a random rotation for our spawned enemies in the **Z** axis because it is the rotation that indicates the direction that the enemy is looking in. So, drag a wire from the **Z (Yaw)** input pin and attach it to a **Random Float** node. The final input for the **Spawn AI From Class** node, **No Collision Fail**, enables or disables a built-in check to see whether or not the intended spawn location of the Actor is blocked by the collision of another object. If the check fails, which means that the Actor would be spawned partially inside another object, then the Actor will fail to spawn. Since we want to ensure that our enemies are not spawning inside other objects, we will leave this input unchecked, ensuring that this test happens. Create a comment container around this series of nodes, describing its utility for finding random rotation and location near the spawnpoint object.

The final step is to increase the enemy count each time an enemy is spawned. Drag a second wire from the **As First Person Character** output pin on the **Cast To FirstPersonCharacter** node, and then attach it to a **SET Current Enemy Count** node. Move this node to the right of the **Spawn AI From Class** node, and then connect the two execution pins. Now, drag a second wire out from the **Get Current Enemy Count** node near the casting node, and then attach it to an **integer + integer** node. Change the bottom input field to 1, and then move the node to the right of **Spawn AI From Class**. Finally, attach the output pin of the **integer + integer** node to the **Current Enemy Count** pin of the **Set Current Enemy Count** node.

After adding a descriptive comment to these nodes, the result should look like this:

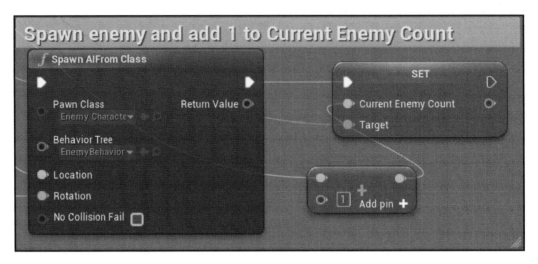

Compile, save, and click on **Play** to test your enemy spawning. Based on what you have set your spawn rate to and where you have placed your spawn point, you should regularly see new enemies appear as you run the game. You will notice, however, that the enemies are not moving once spawned unless they hear or see the player. This is because they are not being created with an established patrol point to pursue. Rather than adding patrol points to our spawned enemies, we will add randomness to our enemy navigation behavior.

Creating enemy wandering behavior

In Chapter 9, *Building Smart Enemies with Artificial Intelligence*, we set the default behavior for enemies as a patrolling movement between two points. While this worked well as a testbed for our hearing and seeing Components, and would be appropriate for a stealth-oriented game, we are going to ramp up the challenge and Action of this game's experience by replacing this behavior with random wandering. This will make avoiding enemies significantly harder, encouraging more direct confrontations. To do this, we are going to return to the EnemyBehavior Behavior Tree. Open EnemyBehavior from the Enemy folder in the **Content Browser**.

Identifying a wander point with a custom task

Once you've opened `EnemyBehavior`, click on the **Blackboard** tab. We need to create a key that will store the location of the next destination that the enemy should wander to. Unlike the **PatrolPoint** key, our destination won't be represented by an in-game Actor, but rather, by vector coordinates. Now, create a new key in the **Blackboard** panel and call this key `WanderPoint`. Change **Key Type** to **Vector**. Next, click on the **Behavior Tree** tab to return to the Behavior Tree.

In the Behavior Tree, we can remove two of the sequences we have already established to handle moving between patrol points and idling. Select the **Move to Patrol** and **Idle** sequence nodes, along with their attached task nodes, and delete them. Now, drag a wire out from the **Selector** node and attach it to a new **Sequence** node. Rename this node to `Wander`, and then move this node to the right of both the **Attack Player** and **Investigate Sound** sequences.

The first task of our `Wander` sequence will be to determine where in the Level the enemy should be wandering. For this, we will need to create another custom task. Click on the **New Task** button and select the **BTTask_BlueprintBase** option from the drop-down menu. Return to **Content Browser** and find the new task object called **BTTask_BlueprintBase_New** in the **Enemy** folder. Rename this task object to `FindWanderPointTask`. Double-click on `FindWanderPointTask` to open the **Event Graph** Editor for the new task.

We will set up nodes that will grab the location of the enemy Actor and generate a random point within a radius around that location. This point will then be stored as our `WanderPoint`. The nodes used to accomplish this can be seen in the following screenshot:

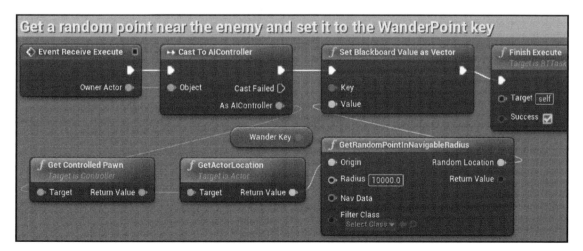

First, we need to create a variable within this task that will allow us to establish a reference to **Blackboard Key**. Add a new variable and call it WanderKey. Set the type to **BlackboardKeySelector** and make sure that the **Instance Editable** checkbox is selected.

Now, add an **Event Receive Execute** node to the Event Graph. Drag a wire from the **Owner Actor** output pin and attach it to a **Cast To AIController** node. Then, attach the two nodes' execution pins. Now that we have access to the AI controller, we can access its controlled Actor's location. Drag a wire out from the **As AIController** output pin of the casting node, and then attach it to a **Get Controlled Pawn** node. Next, drag a wire out from the **Return Value** output pin of this node, and then attach it to a **GetActorLocation** node.

With the enemy Actor's location in hand, we can now generate the random location that will serve as our WanderPoint. Drag a wire out from the **Return Value** output pin of **Get Actor Location**, and then attach it to a **Get Random Point in Radius** node. Set the **Radius** value of this node to a large number that should cover most or all of your Level. I set mine to 10000.

Next, we need to store this vector in the Blackboard. Drag a wire out from the **Random Location** output pin of **Get Random Point in Radius**, and then attach it to a **Set Blackboard Value as Vector** node. Drag the **WanderKey** variable onto the **Key** input of this node, and then attach the input execution pin to the output execution pin of the **Cast To AIController** node. Finally, drag a wire out from the output execution pin of **Set Blackboard Value as Vector**, attach it to a **Finish Execute Node**, and check the **Success** input box.

Add a descriptive comment around these nodes. Then, compile and save this Blueprint. Click on the **EnemyBehavior** tab to return to the Behavior Tree.

Adding wandering to the Behavior Tree

Now that we have our custom task, we can make the task sequence that will cause the enemy to find a WanderPoint, move to it, and wait there for a brief period of time. These Actions are represented by the nodes of the screenshot:

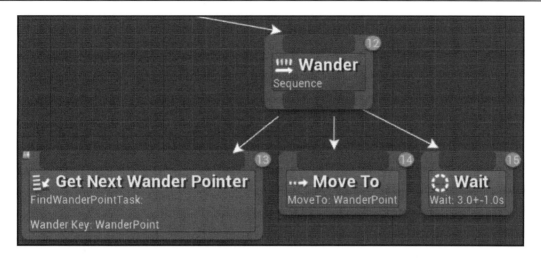

Start by dragging a wire out from the **Wander** sequence node, and then attach it to your new **FindWanderPointTask** task node. Click on the new node and change **Wander Key**, which is in the **Details** panel, to **WanderPoint**. Also, change **Node Name** to Get Next Wander Point in order to be more explicit about its purpose.

Drag another wire down from the **Wander** sequence node, and then attach it to a **MoveTo** task node. Click on this node and change **Blackboard Key** to WanderPoint. Move this node to the right of the **Get Next Wander Point** node. Drag the third wire down and attach it to a **Wait** task node, placing the node to the right of those other two task nodes. In the **Details** panel, change **Wait Time** to 3.0 and **Random Deviation** to 1.0 to give the wait time a bit of variance. Now, save the Behavior Tree.

A few final modifications should be made before we test our work. Return to the Level Editor by clicking on FirstPersonExampeMap. Any enemies you have manually placed in the world can now be removed, as we now have an enemy spawner to serve the Function of creating our enemies. Find the enemy Actors in **World Outliner** and delete them by right-clicking on the object, selecting **Edit**, and then selecting **Delete**. Now, find the FirstPersonCharacter object and select it. In the **Details** panel, scroll down until you see a list of the variables we attached to the character Blueprint. Unless you created a custom category for these variables, they will be listed under the **Default** category. From here, we can easily modify the game values that determine player behavior and our win conditions.

In this case, we want to modify the **Target Goal** value to be higher so that the game can continue for a longer period of time. I set this value to 20 so that the player must eliminate 20 enemies before winning the game:

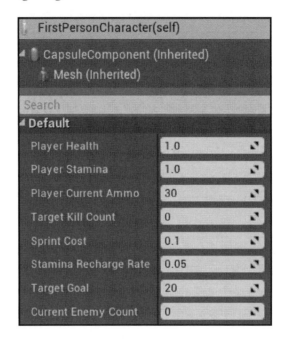

Now, click on **Play** to run the game. You should see the spawned enemies choosing paths in random directions and moving toward them. When enemies reach their WanderPoint, they will pause there briefly before choosing another random point and walking there. You will also notice that the enemies choose their WanderPoint independently of one another. This is because each enemy has its own instance of the Behavior Tree. Thus, every Behavior Tree task, such as the one we just created to find a WanderPoint, is running independently for each enemy. You will also notice that because we chose to have higher-priority sequences abort lower-priority sequences, any time an enemy hears or sees the player, they will end their wander movement and begin approaching the player or the location of the sound.

Summary

In this chapter, we started off on the path of creating a challenging but balanced game experience by enhancing the capabilities of our AI-driven enemies. We gave our enemies zombie-like behavior by allowing them to wander aimlessly around the Level until noticing the player by sight or sound. We also gave them the ability to charge forward when they noticed the player and launch a melee attack, lowering the player's health. Then, we gave the player the chance to fight back by attacking the enemy, eventually destroying them once the enemy's health is depleted. Finally, we gave new flexibility to our game by setting up a system to create new enemies as the game is being played.

At this point, the core content of our game is nearly complete. You should feel proud of the significant progress you have made! You can take some time to tweak the many variables you have created to customize the gameplay to your liking, or you can continue reading if you are ready to move on to the final systems.

In the next chapter, we will add the final Components necessary for a full game experience. We will end the game when the player runs out of health, create a round-based advancement system, and create a save system so that the player can return to a previously saved game state.

11
Game States and Applying the Finishing Touches

In this chapter, we will take the final steps to evolve our game into a complete and fun experience that challenges the player. First, we will introduce player death, which is activated when the player's health is fully drained. Then, we will introduce a round system that will elevate the challenge for the player by requiring increasingly numerous enemies to be defeated as they progress through the rounds. Finally, we will introduce a saving and loading system so that the player can leave the game and later return to the round that they were last playing. With these things accomplished, we will have an arcade-style first-person shooter that a player can continually return to for an increasingly difficult challenge. In the process, we will cover the following topics:

- Branching menus based on player conditions
- Creating scaling difficulty with gameplay modifiers
- Supporting the game state being saved and reloaded at a later time
- Branching level initialization based on the saved data
- Creating transition screens that display gameplay data

Making danger real with player death

In Chapter 10, *Upgrading the AI Enemies*, we made significant progress toward a balanced game in which enemies threaten the player but the player can use skill to overcome that challenge. One missing component glaringly remains. If the player runs out of health, then they should not be able to continue progressing through the game. Instead, we will take what we've learned about from the win screen we created in Chapter 8, *Creating Constraints and Gameplay Objectives*, and apply it to a lose screen. This screen will enable the player to restart the level with full ammo and a freshly filled health bar, but will also negate any progress they had made toward reaching their target goal.

Setting up a lose screen

The lose screen will be presented when the player runs out of health. We will present them with options to restart the last round or quit the game. You may remember the win screen we created; we presented similar options there. Rather than remaking the UI screen from scratch, we can save some time by using our `WinMenu` object as a template.

Go to **Content Browser** and open the `UI` folder inside `FirstPersonBp`. Right-click on `WinMenu` and select the **Duplicate** option. Name this new Blueprint Widget `LoseMenu`. Now, open `LoseMenu` and select the text object showing **You Win**. Look at the **Details** panel and change the **Text** field under **Content** to `You Lose. Try Again?`. Also, change the **Color and Opacity** setting to a dark red color. Finally, you may wish to change the **Shadow Color** setting's alpha value **A** from `0.0` to `1.0` in order to show shadows behind the text, as shown in this screenshot:

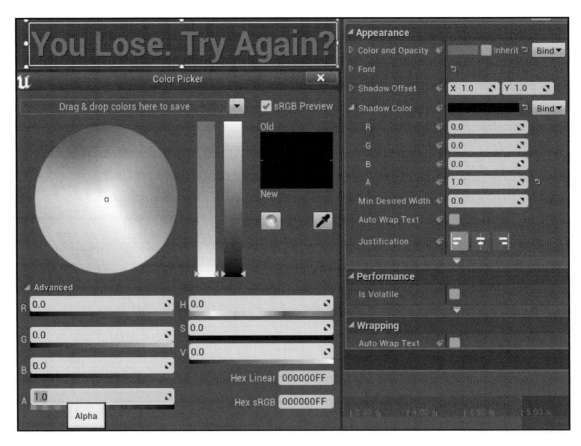

The two buttons, **Restart** and **Quit**, can remain identical to their WinMenu counterparts in appearance and functionality for now. Compile and save this Blueprint, and then return to the **Content Browser**. Open FirstPersonCharacter inside the Blueprints folder.

To track whether or not the player has lost the game, we will need to create a new variable. From the **My Blueprint** panel, add a new variable called Lost Game. In the **Details** panel, set **Variable Type** to **Boolean**. With the variable created, find the series of nodes we used to decrease the player's health, triggering the **Event Any Damage** node.

We will need to extend the **SET Player Health** operation with a **Branch** comparison that will test whether the player's health is less than zero, and if so, set the **Lost Game** variable to **True** and end the game. The nodes used to accomplish this are shown in the following screenshot:

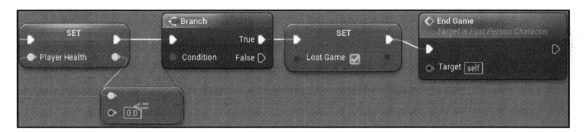

Begin by giving yourself additional room to the right of the **SET Player Health** node. Drag a wire from the output execution pin of this node to a **Branch** node. Then, connect the **Condition** input pin of the **Branch** node to a **float <= float** node. Leave the bottom input field of this new node as 0.0, and then connect the top input pin to the output pin of the **SET Player Health** node.

Now, drag a wire from the **True** output execution pin of the **Branch** node, and then connect it to a **SET Lost Game** node. Check the **Lost Game** input pin box to set this **Boolean** to **True** when the player runs out of health. Then, connect the **SET Lost Game** node to an **End Game** node, which will call our previously created Function to show WinMenu. The next step will be to edit the **End Game** Function so that it will show LoseMenu if the Function is called while the **Lost Game** variable is set to **True**.

Find the block of nodes that triggers the **End Game** Event, where we call our WinMenu screen. After the nodes that pause the game and enable the mouse arrow, we are going to create a branch node that will test the **Lost Game** variable, as seen in the following screenshot:

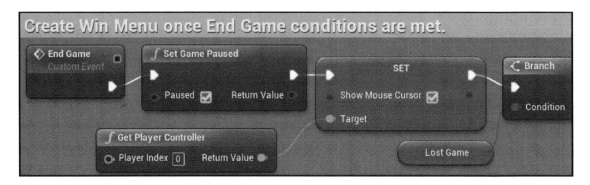

Start by breaking the connection between the **SET Show Mouse Cursor** and **Create WinMenu_C Widget** nodes, and then drag the **Widget** and **Viewport** nodes to the side for now. Then, connect the **Set Show Mouse Cursor** node to a new **Branch** node. Next, drag the **Lost Game** variable onto the **Condition** input pin of the **Branch** node. The next step will be to create and display LoseMenu when **Lost Game** is **True**, and WinMenu when it is **False**, as seen in this screenshot:

Drag a wire from the **True** output execution pin of the **Branch** node, and then connect it to a new **Create Widget** node. Inside this node, select `LoseMenu` from the **Class** input drop-down menu. Then, drag a wire from the **Return Value** output pin to an **Add to Viewport** node. Finish the **True** branch by attaching the Viewport node to a **SET Lost Game** node, and ensure that the **Lost Game** input checkbox is left unchecked. This step is necessary to ensure that the game won't mistakenly think that the player has already lost if they restart or resume playing later. Finally, reconnect the create Widget and Viewport nodes you dragged aside earlier to the **False** output execution pin of the **Branch** node.

Compile, save, and then click on **Play** to test your work. If you stand next to an enemy long enough for it to drain your health to zero, then you should now see `LoseMenu` we created.

Now, the player needs to be more careful with the enemies, so as to not lose the game. The next step to make the game more interesting is to create a round-based experience.

Creating round-based scaling with saved games

We now have a game that supports a full play experience. The game can be won with the appropriate application of skill, but can also be lost by getting overwhelmed by the intelligent enemies we created. However, the gameplay experience is limited to the number of enemies we have set as our target goal. This results in the game feeling shallow. To address this, we can adopt techniques used by arcade games, which increase the difficulty of the game as the player progresses through a series of rounds. This is a way to add depth and fun to your game using the existing assets, without requiring you to spend hours creating custom content.

The rounds we create will serve as the score of the player. The higher the round they reach, the more the player is thought to have achieved. To ensure that the maximum round the player reaches is limited only by their skill, rather than the amount of time for which they play the game in a single sitting, we will implement a save system so that the player can pick up from where they left off if they leave the game and come back to it later.

Storing game information using Save Game Object

The first step we need to perform in order to create a save system is to create a new kind of Blueprint that will store the game data that we want to save. Go to the **Content Browser** and open the `Blueprints` folder. Click on the **Add New** button, select **Blueprints**, and then click on **Blueprint Class**. In the window that appears, search for and select **SaveGame** to create a new Blueprint of that class. Name this Blueprint `SaveSystem`, and then double-click on it to open the Blueprint.

This Blueprint will contain our variable stored for the saved data:

In our case, we are going to implement a series of increasingly difficult rounds, so we want to track which round the player was on before they quit the game. We do not need to store any data on how many enemies the player has killed because it would make more sense to the player for each game session to start at the beginning of a round. To track the current round, create a new variable called `CurrentRound` from the **My Blueprint** panel. Change **Variable Type** to **Integer**, and then mark the variable as **Instance Editable**. Compile the Blueprint and set its **Default Value** to **1**. That's all we need to do in `SaveSystem`. Compile again and save the Blueprint now.

Storing and loading the saved data when starting the game

Now that we have a container for our saved data, we need to ensure that the data is stored somewhere on the player's machine and that it is retrieved when the player returns to the game. We also want the saved data to be updated each time the level loads because we will increase the current round number each time the player wins a round. Like the rest of our gameplay settings, we will add this process to the `FirstPersonCharacter` Blueprint. Now, go to **Content Browser**, open the `Blueprints` folder, and open `FirstPersonCharacter`.

In addition to the `SaveSystem` Blueprint, which will store information about what gameplay data to save, we are going to need **Save Game Object** that will actually contain the particular data for that user. To easily reference this saved data, we will save it in a variable that we can reference throughout `FirstPersonCharacter`. From the **My Blueprint** panel, create a new variable called `SaveGameInstance`. In the **Details** panel, click on the **Variable Type** drop-down menu and search for `Save System`. Select the **Save System** option to allow this variable to contain an instance of the `SaveSystem` Blueprint that we just created, as shown in the following screenshot. This variable does not need to be editable, and you should leave the default value to **None**:

Now, find the block of Blueprint nodes that draws the **Heads-Up Display (HUD)** on the screen when the gameplay begins, triggering the **Event BeginPlay** node. Similar to what we did with the `WinMenu` sequence, break the connections between **Event BeginPlay** and **Create HUD Widget**. Then, drag the Widget node and its connections to the side to make room for a significant number of new nodes. Back at the **Event BeginPlay** node, drag a wire out from its output execution pin, and then attach it to a **Does Save Game Exist** node.

When the game begins, we are going to use **Does Save Game Exist** to check for the existence of a save game file that features the save slot and user we specify in the node. We are going to save our data in a single save slot only so that each save operation will overwrite the previously saved data. Additionally, we will not create a user system for our game, so anyone playing the game on a particular machine will be assumed to be the only player. A **Branch** node will direct the game operations, depending on whether or not a saved game is found. If no saved game exists, then a new **Save Game Object** of `SaveSystem` type will be created. If one already exists, then we will load the saved data from it.

The nodes used to accomplish this can be seen in this screenshot:

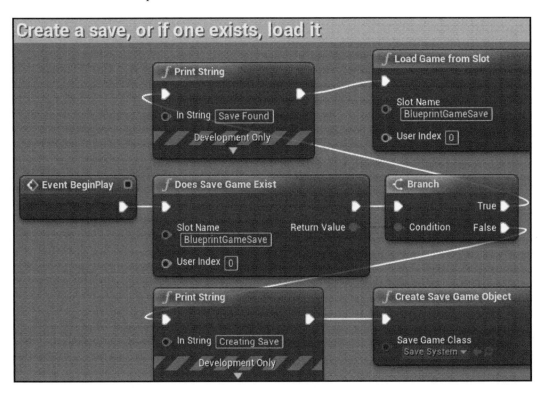

First, we must determine what our saved game slot is going to be called. In the **Slot Name** input field of **Does Save Game Exist**, type `BlueprintGameSave`. Leave the **User Index** input at 0. This combination asks the player whether there is a saved game by the first user in the user index, which will be our only user, and in the save slot called `BlueprintGameSave`, which will be our only save slot. Next, drag a wire from the **Return Value** output pin of **Does Save Game Exist**, and then attach it to a **Branch** node.

Whenever you are constructing a complex system, such as our save structure, it is wise to use the **Print String** nodes, as shown in the previous screenshot, to evaluate whether your Blueprint logic is behaving the way you think it should during gameplay. In the preceding case, we are finding out whether or not a saved game was found and printing the result.

From the **Branch** node, we will create a path to load content from a saved game, and another path to create a save game file. Drag a wire from the **True** output execution pin of the **Branch** node. If you wish to see a debug message printed on the screen when a saved game is supposed to be loaded, then you can first route the **True** path of the **Branch** node through a **Print String** node, as seen in the preceding example. But this is not necessary to make the save system work. Whether you choose to use a **Print String** node or not, ensure that the **Branch** node is connected to a **Load Game from Slot** node, and then enter `BlueprintGameSave` in the **Slot Name** input field.

Next, drag a wire from the **False** output execution pin of the **Branch** node. Again, you have the choice of attaching the wire to a **Print String** node to aid in debugging or just attaching it directly to a **Create Save Game Object** node. Within this node, click on the **Save Game Class** input dropdown, and then select **Save System** from the options presented.

Now, we need to ensure that the saved data, whether we just created it or are loading it from an existing file, is stored inside our `SaveGameInstance` variable. This can be accomplished through casting, as seen here:

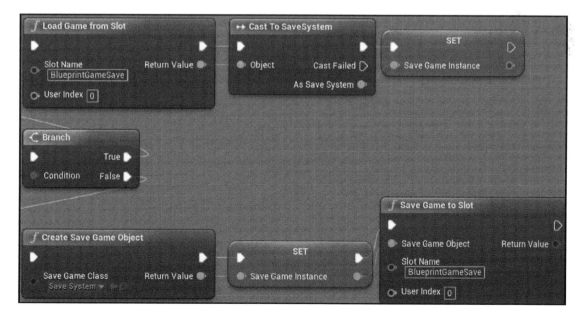

Start by dragging a wire from the **Return Value** output pin of the **Load Game from Slot** node, and then attach it to a **Cast To SaveSystem** node. Also, connect the execution pins of these two nodes. Then, drag the `SaveGameInstance` variable onto the **As Save System** output pin of the casting node to both create and attach a **SET Save Game Instance** node.

Next, attach the same variable data-storing nodes in the branch where we are creating a new **Save Game Object**. Drag the `SaveGameInstance` variable onto the **Return Value** output pin of the **Create Save Game Object** node. The cast node is not needed because the **Create Save Game Object** node returns an instance of the **Save System** class used as an input parameter.

With our **Save Game Object** created and stored in a variable, we need to save this data in a file that will be stored on the player's machine. Drag a wire from the output pin of the **SET Save Game Instance** node we just created, and then drop it onto a **Save Game to Slot** node. Inside this node, enter `BlueprintGameSave` in the **Slot Name** input field. This will complete the steps necessary to create or load a save file when the game starts playing. Select all these nodes and wrap them in a comment box in order to leave a note about their functionality for yourself.

Increasing the enemy target goal

Our next goal is to take advantage of the data we can store in the save file to change the gameplay for the player as they progress. We will do this by extracting the current round from the save file and multiplying the number of enemies that need to be defeated in order to complete a round by a new multiplier variable we will create. This is shown in the following screenshot:

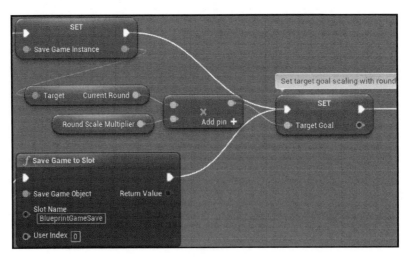

Begin by creating a new variable in the **My Blueprint** panel, and then rename it to
RoundScaleMultiplier. Change its **Variable Type** to **Integer**, and then set the default
value to a low number, such as 2. With a multiplier of 2, each round will add two more
enemies that need to be defeated before the player can progress to the next round.

Now that we have a multiplier variable, we will multiply it with the current round
information stored in the save file, and then use the result for TargetGoal. First, drag a
wire from the **Save Game to Slot** node's output execution pin, and then attach it to a **SET
Target Goal** node. Also, connect the output execution pin of the **SET Save Game Instance**
node that ends the loading sequence to the same **SET Target Goal** node so that both the
save object creation and save object loading branches end on the same node.

Next, drag a wire from one of the **SET Save Game Instance** nodes' output pins, and
then attach it to a **GET Current Round** node. Attach the output pin of this node to an
Integer * Integer node. Then, drag the RoundScaleMultipler variable onto the bottom
input pin of the newly created **Integer * Integer** node. Finally, attach the output pin of this
node to the input **Target Goal** pin of **SET Target Goal**. Even though these nodes are
connected to our save system, scaling the target goal is a relatively independent Function
that happens to trigger in the same Event. As such, select all four nodes that you just
created and give them their own comment box in order to leave you with a reminder of
their purpose.

The final step for establishing our game initialization logic is to reconnect the HUD creation
and drawing nodes to the sequence we have just concluded. Connect the output execution
pin of the **SET Target Goal** node to the **Create HUD Widget** node's input execution node,
as seen in this screenshot:

We already have the initialization needed for the round-based system. Now, we need a
transition screen to be shown between rounds.

Creating a transition screen to be shown between rounds

Currently, when the player defeats enough enemies to meet the requirements displayed by `TargetGoal`, they are presented with `WinMenu`. It congratulates them and offers them the opportunity to restart the game or quit the application. Now that we are adopting round-based gameplay, we want to replace this `WinMenu` screen with a transition screen that will bring the player into the next round of gameplay.

We will start by making substantial modifications to our `WinMenu` Blueprint Widget. Go to **Content Browser** and open the **UI** folder. Rename the `WinMenu` Blueprint to `RoundTransition` so that it more accurately reflects its new purpose. Now, open the `RoundTransition` Blueprint.

First, go to the **Hierarchy** panel and select the `Quit` button object. Delete this button, as we will not need to present an option to quit during the round transitions. Next, click on the **Restart** button object and rename it to `Begin Round`. Click on the **Text** object (nested underneath the button object) and in the **Details** panel, change the text from `You Win!` to `Begin Round`. Finally, move this button to the lower-middle part of the canvas.

After that, select and delete the **You Win!** text block object. From the **Palette** panel, search for and drag down a new **Horizontal Box** object. Name this box `Round Display` and check the **Size To Content** property. Back in the **Palette** panel, search for a **Text** object, and then drag two of them down to the **Hierarchy** panel, placing them both on top of the **Round Display** object we created.

Select the first of these **Text** objects, and then look at the **Details** panel. Change the **Text** field to `Round`, including the space. Also, change the font size to `150`. Now, select the other **Text** object. Change its font size to `150` as well, and change its **Text** field to any two-digit number. Finally, select the `Round Display` parent object again, and then resize the box until both the round text and the two-digit number can be seen fully. Place this object above the `Begin Round` button on the canvas. The final result of this layout should resemble the following screenshot:

Now, we need to add behavior to this screen. Because the `Begin Round` button is merely a renamed version of the old `Restart` button, and we want the functionality of reloading the level to remain the same, we can leave this button alone. The additional binding behavior we need is to adjust the round number to match the round stored in the current save file. To start this process, click on the numbered text object, which is shown as **10** in the preceding screenshot, and then click on the **Bind** button next to the **Text** field in the **Details** panel. Next, click on the **Create Binding** option.

Our goal for this binding is to extract the current round from the saved game and show it on the screen in the form of text. The nodes used to accomplish this can be seen in the following screenshot:

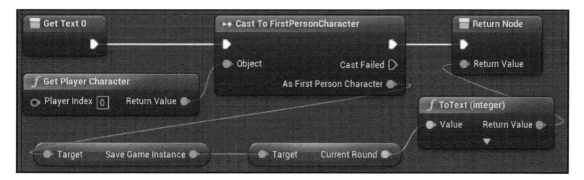

The current round is accessible through the **Save Game Instance** variable attached to our player character, so we must first cast to that Blueprint to extract the save game information. Attach a **Cast To FirstPersonCharacter** node to the initial **Get Text 0** node, and then connect the output execution pin of that node to **Return Node** that concludes this binding. Now, drag the **Object** input pin of the casting node out, and attach it to a **Get Player Character** node.

With the player character referenced, we drag a wire from the **As First Person Character** output pin and attach it to a **GET Save Game Instance** node. Then, we attach the output pin of this node to a **GET Current Round** node. With this information in hand, we can convert the data to text. If we attach the output pin of the **GET Current Round** node to the **Return Value** input pin of **Return Node**, then a **To Text (Int)** translation node will be created for us automatically. Compile and save the RoundTransition Blueprint to finish your work here.

Transitioning to a new round when the current round is won

Now that we have a transition screen to display, we want to integrate it into our **End Game** sequence and combine it with the nodes that will increment the round each time the player beats their target goal. Return to the FirstPersonCharacter Blueprint, which is located inside the Blueprints folder of the **Content Browser**, to start working toward this goal.

Find the sequence of nodes you modified to branch between the win and lose menus that are triggered by the **End Game** Event. In the **Branch** node, disconnect the **Create Round Transition Widget** and **Add to Viewport** nodes from the **False** output execution pin, and then move them to the right. We will add nodes that increase the round by one and save that new round number in the save file, before displaying the transition screen. The Blueprint nodes meant for calculating and saving the current round number can be seen in the following screenshot:

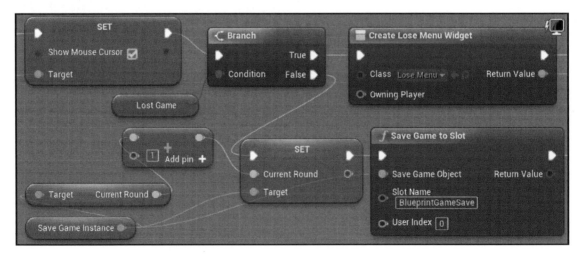

Begin by dragging and dropping the **Save Game Instance** variable onto the grid below the **Branch** node, and then selecting the **Get** option from the menu that appears. Then, drag a wire out from this node and attach it to a **SET Current Round** node. Attach the input execution pin of this node to the **False** output execution pin of the **Branch** node. Next, we need to calculate the integer that will be set as the current round.

Drag a second wire from the **GET Save Game Instance** node and attach it to a **GET Current Round** node. Now, attach this node to an **integer + integer** node. Fill in the bottom input field with the number 1, and then attach the output pin of this node to the **Current Round** input pin of the **SET Current Round** node. Finally, store this information in the save file by dragging the third wire from the **GET Save Game Instance** node and attaching it to a **Save Game to Slot** node. Attach the input and output execution pins of this node and the **SET Current Round** node, and then fill in the **Slot Name** input field with
`BlueprintGameSave`.

Next, we need to connect the **Save Game to Slot** node to the **Create Round Transition Widget** node, as seen in the following screenshot. We are now ready to test whether our round system is functional. Compile and save this Blueprint, and then click on the **Play** button to test:

When you load the game, you should notice that the target goal counter at the top of the game has a low number of enemies as the goal. Defeat the number of enemies indicated by the goal and you should see the round transition screen appear, displaying **Round 2**. When you press the **Begin Round** button, you will reload the level with your health and ammo restored, but with a higher number of enemies as the target. Defeat the number of enemies shown by the new target, and then you should be presented with the **Round 3** transition screen. Finally, if you quit the game and then click on the **Play** button again, you should find that the game loads the round that you were last on.

Pausing the game and resetting the save file

Now that we have the ability to track the player's progress, we should offer them the ability to reset his save file if they wish to begin the game from the start. We can accomplish this through the addition of a pause menu, which has the added benefit of allowing the player to take a temporary break from the Action.

Creating a pause menu

First, we will create a pause menu that will present the player with options to resume playing the game, to reset the game to round one, or to quit the application. Begin by going to the UI folder in **Content Browser**. Right-click on LoseMenu and select the **Duplicate** option. Rename this new Blueprint Widget to PauseMenu and open it.

Select the text displaying **You Lose. Try Again?** and, in the **Details** panel, change the **Text** field to say Paused.... Change the text color to a color you feel is appropriate for a pause message. Now, select the **Restart** button's text object, and then change the **Text** field to Resume.

Next, we will add a third button to allow the player to reset the save file. From the **Palette** panel, drag down a **Button** object into **Hierarchy**, dropping it onto the **CanvasPanel** object. Rename the button object to the Reset button. Then, drag a **Text** object down from **Palette** and drop it onto the Reset button.

Select the text object on the Reset button, and then change the **Text** field to Reset All. Also, change the font size to 60, the font color to black, and set **Justification** to center alignment. Now, click on the Reset button object and, in the **Details** panel, change the **Size X** field to 400.0 and the **Size Y** field to 150.0. Next, select the other two buttons and change their **X** and **Y** sizes to the same values.

Now, arrange all the three buttons along the center of the canvas, inserting the Reset All button between the Resume and Quit buttons. The final layout should resemble the following screenshot:

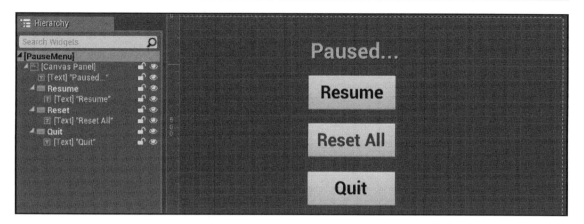

Resuming and resetting the save file

The next step is to modify the functionality of the pause screen buttons so that they can properly resume the game or reset the save file on the player's machine. Click on the Reset All button, and in the **Details** panel, click on the + button next to **On Clicked** in order to create a new button Event. We will start by setting up the series of nodes needed to resume the game from a paused state, as seen in this screenshot:

In the **Graph** view, delete the **Open Level** node attached to the Resume button Event, and then connect the **Remove from Parent** node directly to the **On Clicked (Resume)** node. In addition to removing the pause menu when **Resume** is clicked on, we need to resume the game and disable the mouse arrow.

Create a **Get Player Controller** node. Drag a wire from the **Return Value** output pin of this node and attach it to a **SET Show Mouse Cursor** node. Ensure that this node's **Show Mouse Cursor** input checkbox is unchecked, and then attach the input execution pin of this node to the output execution pin of the **Remove from Parent** node. Finally, attach the output execution pin of the **SET Show Mouse Cursor** node to a **SET Game Paused** node, while ensuring that the **Paused** input checkbox is left unchecked. That will complete the functionality of the Resume button.

Now, turn your attention to the **On Clicked (Reset)** node. First, we will check for the existence of a saved game to be reset and, if one is found, we will use the player character to set the new saved data. The nodes needed to handle the save game branch and player character casting can be seen here:

Drag a wire from the output execution pin of the **On Clicked (Reset)** node, and then attach it to a **Does Save Game Exist** node. In the **Slot Name** input of this node, type BlueprintGameSave, ensuring that your spelling is consistent with the slot names given in the core logic within FirstPersonCharacter.

Next, drag a wire from the **Return Value** output pin and attach it to a **Branch** node. Attach the **True** output execution pin of the **Branch** node to a **Cast To FirstPersonCharacter** node. Finally, drag a wire from the **Object** input pin of the casting node and attach it to the **Get Player Character** node.

Now that we have the player character, we need to grab its **Save Game Instance** and reset the current round to the first round. We will then need to save this updated save game information to the BlueprintGameSave slot on the player's machine.

Start by dragging a wire from the **As First Person Character** output pin of the **Cast To FirstPersonCharacter** node and attaching it to a **GET Save Game Instance** node. Next, drag a wire from the output pin of this node to the **Set Current Round** node. Ensure that the execution pins between this node and the **Cast To FirstPersonCharacter** node are connected, and then set the input **Current Round** field to 1. Because the only data we intend to persist across play sessions is the current round the player is on, this is the only information we need to overwrite in order to represent a fresh save game.

Now, we need to ensure that our updated round data is actually stored in the player's machine. Drag a second wire from the output pin of the **GET Save Game Instance** node, and then attach it to a **Save Game to Slot** node. Connect the input execution pin of this node to the output execution pin of the **SET Current Round** node, and for the **Slot Name** input field, write `BlueprintGameSave`. The results of this should look like the following screenshot:

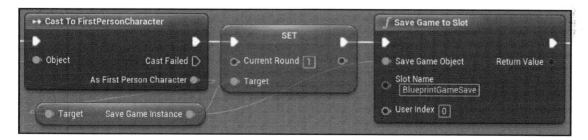

The final step for our `Reset` button is to reload the game map and remove the pause menu at the end of the sequence, as shown in this screenshot:

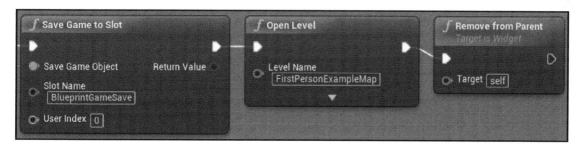

Drag a wire from the output execution pin from the **Save Game to Slot** node to an **Open Level** node. Then, look all the way back to the **Branch** node described earlier, drag a wire from the **False** output execution pin of that node, and connect it to the **Open Level** node. This will ensure that even if there is no save game data to overwrite, the button will still give some feedback by starting the game with the first round. For the **Level Name** input field of the **Open Level** node, enter either `FirstPersonExampleMap`, or the name of your Level if you have chosen to rename it differently from our example. Finally, connect a wire from the output execution pin of the **Open Level** node to a new **Remove from Parent** node. Congratulations! That concludes our work on the pause menu functionality. Create a helpful comment for the `Reset` button nodes, and then compile and save the Blueprint to finish.

Triggering the Pause menu

Now that we have created our **Pause** menu, we need to create a way for the player to bring up the menu. Traditionally, computer games use the *Esc* key to pause the game and return to a menu, so we will follow that trope here. First, we will bind the *Esc* key to a pause Action. Just as we did in Chapter 6, *Enhancing Player Abilities*, we will add a new Action mapping to **Project Settings**. On the **Edit** button in the Unreal Editor menu, select the **Project Settings** option. On the left side of the window that appears, look for the **Engine** category and select the **Input** option. Click on the + sign next to **Action Mappings**, and then name the mapping as **Pause**. Use the drop-down menu to select the **Escape** key mapping, as seen in this screenshot:

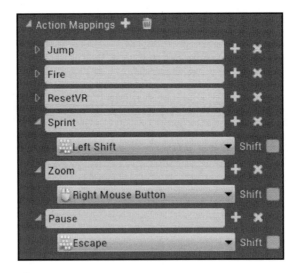

Like all other Actions the player can take, we want to establish the functionality of this Action within the `FirstPersonCharacter` Blueprint. Go to the **Content Browser** and open the `FirstPersonCharacter` Blueprint inside the `Blueprints` folder. In the following screenshot, you can see the nodes we will build in order to create and show the **Pause** menu:

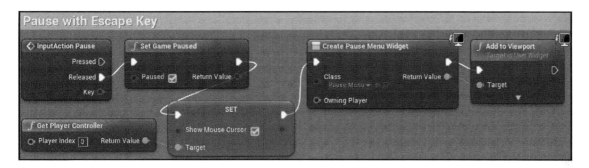

First, find some empty grid space and add an **InputAction Pause** Event node. Since bringing up the **Pause** menu will disrupt the gameplay, it will feel better if the Action is taken only when the user releases the *Esc* key, as opposed to when they first press it. Drag a wire from the **Released** output pin of the **Escape** node, and then attach it to a **SET Game Paused** node. Ensure that the **Paused** input checkbox of this node is checked.

With the game paused, we need to enable the mouse arrow so that the player can click on the menu buttons. Start by creating a **Get Player Controller** node, and then drag a wire from its **Return Value** output pin to a **SET Show Mouse Cursor** node. Check the **Show Mouse Cursor** input box to set the mouse arrow to appear on the screen. Then, connect the input execution pin of this node to the output execution pin of the **SET Game Paused** node.

With the game paused and the cursor enabled, we can bring up the **Pause Menu** UI we created. Drag a wire from the output execution pin of the **SET Show Mouse Cursor** node and attach it to a **Create Widget** node. Select **Pause Menu** from the **Class** input drop-down menu. Then, drag a wire from the **Return Value** output pin of this node and attach it to an **Add to Viewport** node. Connect the execution pins between these two nodes in order to finish this series of nodes. Remember to add a helpful comment box around the nodes, and then compile and save this Blueprint.

We will have to make a slight alteration to our testing strategy in order to test the pause menu. The *Esc* key, by default, closes any active windows that are currently playing the game within the Editor. Thus, the game would close before we could see the pause menu we created. There are two ways by which we can get around this. We can change the key to bring up the pause menu to something other than *Esc*, such as the *P* key. Alternatively, we can change the **Play** mode in the Editor to generate a standalone game window. To follow the latter option, click on the downward-facing arrow next to the **Play** button, and then select the **Standalone Game** option, as seen in the following screenshot:

Now, while playing, you should be able to press the *Esc* key you set up to bring up the pause menu. Clicking on the Resume button should close the pause menu and return you to the game. If you progress several rounds through the game and then press the Reset All button from the pause menu, then you should automatically reload the level, with your progress reset to the first round of the game. If this is what you see, then congratulations! You have accomplished a significant achievement in creating SaveSystem that is able to store, load, and reset progress across multiple rounds of gameplay. If the save system does not work, then check whether BlueprintGameSave is spelled correctly in all **Slot Name** input fields.

Summary

In this chapter, we have made significant strides toward making our game a complete experience that can be played and enjoyed by other people. You learned how to branch the end states of the game based on whether the player has won or lost. You also learned about how to implement a save system that allows the player to return to their earlier game sessions, with their progress intact. Then, we implemented a round system that modifies the gameplay goal each time the player progresses to a new round. Finally, we implemented additional menu systems that give the player information about which round they are on, and give them the opportunity to pause the gameplay and even reset their own save file.

This represents the entire game experience we will create in the book. In the next chapter, we will explore making and publishing builds of the game we created so that we can share the experience with others. In addition, we will look back at how far your skills have developed, and then look forward and discuss how you can pursue further learning and extend this game to be even better.

12
Building and Publishing

One of the best ways to grow as a game developer is to share your work with others so that you can get feedback on how to evolve your designs and content. An early priority should be to create sharable builds of your game so that other people can play the experience for themselves. Fortunately, Unreal Engine 4 makes it extremely simple to create builds of your game that can work across multiple platforms. In this chapter, we will look at how to optimize the settings of our game, the process of building for your target desktop platform, and how you might approach developing for mobile devices, game consoles, and web browsers. In the process, we will cover the following topics:

- Optimizing graphics settings
- Setting up our game to be played by others
- Packaging the game into a build

Optimizing your graphics settings

Prior to creating a build, or a version of our game that has been optimized to play on a particular platform, you should change the graphics settings of our game to ensure that they are suited to your target machines. The graphics settings in Unreal Engine 4 are identified as **Engine Scalability Settings**. This setting interface is composed of several graphics settings, each of which determines the final visual quality of one element of the game. With any game, there is a trade-off between high-quality effects and visuals, and the performance of that game in terms of frame rate.

Games that struggle with low frame rates feel bad from a gameplay perspective, even if the mechanics are otherwise solid. As such, it is important to balance the desire to make your game look as good as it can with the need to understand what the performance impact will be on the machines that your players will be running the game on. Because of the varying hardware performance of PCs and macOS computers, many games targeting those platforms use custom menu settings to allow the player to tweak the graphics settings of the game themselves. However, the game we have created only uses very simple assets and a relatively constrained level size, so we are simply going to define some workable defaults before generating a build to distribute.

To access **Engine Scalability Settings**, go to the `FirstPersonExampleMap` tab and look at the Level Editor toolbar at the top. Click on the **Settings** button, and hover over **Engine Scalability Settings** to see a pop-out display of the **Quality** settings that you can tweak, as seen in the following screenshot:

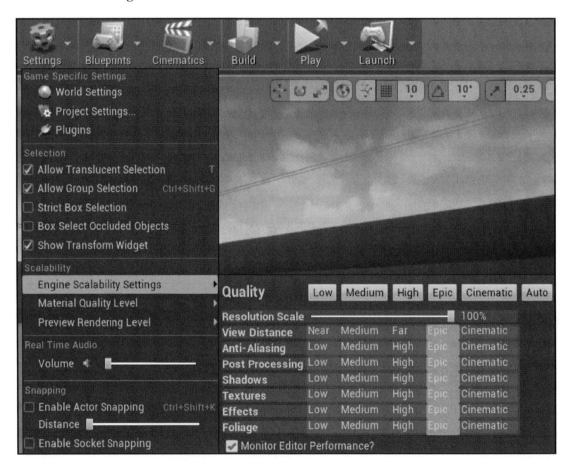

The buttons along the top of this menu, ranging from **Low** to **Epic**, serve as presets of the settings based on the broad level of performance versus quality that you want to target at runtime. Clicking on the **Low** button will set all the quality settings to the minimum, giving you the best possible performance, in exchange for the least visually attractive settings. **Epic** is the opposite end of the spectrum, raising all of the engine quality settings to their maximum, at the sacrifice of significant performance, depending on the assets you have chosen to use.

The **Cinematic** button will set all the quality settings to cinematic quality, which is used for offline rendering of cinematics only. This setting is not intended for use during gameplay or at runtime.

The **Auto** button will detect the hardware of the machine you are currently running the Editor on, and adjust the graphics settings to a level that strikes a good balance between performance and a graphical quality that is suitable for your machine. If you are intending to target hardware that is roughly equivalent to the machine you are developing on, using the **Auto** setting can be a simple way to establish the graphics settings for your build. If you wish to tweak these settings individually, you can use this brief description of their functions to help you:

- **Resolution Scale**: This setting causes the engine to render the game in a lower resolution than the resolution that your player will be targeting, and uses software to upscale the game to the targeted resolution. This improves the performance of the game, at the cost of perceived fuzziness at lower resolution scales.
- **View Distance**: This determines the distance from the location of the camera that objects will be rendered. Objects beyond this distance will not be rendered. Shorter view distances increase performance but can cause objects to pop into view suddenly as they cross the view distance boundary.
- **Anti-Aliasing**: This setting softens the jagged edges of 3D objects in the world, which can dramatically improve the look of your game. At the higher settings, you will see less jagged edges, but it will decrease performance.
- **Post Processing**: This setting changes the baseline quality settings of several filters that get applied to the screen after the scene is created, such as motion blur and light bloom effects.
- **Shadows**: This changes the baseline quality of several bundled settings that combine to determine the look of shadows in the game. Highly detailed shadows often have a dramatic impact on performance.

- **Textures**: This setting will affect the process by which the textures used in your game are managed by the engine. If you have many large textures in your game, reducing this setting can help avoid running out of graphics memory and thus increases performance.
- **Effects**: This setting changes the baseline quality settings of several special effects applied to the game, such as material reflections and translucency effects.
- **Foliage**: This setting will affect the quality of foliage used in the game.

Ultimately, the best way of optimizing the performance of your game is to regularly test it on the machines you intend for people to play it on. If you notice sluggish performance, take note of where you see it occur. If the performance of your game is always low, you might need to reduce some of the post-processing or anti-aliasing effects. If performance is low only in certain areas of your level, you might need to look at reducing the object density in that area or reduce the quality of a particular game model.

Setting up our game to be played by others

Unreal Engine 4 offers a wide variety of platforms that you can choose from to build your game, and this list will continue to expand as newer versions of the engine are released and new technologies emerge. Currently, you can deploy your game on Windows PC, macOS, iOS, Android, Linux, SteamOS, and HTML5. This engine also supports the creation of content that utilizes the various emerging virtual reality platforms, such as **Oculus Rift**. If you are a registered console developer with the appropriate development kit, you will be pleased to know that Unreal Engine 4 also supports the creation of games for the Xbox One and PlayStation 4. Each platform has its own unique requirements and best practices associated with it for game development. Mobile and web (HTML5) games, in particular, have higher optimization requirements in order to get games to perform well on those platforms.

Creating a distributable form of your game for one of these platforms involves a process called **packaging**. Packaging takes all of the code and assets of the game and sets them up in the proper format to be able to perform on the selected platform. We will be following the path to making a Windows PC or macOS release of your game.

It is important to note that Unreal Engine 4 can only create Windows builds from a copy of the engine running on a Windows PC, and OS X builds from copies installed on a macOS running OS X. Thus, the platforms that you can target with your game will be partially limited by the machine you are developing the game on. If you are developing on a Windows PC and wish to create an OS X build of the game, you can install another copy of Unreal Engine 4 on a macOS, and copy your project files to this new machine. From there, you will be able to generate an OS X build, with no further changes required.

First, we may want to customize some of the settings that will determine how our project appears on the target machine. To do so, click on the **Settings** button in the Level Editor toolbar, and then click on **Project Settings...**, as shown here:

Inside **Project Settings...**, you will see a wide variety of options in the left panel for the customization of different aspects of the game, engine, and platform interactions. By default, the **Project – Description** page will open.

Here, you can customize the project name, the thumbnail as it will appear in the Unreal Engine project selector, and a brief description of the project and its creator or **Publisher**, as shown in this screenshot:

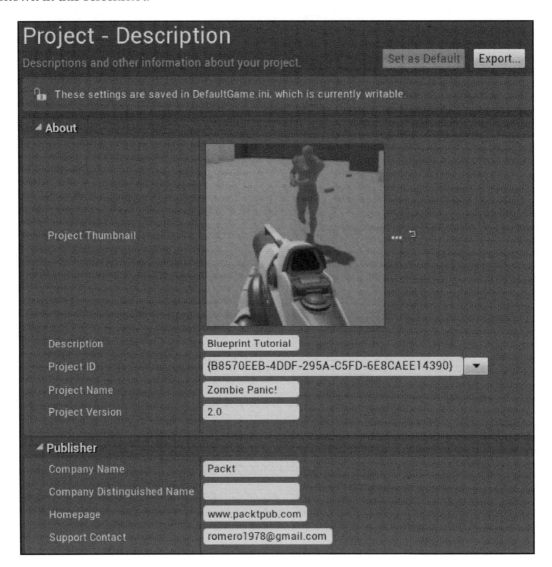

Clicking on **Maps & Modes** will bring you to a page where you can determine which map the game will load by default. Our game has only one map, so that makes this choice easy, but you will often need to designate a map dedicated to your main menu screen to be the first map to load. When you create games with multiple maps, you will need to ensure that the first map loaded is able to manage which map is loaded next in the play experience. This is similar to how we determined in Chapter 11, *Game States and Applying the Finishing Touches*, which round to activate when we loaded our game from an existing saved file:

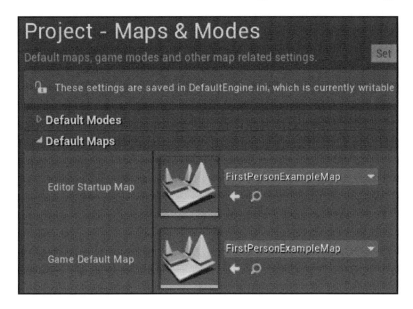

Finally, clicking on the platform you are targeting with this build will bring you to that platform's customization page.

In the **Windows** example shown in the following screenshot, the **Splash** screens and the game **Icon** image are available for changing. Mobile and console platform targets will have more options to change, which will be specific to each of those platforms:

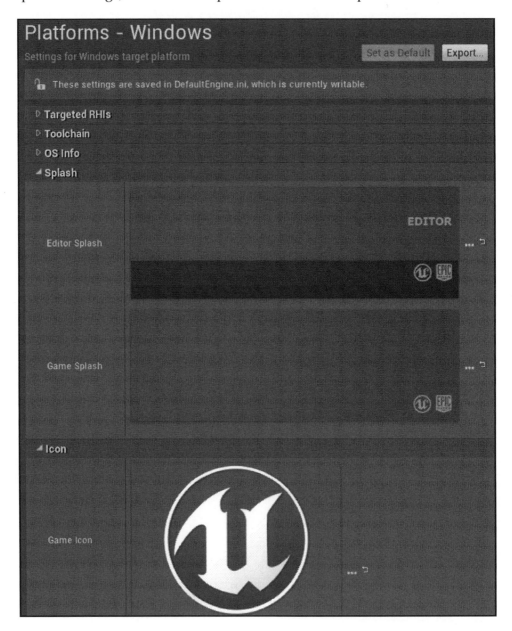

Replace the default **Splash** and **Icon** settings with the images you would like to use for your game. This can be as simple as an edited screenshot from the game, or you can show off a custom piece of art made specifically for icons and splash screens. Once you are satisfied with your project settings, leave the **Project Settings** window.

Packaging the game into a build

To package your game to be played on a particular platform, click on **File** in the main menu, then on **Package Project**, and finally, on the relevant platform that matches the build you want to make, as follows:

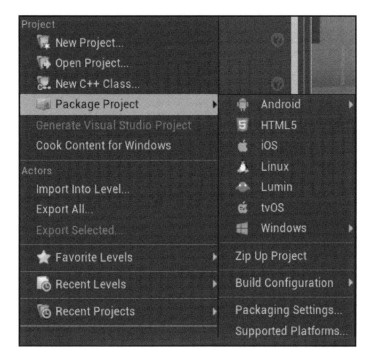

Once you click on a platform, you will be prompted to select a location on your hard drive to store the build you make. After selecting a location, you will see a popup that tells you that the engine is packaging the project. If something goes wrong in the packaging process, you will be shown the details of the error in the output log window that pops up. Packaging a project can take a bit of time, depending on how complex and large the project is, but if you don't encounter any errors, then you will eventually see a message saying that the packaging is complete. Congratulations, you have created a packaged copy of your game!

Navigate to the folder where you chose to store your build. On a macOS, open the folder called **MacNoEditor** and double-click on the application to launch it. For Windows, open the **WindowsNoEditor** folder and double-click on the executable to run the game. Take a moment to go through the game you created in its final form, and reflect on just how far you have come. You now have a functional game that other people can play and enjoy. Making even simple games is no easy feat, so you should feel proud of your accomplishment!

Build configurations and packaging settings

The **Package Project** menu has some more options for configuring the package that are described as follows:

- **Zip Up Project**: Compresses the project edit files into a ZIP file. This is useful for moving the project to another computer or for passing the project to someone else.
- **Build Configuration**: Defines how the build will be done. In Blueprint-only projects, you have two options: **Development** and **Shipping**. Development builds contain information that is used in debugging to help you find errors. Shipping builds are cleaner as they do not have debug information and should be used to create the final version of the game that will be distributed.
- **Supported Platforms**: In this option, we are informed which platforms will be supported by the project.
- **Packaging Settings**: Displays the project packaging configuration options that can be modified. The next screenshot shows these options:

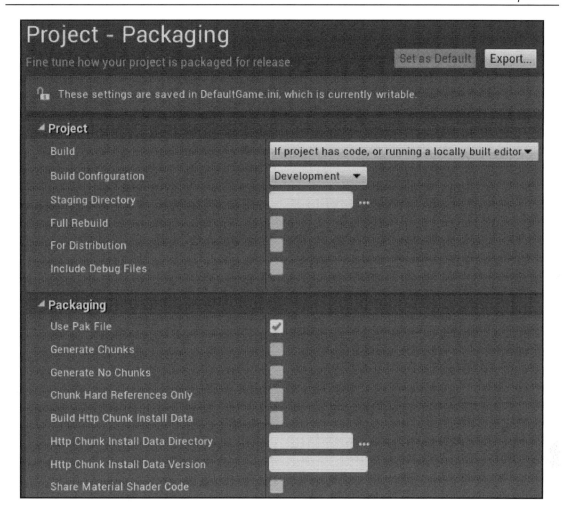

The **Staging Directory** property is used to define the folder where the packaged build will be stored. The **For Distribution** option is required when submitting a game to the App Store or Google Play Store. The **Use Pak File** option defines whether the project files will be gathered into a single `.pak` file or will be available individually.

Summary

In this chapter, we discussed creating playable builds of the game we created across multiple platforms. We learned how to optimize the graphics settings and also discussed how to set up the game to be played by others. Finally, we saw how to change the build configurations and packaging settings.

With what you've learned in this chapter, you will be able to better present your project and distribute it on different platforms so that others can enjoy it.

This chapter concludes section 3 and ends our implementation of the playable shooter game. Section 4 will cover advanced Blueprints concepts. In the next chapter, we will learn about data structures and flow control.

Section 4: Advanced Blueprints

4

This section will explore advanced Blueprints concepts that will help you when you are developing complex games. We will examine data structures, flow control, math nodes, trace nodes, and Blueprints tips to increase the quality of Blueprints. The final chapter explains some **Virtual Reality (VR)** concepts and explores the VR template.

This section includes the following chapters:

- Chapter 13, *Data Structures and Flow Control*
- Chapter 14, *Math and Trace Nodes*
- Chapter 15, *Blueprints Tips*
- Chapter 16, *Introduction to VR Development*

13
Data Structures and Flow Control

In section 3, we learned how to create a basic AI game using Behavior Trees, how to add game states, and how to build and publish a game.

Section 4 will teach you about advanced Blueprints concepts that will help when developing complex games. We will learn about data structures, flow control, math nodes, Blueprints tips, and gain an understanding of virtual reality development.

This chapter will explain what data structures are and how they can be used to organize data in Blueprints. We will learn about the concept of containers and how to use arrays, sets, and maps to group multiple elements, as well as other ways to organize data using enumerations, structures, and data tables. In this chapter, we will also see how to control a Blueprint's flow of execution by using various types of flow control nodes.

These are the topics of this chapter:

- Containers
- Other data structures
- Flow control nodes

Containers

A container is a type of data structure whose instances can store collections of values or instances. The values in a container must be of the same type. An element of a container can be retrieved later by using a label that the container associated with it.

The containers available in Blueprints are arrays, sets, and maps. To turn a variable into a container, click the icon next to **Variable Type** and choose one of the containers that appear, as shown in the next screenshot:

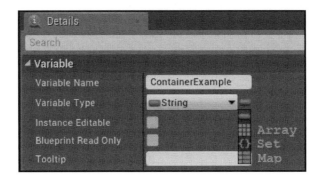

Arrays

An array is a type of container that stores one or more values of a specific data type. Thus, a single variable can be used to store multiple values instead of using separate variables for each value.

Arrays provide indexed access to their elements, so the label used to retrieve an element is the element's sequential index in the container.

To create an array, first create a variable and define its type. Then, click the icon next to the **Variable Type** drop-down menu and select the icon of an array, as shown in this screenshot:

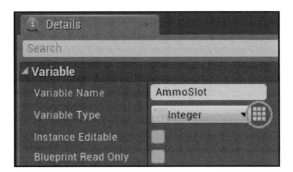

Compile the Blueprint to be able to add the default values of the array. In the **Default Value** panel of the variable, click the **+** icon to add elements to the array. The next screenshot shows an example of an **Integer** array named **Ammo Slot** with four elements used to store the amount of ammunition the player has. Each element of the array stores the amount of ammunition of one type of weapon:

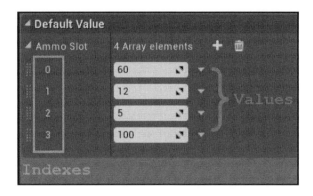

Arrays always start from index 0. So, in the previous example with 4 elements, the index of the first element is **0**, and the index of the last element is **3**.

To get a value from an array, use the **Get (a copy)** node. This node has two input parameters, which are a reference to an array and the index of the element, as shown in this screenshot:

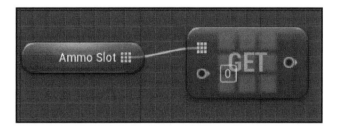

To modify an element of an array, use the **Set Array Elem** node. The example in the next screenshot sets the **Item** value in the element to 75, with an **Index** value of 3:

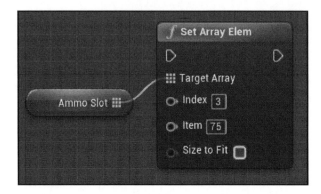

Two nodes can be used to add elements to an array. The **ADD** node adds an element to the end of the array. The **INSERT** node adds an element at the index passed as an input parameter:

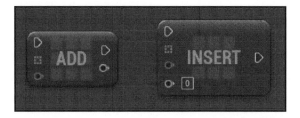

You can get the number of elements in an array by using the **LENGTH** node. The **LAST INDEX** node returns the index of the last element of the array. The following screenshot shows these two nodes:

Let's create an example to examine the use of arrays that store instances of Actors. In this example, we'll create a Blueprint called `BP_RandomSpawner`, which will have an array of **Target Points**. The elements of the **Target Points** array can be set in the Level Editor. When the level starts, the `BP_RandomSpawner` Blueprint will randomly select one element of **Target Points** and spawn an instance of a Blueprint in this location.

These are the steps to create this example:

1. Create or use an existing project that has the starter content.
2. Click the **Add New** button in **Content Browser** and choose the **Blueprint Class** option.
3. On the next screen, choose **Actor** as the parent class.
4. Name the Blueprint `BP_RandomSpawner` and double-click it to open the Blueprint Editor.
5. In the **My Blueprint** panel, create a new variable named `TargetPoints`. In the **Details** panel, click the **Variable Type** drop-down menu and search for `target point`. Hover over **Target Point** to display a submenu and then choose **Object Reference**. Click the icon to the right of **Variable Type** and select the **Array** icon. Check the **Instance Editable** attribute, as shown in the next screenshot:

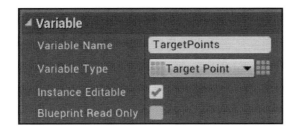

6. Right-click on **Event Graph** and add **Event BeginPlay**. Drag the `TargetPoints` variable from the **My Blueprint** panel and drop it into **Event Graph**. Choose the **GET Target Points** option to create a node. Add the Actions shown in the next screenshot. The **Random Integer in Range** function returns a random integer between the value of 0 and the last index of the **Target Points** array. This value is used as the index in the **GET** node. The transform of the selected **Target Points** is used to define the location where an instance of a Blueprint will be spawned. In this example, the Blueprint spawned is **SpawnActor Blueprint Effect Smoke**, which is from the starter content. To use another Blueprint, change the **Class** input parameter in the **SpawnActor** Action:

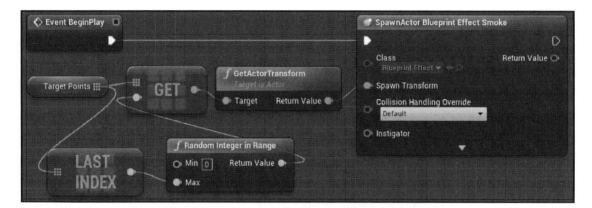

7. In the Level Editor, look at the **Modes** panel on the left. Search for `target`, as shown in the next screenshot. Drag **Target Point** and drop some instances in different locations of the level:

8. Drag `BP_RandomSpawner` from **Content Browser** and drop it on the level. The `TargetPoints` variable appears in the **Details** panel because we checked the **Instance Editable** attribute. Click the + icon to add elements to the array. Click the drop-down menu of each element and select one of the **TargetPoint** instances that are in the level. The next screenshot shows the array with 5 elements:

9. Click the **Play** button of the Level Editor. `BP_RandomSpawner` will spawn an instance of `Blueprint Effect Smoke` at one of the **TargetPoint** instances.

Sets

A set is another type of container. It is an unordered list of unique elements. The search for an element of the set is based on the value of the element itself. There is no index. The elements of a set must be of the same type, and repeated elements are not allowed.

To create a set, first create a variable and define its type. Then, click the icon next to the **Variable Type** drop-down menu and select the icon of a set, as shown in this screenshot:

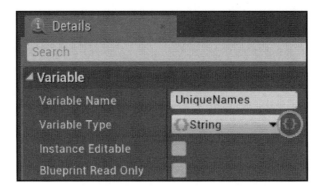

Compile the Blueprint so that you can add default values to the set. In the **Default Value** panel of the variable, click the **+** icon to add elements to the set. The following screenshot shows an example of a **String** set with four elements:

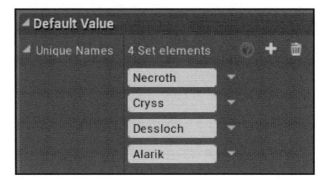

The next screenshot shows some of the Actions of the set container. Here is a brief description of each Action:

- **ADD**: Adds an element to a set.
- **ADD ITEMS**: Adds elements from an array to a set. The array must be of the same type as the set.

- **CONTAINS**: Returns true if the set contains the element.
- **LENGTH**: Returns the number of elements in a set:

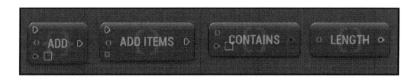

A set does not have a **GET** element node, so if you need to iterate through the elements of a set, then you can copy the elements of a set to an array. The next screenshot shows the **TO ARRAY** node and other nodes that are used to remove elements:

- **TO ARRAY**: Copies the elements of a set to an array
- **CLEAR**: Removes all elements of a set
- **REMOVE**: Removes an element of a set, or returns **True** if an element was removed and **False** if the element was not found
- **REMOVE ITEMS**: Removes the elements specified in an array from a set:

Some nodes perform operations with two sets and return a different set. These nodes are shown in the next screenshot:

- **UNION**: The resulting set contains all the elements from the two sets. Since the result is a set, all duplicates will be removed.
- **DIFFERENCE**: The result set contains the elements of the first set that are not in the second set.
- **INTERSECTION**: The result set contains the elements that exist in the two sets:

The next screenshot shows a simple example of the use of a set. There is a set named **Unique Names** that keeps the names of the players who have won a round. In this case, we want to know the players who have won at least one round. We do not need to know how many rounds a player has won:

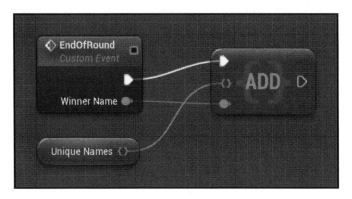

Maps

There is another type of container: a map. A map uses a key-value pair to define each element. The key type can be different from the value type. A map is unordered and is searched by using the key value, so duplicate keys are not allowed.

To create a map, first, create a variable, click the icon next to the **Variable Type** drop-down menu, and select the icon of a map, as shown in the next screenshot. After that, you need to choose the key type on the left and the value type on the right. The example in the screenshot uses **String** as the key type and **Float** as the value type:

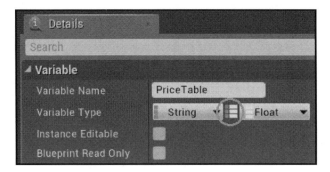

Just like any other new variable in Blueprints, it is necessary to compile the Blueprint before adding the default values of the map. In the **Default Value** panel of the variable, click the **+** icon to add elements to the map. The next screenshot shows an example of a map with four elements. Each element has a **String** key and a **Float** value:

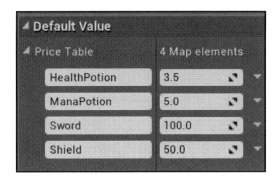

The next screenshot shows some map nodes to add an element, remove an element, or remove all elements of a map:

- **ADD**: Adds a key-value pair to a map. If the key already exists in the map, then the value associated with the key will be overwritten.
- **REMOVE**: Removes a key-value pair from a map. Returns **True** if the key-value pair was removed. If the key was not found, then the node returns **False**.
- **CLEAR**: Removes all elements of a map:

The following nodes are used to get the length of a map, check whether a key exists, and get the value associated with a key in the map:

- **LENGTH**: Returns the number of elements in a map.
- **CONTAINS**: Receives a key as an input parameter and returns **True** if the map contains an element that uses that key.

- **FIND**: The **FIND** node is like the **CONTAINS** node, but it also returns the value associated with the key used in the search:

The following nodes are used to copy the keys and values of a map to arrays:

- **KEYS**: Copies all the keys of a map to an array
- **VALUES**: Copies all the values of a map to an array:

The following screenshot shows an example usage of a map. **Price Table** is a map that uses **Product Name** as its key and the price of the product as its value. There is a function named **Calculate Total Price** that receives **Product Name** and **Amount**, which will be bought as input parameters. **Product Name** is searched in the **Price Table** map to get the price of the product. The price of the product is multiplied by **Amount** to find **Total Price**:

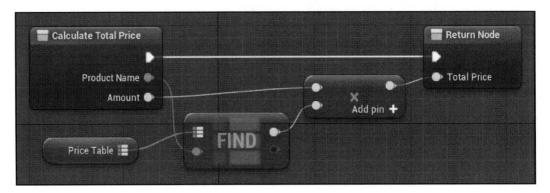

Other data structures

There are other data structures that help organize data within a game or application. These data structures are not created within a Blueprint class. They are independent auxiliary assets that can be used in a Blueprint.

Let's learn how to create and use enumerations, structures, and data tables.

Enumerations

An **enumeration**, also known as an **enum**, is a data type that contains a fixed set of named constants and can be used to define the type of a variable. The value of a variable whose type is an enumeration is restricted to the set of constants defined in the enumeration.

To create an enumeration, click the **Add New** button in **Content Browser**, and in the **Blueprints** submenu, select **Enumeration**, as shown in the following screenshot:

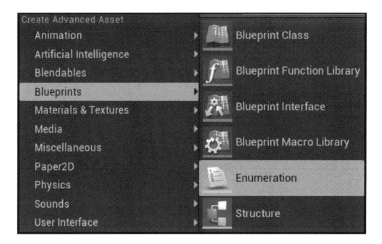

Give a name to the enumeration created and double-click it to edit its values. In the Enumeration Editor, click the **New** button to add a named constant to this enumeration. The next screenshot shows the Enumeration Editor with five named constants of an enumeration named `WeaponCategory`. You can add descriptions to the enumeration and for each constant:

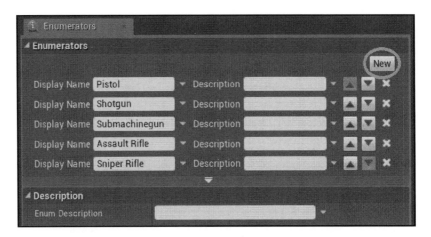

To use the enumeration data type, create a variable in the Blueprint Editor, click the **Variable Type** drop-down menu, and search for the name of the enumeration, as shown in the following screenshot:

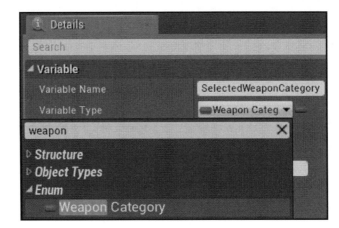

The next screenshot shows that a variable defined with an enumeration type is restricted to the constants of the enumeration:

For each enumeration type, there is a **Switch On** node that is used to change the execution flow based on the enumeration value, as shown in the next screenshot:

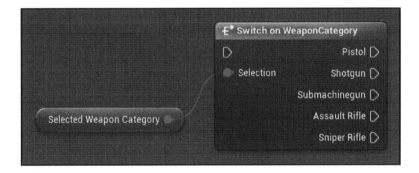

Structures

A **structure**, also known as a **struct**, is a composite data type that can group variables of different types into a single type. An element of a structure can be of a complex type, such as a structure, array, set, map, or object reference.

To create a structure, click the **Add New** button in **Content Browser**, and in the **Blueprints** submenu, select **Structure**, as shown in the following screenshot:

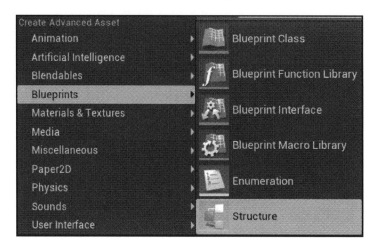

Give a name to the structure created and double-click it to define its variables. In the Structure Editor, click the **New Variable** button to add variables to the structure. Each variable can be of a different type, and you can click on the container icon to turn the variable into a container, such as an array, set, or map. The following screenshot shows the variables of a structure named **Weapon Type** in the Structure Editor. Note that the **Category** variable is of the enumeration type, like the **Weapon Category** variable that we previously created:

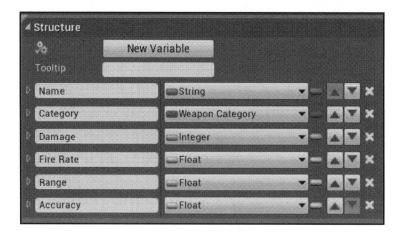

To use the **Structure** data type, create a variable in the Blueprint Editor, click the **Variable Type** drop-down menu, and search for the name of the structure, as shown in the following screenshot:

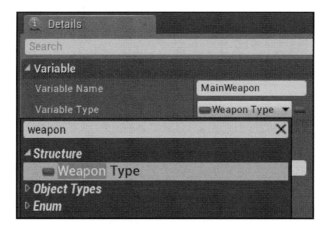

Compile the Blueprint so you can edit **Default Value**. The next screenshot shows the structure, filled with example values of weapons:

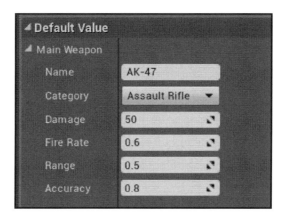

The float variables in the previous screenshot use relative values that represent percentages. For example, *0.5* is *50%* and *1.0* is *100%*.

For each structure type, there are **Make** and **Break** nodes available for use in a Blueprint. The **Make** node receives the separate elements as input and creates a new structure. The **Break** node receives a structure as input and separates its elements. The next screenshot shows the **Make** and **Break** nodes of the **Weapon Type** structure:

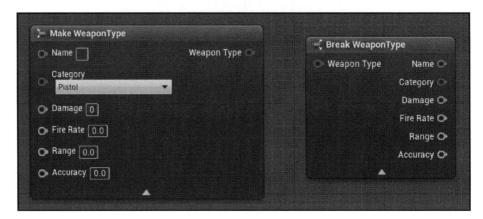

Data tables

A **data table** is a table of values based on a structure. It can be used to represent a spreadsheet document. This is useful for data-driven gameplay where game data needs to be constantly modified and balanced. In these cases, the data can be modified in a Spreadsheet Editor, and then imported into the game.

To create a data table, click the **Add New** button in **Content Browser**, and in the **Miscellaneous** submenu, select **Data Table**, as shown in the next screenshot:

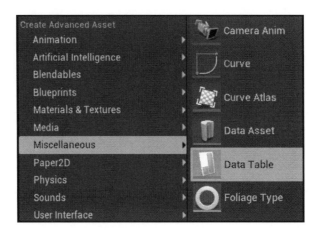

After selecting **Data Table**, the Unreal Editor will ask you to choose a structure that represents the data type of the table. The next screenshot shows that the data table will be created based on the **Weapon Type** structure:

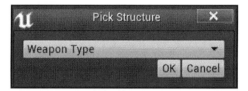

Give a name to the data table created and double-click it to open the Data Table Editor. The next screenshot shows a data table named `WeaponTable` with some sample data. Click the + icon to add a row to the table. Each row has **Row Name** that identifies the row, so this **Row Name** must be unique. In the screenshot example, the **Row Name** is a simple index:

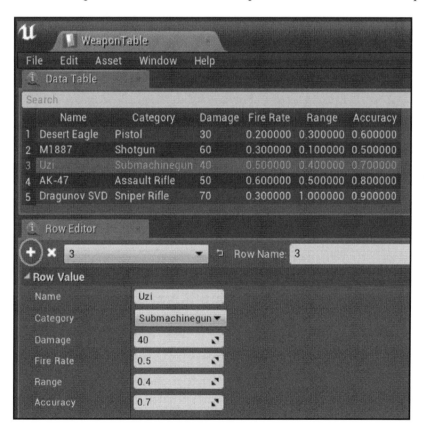

The data table can also be imported from a plain text **comma-separated values (CSV)** file. The next screenshot shows an example of a CSV file. A Spreadsheet Editor can export a spreadsheet to the CSV format:

```
---,Name,Category,Damage,Fire Rate,Range,Accuracy
1,"Desert Eagle","Pistol","30","0.200000","0.300000","0.600000"
2,"M1887","Shotgun","60","0.300000","0.100000","0.500000"
3,"Uzi","Submachinegun","40","0.500000","0.400000","0.700000"
4,"AK-47","Assault Rifle","50","0.600000","0.500000","0.800000"
5,"Dragunov SVD","Sniper Rifle","70","0.300000","1.000000","0.900000"
```

To import a CSV file, click the **Import** button of **Content Browser** and select the CSV file. A dialog box will appear, asking you to select a structure in the field **Choose DataTable Row Type**, as shown in the following screenshot:

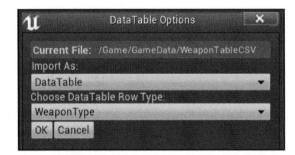

To use a data table in a Blueprint, create a variable in the Blueprint Editor and select **Data Table** as **Variable Type**. Compile the Blueprint, and in **Default Value**, select one data table, as shown in the following screenshot:

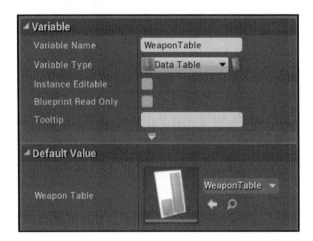

The following screenshot shows some Actions to get data from a data table:

- **Get Data Table Row**: Returns a structure with the data of a specific row
- **Get Data Table Row Names**: Copies all the **Row Names** of a data table to an array
- **Get Data Table Column as String**: Copies all the values of a column to an array of strings:

The following screenshot shows an example usage of a data table. **Select Weapon** is a function that receives **Weapon ID** as an input parameter and searches in **Weapon Table** for a weapon whose **Row Name** is equal to **Weapon ID**. If it finds the weapon, then it copies the weapon data to the **Current Weapon** variable:

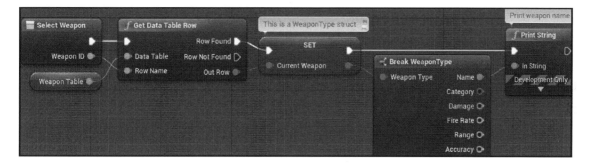

Flow control nodes

There are some nodes that control the flow of the execution of a Blueprint. These nodes determine the execution path based on conditions. Let's learn about the main types of flow control nodes.

Switch nodes

A **switch node** determines the flow of execution based on the value of an input variable. There are different types of switch nodes. The next screenshot shows an example of the **Switch on Int** node:

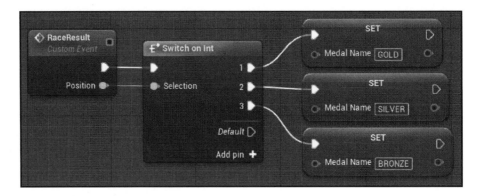

The **Selection** input parameter receives an integer value that determines the output pin that will be executed. If the input value has no pin, then the **Default** pin will execute. You can change the start index in the **Details** panel of **Switch on Int**. The output pins are added by using the **Add pin +** option.

Another type of switch is the **Switch on String** node, which is shown in the following screenshot. The output values must be added in the **Details** panel of the **Switch on String** node, under **Pin Options | Pin Names**:

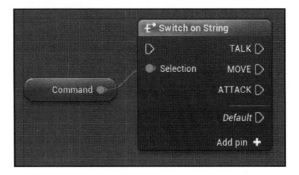

There is also **Switch on Enum**, which uses the values of an enumeration as the available output pins.

FlipFlop

Every time a **FlipFlop** node is executed, it toggles between the two output pins: **A** and **B**. There is a Boolean output parameter named **Is A**. If the parameter **Is A** is **True**, then it indicates that pin **A** is running. If it is **False**, then pin **B** is running.

The following screenshot shows an example of the **FlipFlop** node. If the player is using dual wield pistols, then when they fire, only one of the pistols fires. In the next shot, the other pistol fires. **Fire Left Pistol** and **Fire Right Pistol** are custom Macros that are being used to simplify this example:

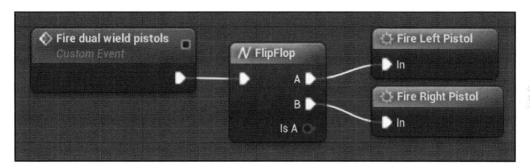

Sequence

When a **Sequence** node is triggered, it executes all the Actions connected to the output pins in order. Thus, it executes all the Actions of a pin, then all the Actions of the next pin, and so on. It is useful to organize groups of Actions.

The next screenshot shows the **Sequence** node in use. The **Print String** functions are being used to show the order of execution. Note that if the **Branch** node returns **False**, then the execution continues on the next output pin of the **Sequence** node.

The **Add pin +** option adds output pins. To remove a pin, right-click on the pin and choose the **Remove execution pin** option:

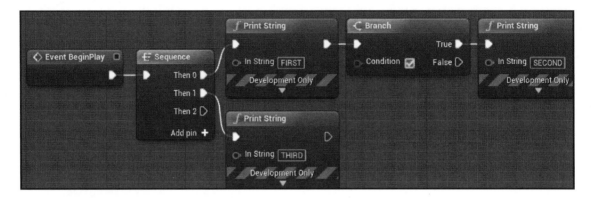

ForEachLoop

A **ForEachLoop** node receives an array as an input parameter and performs the Actions of the **Loop Body** output pin for each element of the array. The current **Array Element** and **Array Index** are available as output pins. The **Completed** output pin is executed when **ForEachLoop** finishes its execution.

In the next screenshot, the **ForEachLoop** node is used to iterate through an array that contains the lamps of a room. It turns on each lamp by using the **Set Visibility** function:

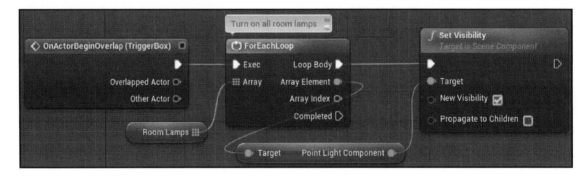

DoOnce

The **DoOnce** node executes the output pin only once. If it is triggered again, then its output pin will not be performed. The **Reset** input pin needs to be triggered to allow the **DoOnce** node to run the output pin again.

The following screenshot shows an example of its usage. When the player presses **Space Bar**, the **DoOnce** node is triggered, and a charged weapon is used. After that, a timer is created to execute the **Full charge Custom Event** that resets the **DoOnce** node after 30.0 seconds. If the player presses **Space Bar** again before 30 seconds have elapsed, then the **DoOnce** node will not execute its output pin:

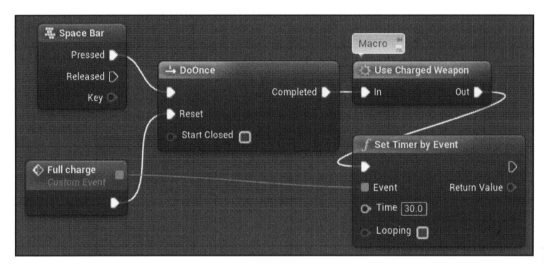

Do N

The **Do N** node allows you to specify how many times the output pin can execute. After the number of executions has completed, the Actions of the output pin will only be executed again if the **Reset** pin is triggered.

In the following screenshot, the player can press **Space Bar** to fire a special weapon. After the third shot, they need to press the **R** key to reset the **Do N** node in order to be able to fire three more times:

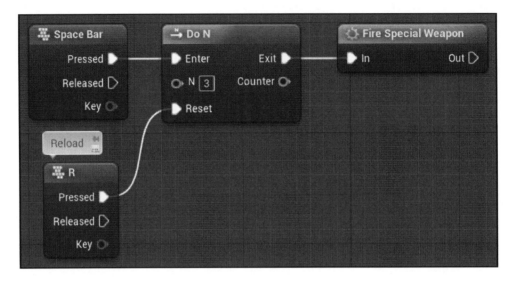

Gate

The **Gate** node has an internal state. It can be opened or closed. If it is open, then the output pin will execute when the **Gate** node is triggered. If it is closed, then the output pin will not execute.

These are the input pins of the **Gate** node:

- **Enter**: Execution pin that receives the flow of execution
- **Open**: Execution pin that sets the state of **Gate** to open
- **Close**: Execution pin that sets the state of **Gate** to closed
- **Toggle**: Execution pin that toggles the state of the **Gate** node
- **Start Closed**: Boolean variable that determines whether the **Gate** node should start in the closed state

The example in the next screenshot has an Actor called **DamageZone**. When the player is overlapping this Actor, the **Gate** node stays open, and damage is applied to the player on every **Tick**. If the player stops overlapping the **DamageZone** Actor, then the **Gate** node will close and the damage will no longer be applied:

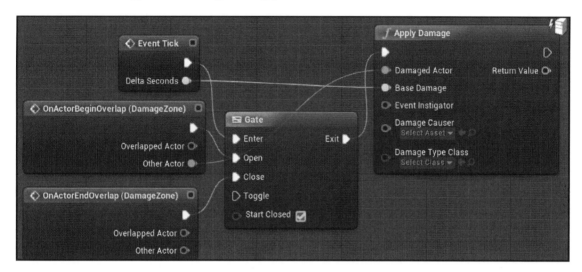

MultiGate

When a **MultiGate** node is triggered, one of the output pins is executed. A **MultiGate** node can have multiple output pins. To add another output pin, use the **Add pin +** option.

These are the input pins of the **MultiGate** node:

- **Reset**: An execution pin used to reset the **MultiGate** node and allow new executions of the output pins.
- **Is Random**: A Boolean variable. If the value is **True**, then the order of execution of the output pins is random.
- **Loop**: This is a Boolean variable that indicates how the **MultiGate** node will behave after the last output pin is executed. If the value is **True**, then the **MultiGate** node continues to execute the output pins. If **False**, then the **MultiGate** node will stop executing the output pins.
- **Start Index**: An integer value indicating the first output pin to be executed.

The following screenshot shows an example of the **MultiGate** node. When the **Tab** key is pressed, a **MultiGate** node is used to set a different **Static Mesh** at each execution. The **Loop** parameter is checked, so **MultiGate** will continue executing the output pins after the last output pin is executed:

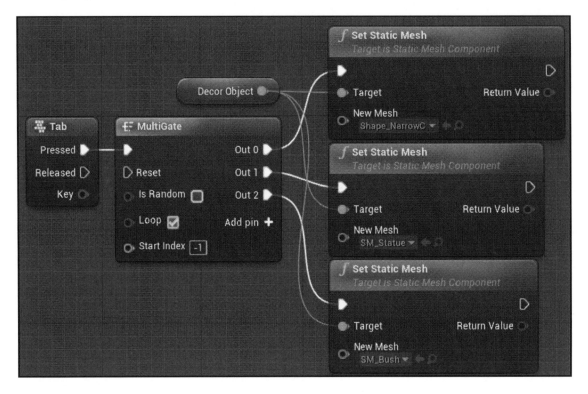

Summary

In this chapter, we learned how to use data structures to organize data in Blueprints. We learned how to store various elements in an array and how to retrieve any of those elements. We learned how to use other types of containers, such as sets and maps, to store data.

After that, we learned how to create and use enumerations, structures, and data tables, and we saw examples of how they can be related. It was presented to us as several flow control nodes, such as **Switch**, **Gate**, and **ForEachLoop**.

This chapter showed various Blueprint features that will help us to organize data so that it can be used effectively. The flow control nodes can simplify the Event Graph because, for each situation, there may be a more suitable node.

In the next chapter, we will learn about world and local coordinates, vector operations, and the use of traces to test collisions.

14
Math and Trace Nodes

The representation of a 3D world is based on mathematical concepts. If you do not know these concepts, then it will be more difficult to understand certain operations performed in a 3D game. This chapter explains some math concepts that are needed for 3D games. We will learn about the difference between world and relative transforms, and how to use them when working with Components. We will learn about how to use vectors to represent position, direction, velocity, and distance. The concept of traces is explained, and various types of traces are presented. This chapter also shows how to use traces to test collisions in a game.

These are the topics covered in this chapter:

- World and relative transforms
- Points and vectors
- Traces

World and relative transforms

The Actor class has a **Transform** structure. This structure has three variables, which are used to represent **Location**, **Rotation**, and **Scale**. The **Transform** structure of an Actor that is on the Level can be modified by using the **Details** panel or the transformation Widget that appears when you select an Actor.

In the Level Editor, there are buttons that we can use to select the type of transformation to apply to an Actor, as we can see in the next screenshot:

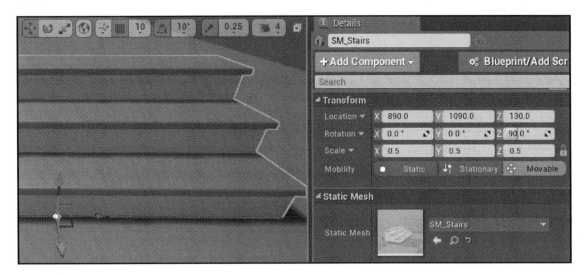

The 3D space is represented by three axes: **X**, **Y**, and **Z**. These axes are represented by colors: the color red is the *x* axis, the color green is the *y* axis, and the color blue is the *z* axis.

The **Location** variable of the **Transform** structure has a set of values for **X**, **Y**, and **Z**, which determine the position on each axis. These values are also known as the world location of the Actor. The next screenshot shows some Actions that we can use to get and set an Actor's location:

- **GetActorLocation**: Returns the current location of the Actor
- **SetActorLocation**: Sets **New Location** for the Actor
- **AddActorWorldOffset**: Uses the **Delta Location** input parameter to modify the current location of the Actor:

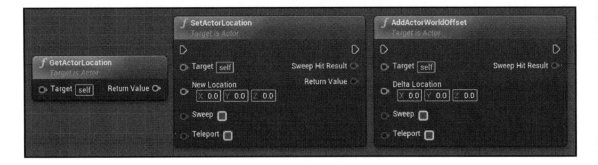

The **Rotation** variable of the **Transform** structure has a set of values for **X**, **Y**, and **Z** in degrees, which determines the rotation on each axis. The following screenshot shows the following rotation nodes:

- **GetActorRotation**: Returns the current rotation of the Actor
- **SetActorRotation**: Sets **New Rotation** for the Actor
- **AddActorWorldRotation**: Adds the **Delta Rotation** input parameter to the current rotation of the Actor:

The **Scale** variable of the **Transform** structure has a set of values for **X**, **Y**, and **Z**, which determines the scale on each axis. The following screenshot shows the nodes that are used to get and set an Actor's scale:

When a Blueprint has Actor Components, the transforms of those Components are known as **relative transforms**, because they are relative to the Component's parent. The next screenshot shows an example of Components. **DefaultSceneRoot** is a small white sphere, which is hidden in the game and used to store the Actor's position in the world. It can be replaced with another Scene Component.

Below it, in the Component's **Hierarchy** of the screenshot, there is a **Static Mesh** Component named **Table**, and below the **Table** Component in **Hierarchy**, there is another **Static Mesh** Component named **Statue**. The transform of the **Table** is relative to the **DefaultSceneRoot** transform, and the transform of the **Statue** Component is relative to the **Table** transform. So, if you move the **Table** Component in the **Viewport**, then the **Statue** Component will move too, but if you change the relative transform of the **Statue** Component instead, then the **Table** Component will remain where it is:

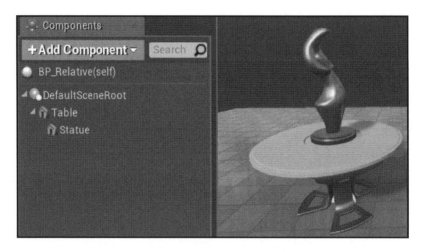

There are nodes to get and set a Component's **Relative Location**. You can also get a Component's **World Location**, as you can see in the following screenshot:

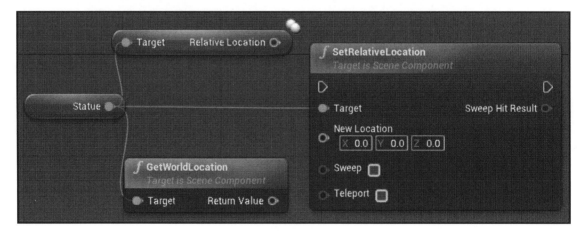

Points and vectors

There is a structure in Unreal Engine named **Vector**, which has three variables of the float type: **X**, **Y**, and **Z**. These values can be used to represent a point (or location) in 3D space. They can also be used as a mathematical vector and represent movement.

Let's first look at an example of using **Vector** as a point. The following screenshot has two Actors. One Actor represents a character and the other represents a couch:

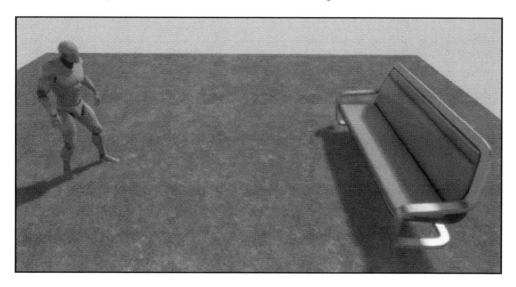

The next screenshot shows the character's **Location**. The **Location** variable of the **Transform** structure is of the **Vector** type, and one Unreal unit equals 1.0 cm by default:

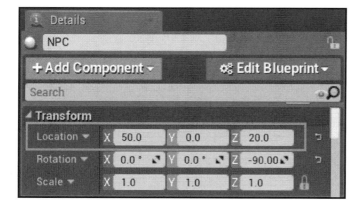

We can represent the character's **Location** simply as (50.0, 0.0, 20.0). The couch's **Location** is (450.0, 0.0, 20.0), which can be seen in the next screenshot:

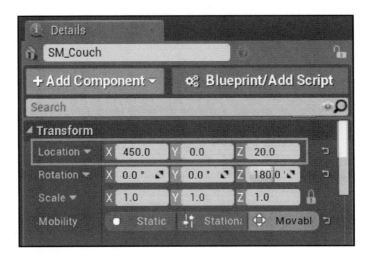

Now, let's see how to use a vector to represent movement. We are going to instruct our character on how to get to the couch. They need to know the direction and distance in which they must move. The next screenshot shows that we are instructing the character to move **400 cm** on the *x* axis:

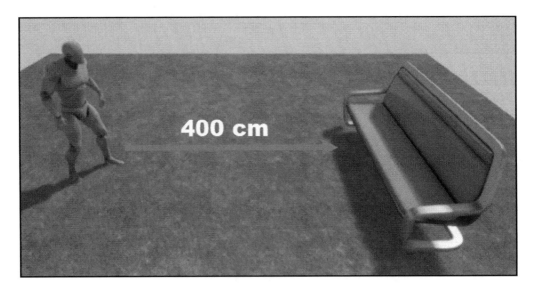

Both the direction and distance are represented by a single vector, using **X**, **Y**, and **Z** values. In the previous screenshot, the value of the vector that describes the movement is (400, 0, 0).

If we take the character location vector and add it to the vector that represents this movement, then the result is the couch location vector. To add two vectors, add each of their elements:

```
couch_location = character_location + vector_movement
couch_location = (50, 0, 20) + (400, 0, 0)
couch_location = (50 + 400, 0 + 0, 20 + 0)
couch_location = (450, 0, 20)
```

If we have a start point and a destination point, and we want to find out the movement vector, then we just need to get the destination point and subtract the start point.

For example, if we want to know the vector that leads from the start point of (25, 40, 55) to the destination point of (75, 95, 130), then we need to solve this expression:

```
vector_movement = destination_point - start_point
vector_movement = (75, 95, 130) - (25, 40, 55)
vector_movement = (75 - 25, 95 - 40, 130 - 55)
vector_movement = (50, 55, 75)
```

A vector has a magnitude (or length) and a direction and is usually represented by an arrow. Vectors are widely used in game programming; they can be used to indicate directions and to represent speed, acceleration, and a force acting on an object.

Vector operations

Several mathematical operations can be done with vectors. Understanding these operations is fundamental to manipulating objects in 3D space:

- **Vector addition**: The sum of two vectors is determined by adding each of their elements. The next example shows the sum of vectors (3, 5, 0) and (5, 2, 0):

```
V1 = (3, 5, 0)
V2 = (5, 2, 0)
V1 + V2 = (3 + 5, 5 + 2, 0 + 0)
V1 + V2 = (8, 7, 0)
```

The following diagram is a graphical representation of the previous example of vector addition:

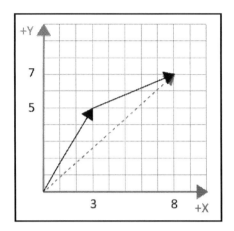

The following screenshot shows the vector addition node:

- **Vector subtraction**: The subtraction of one vector from another is determined by subtracting each of its elements. This is an example of vector subtraction using the vectors (6, 8, 0) and (1, 4, 0):

```
V1 = (6, 8, 0)
V2 = (1, 4, 0)
V1 - V2 = (6 - 1, 8 - 4, 0 - 0)
V1 - V2 = (5, 4, 0)
```

The following diagram is a graphical representation of the previous example of vector subtraction :

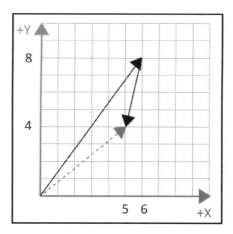

The vector subtraction node is shown in the following screenshot:

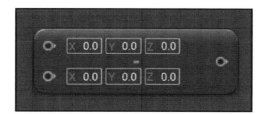

- **Length of a vector**: The length (or magnitude) of a vector can be used to represent the distance between two points. It can be calculated using the Blueprint node of the next screenshot:

- **Normalizing vectors**: We use vector normalization to find a unit vector. The unit vector has a length equal to one. It is often used when direction needs to be indicated. There is a node named **Normalize** that receives a vector as input and returns the normalized vector:

- **Scalar vector multiplication**: An integer or float number is also known as a **scalar value**. The multiplication of a vector by a scalar value is done by multiplying each of its elements by the scalar value. This operation changes the length of the vector, but the direction remains the same unless the scalar is negative, in which case, the vector will point in the opposite direction after the multiplication:

- **Dot product**: The dot product is a projection of one vector onto another vector. The dot product of two normalized vectors is equal to the cosine of the angle formed between the vectors and can range from -1.0 to 1.0:

The dot product can be used to verify the relationship between two vectors, such as whether they are perpendicular or parallel. The following diagram shows some examples of a dot product between two vectors, **A** and **B**:

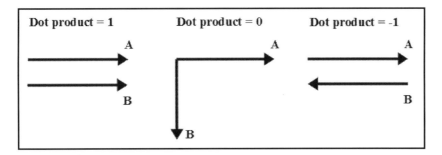

- **Actor vectors**: Some Functions return the forward, right, and up vectors of an Actor. The returned vectors are normalized (*length = 1*). The following screenshot shows these Functions, which are often used to direct movement:

Traces

Traces are used to test whether there are collisions along a defined line segment. A trace can be done by channel or by object type, and can return the single or multiple objects that have been hit.

The channels available are **Visibility** and **Camera**. The object type can be **WorldStatic, WorldDynamic, Pawn, PhysicsBody, Vehicle, Destructible**, or **Projectile**.

The next screenshot shows the collision responses of a **Static Mesh** Actor. There are **Collision Presets** that can be selected, such as **BlockAll**, **OverlapAllDynamic**, and **Pawn**. Or, you can choose **Custom...** as **Collision Presets** and define the **Collision Responses** properties individually. The object type is set via the **Object Type** property dropdown, while the **Visibility** and **Camera** channels are defined in the **Trace Responses** section of the **Collision Responses** table:

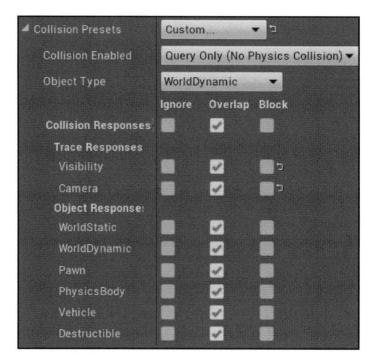

When a trace Function collides with something, it returns one or more **Hit Result** structures. The **Break Hit Result** node can be used to access the **Hit Result** variables, as seen in the following screenshot:

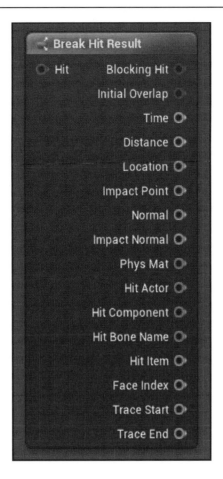

These are some of the variables of the **Hit Result** structure:

- **Blocking Hit**: A Boolean value that indicates whether the trace hit something
- **Location**: The location of the hit
- **Normal**: The normal vector that is perpendicular to the surface that was hit
- **Hit Actor**: The reference to the Actor hit by the trace

Traces for objects

The **LineTraceForObjects** Function tests for collisions along a defined line and returns a **Hit Result** structure with data for the first Actor hit that matches one of the **Object Types** values specified in the input parameter.

The **MultiLineTraceForObjects** Function has the same input parameters as the **LineTraceForObjects** Function. The difference between the functions is that the **MultiLineTraceForObjects** Function returns an array of **Hit Result** structures, rather than a single result, making it more expensive to perform. The next screenshot shows the two **TraceForObjects** Functions:

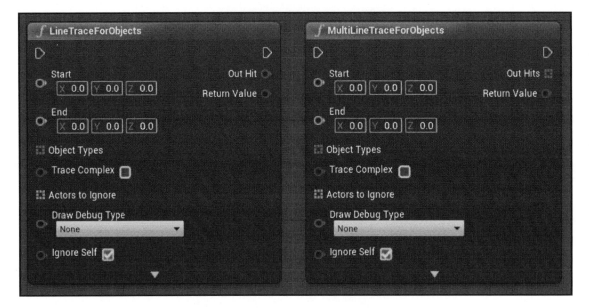

These are the input parameters of the two **TraceForObjects** Functions:

- **Start**: The location vector that defines the start of the line to be used for the collision test.
- **End**: The location vector that defines the end of the collision test line.
- **Object Types**: An array that contains **Object Types** that will be used in the collision test.
- **Trace Complex**: A Boolean value. If it is **True**, then the trace will test against the actual Mesh. If it is **False**, then the trace will test against simplified collision shapes.
- **Actors to Ignore**: An array with Actors that should be ignored in the collision tests.
- **Draw Debug Type**: This allows the drawing of a 3D line that represents the trace.
- **Ignore Self**: A Boolean value that indicates whether the Blueprint instance that is calling the Function should be ignored in the collision test.

Traces by channel

The **LineTraceByChannel** Function tests for collisions along a defined line using **Trace Channel**, which can be **Visibility** or **Camera**, and returns a **Hit Result** structure with data for the first Actor hit in the collision test. There is also the **MultiLineTraceByChannel** Function, which returns an array of **Hit Result** structures:

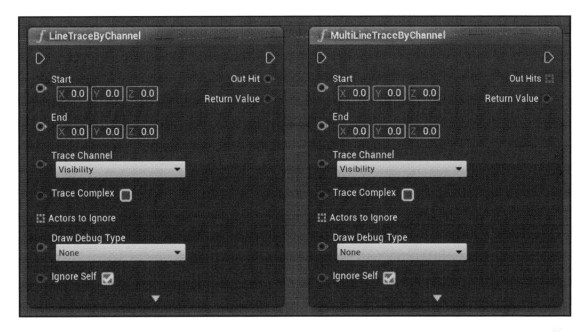

The input parameters of these Functions are as follows:

- **Start**: The location vector that defines the start of the line to be used for the collision test.
- **End**: The location vector that defines the end of the collision test line.
- **Trace Channel**: A channel used for the collision test. It can be **Visibility** or **Camera**.
- **Trace Complex**: A Boolean value. If it is **True**, then the trace will test against the actual Mesh. If it is **False**, then the trace will test against simplified collision shapes.
- **Actors to Ignore**: An array with Actors that should be ignored in the collision tests.

- **Draw Debug Type**: This allows the drawing of a 3D line that represents the trace.
- **Ignore Self**: A Boolean value that indicates whether the Blueprint instance that is calling the Function should be ignored in the collision test.

Shape traces

You can also use shapes to do the traces. There are trace Functions for the sphere, capsule, and box shapes, but these Functions are more expensive to perform than line traces.

For all these shapes, there are Functions to trace by channel and by object type. There are also Functions that return a single hit or multiple hits.

The next screenshot shows the **SphereTraceForObjects**, **CapsuleTraceForObjects**, and **BoxTraceForObjects** Functions:

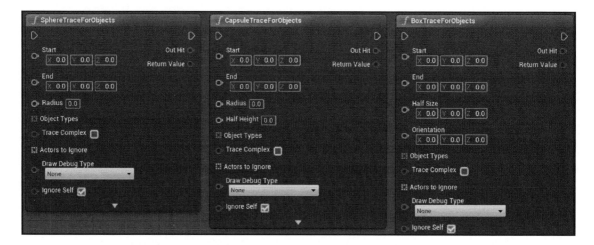

Debug lines

The trace Functions have an option to draw debug lines that help when testing traces. Click on the small arrow at the bottom of the trace Functions to display the **Trace Color**, **Trace Hit Color**, and **Draw Time** parameters, as shown in the following screenshot:

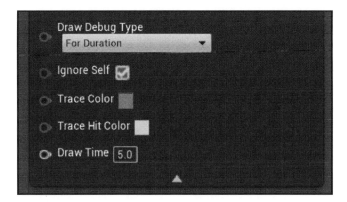

The **Draw Debug Type** parameter can be set to one of the following values:

- **None**: Don't draw the line
- **For One Frame**: The line only appears for one frame
- **For Duration**: The line stays for the time specified in the **Draw Time** parameter
- **Persistent**: The line does not disappear

Example of vectors and trace nodes

Let's do an example to see the use of vectors and trace nodes. We will modify the Player Character to use a line trace to find and toggle the light of another Blueprint:

1. Create a new project using the **First Person** template with starter content.
2. Open the FirstPersonCharacter Blueprint, which is located in the /FirstPersonBP/Blueprints folder.

3. In the **My Blueprint** panel, create a new **Macro** and name it `Trace Locations`. In the **Details** panel, add two output parameters of the `Vector` type. Name the parameters `Start Location` and `End Location`, as shown in the next screenshot. We do not need input parameters:

4. Double-click the name of the Macro to edit it. Add the Actions of the following screenshot. This Macro calculates the **Start** and **End** locations that will be used by **Line Trace**. Since this is a first-person game, we are using the camera as **Start Location**, and **End Location** is `300` cm ahead of **Camera**:

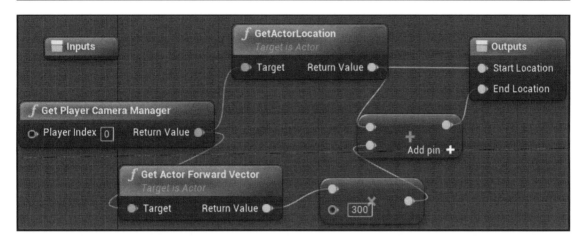

5. Click on the **Event Graph** tab and add an input Event for the *Enter* key. Add a
   LineTraceByChannel node and add the **Trace Locations** Macro to the **Event
   Graph**. Connect the outputs of the Macro to the **Start** and **End** inputs of **Line
   Trace**, as shown in the next screenshot:

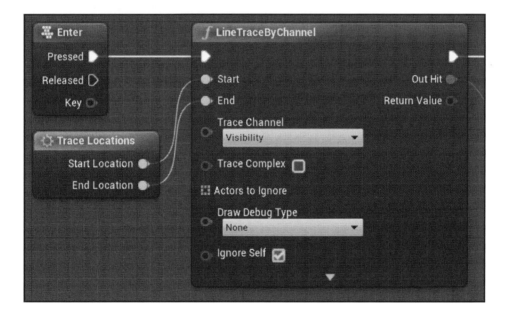

6. Connect the Actions of the following screenshot to the output of the
LineTraceByChannel node. These Actions test whether **Hit Actor** is of
the **Blueprint_WallSconce** type. If it is, then the light of **Blueprint_WallSconce** is
toggled. Compile the Blueprint to apply the changes.

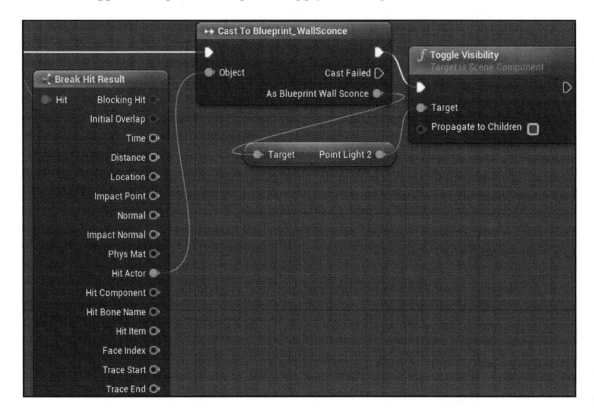

7. Add an instance of `Blueprint_WallSconce` (which is in
the `/StarterContent/Blueprints/` folder) to the Level, and then play the
Level. Move your character close to the instance of `Blueprint_WallSconce`,
look at it, and press the *Enter* key to toggle the light. The next screenshot shows
the Player Character and `Blueprint_WallSconce`:

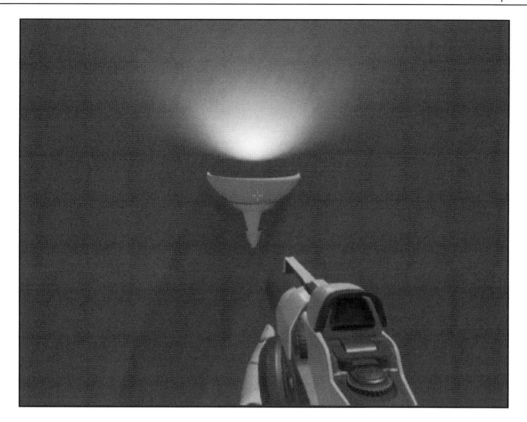

Summary

This chapter presented some math concepts and showed you how to use world and relative transforms. We saw how several Blueprint nodes are used to modify an element of a transform, such as **Location**, **Rotation**, and **Scale**.

This chapter has shown that a vector structure can be used to represent a point in 3D space or a mathematical vector. We learned how to do several vector operations using Blueprint nodes.

Finally, we saw how to test collisions using the trace nodes. There are many trace nodes, which are based on the type of collision response, the shapes used, and whether the trace nodes return single or multiple hits.

In the next chapter, we will learn several tips for dealing with the complexity of Blueprints and increasing the quality of Blueprints.

15
Blueprints Tips

This chapter contains several tips on how to improve the quality of Blueprints. We will learn about how to use various Editor shortcuts that speed up our work. We will also learn about some Blueprint best practices that will help you decide what type of implementation should be done and where. Finally, we'll learn about more useful miscellaneous Blueprint nodes.

These are the topics covered in this chapter:

- Blueprint Editor shortcuts
- Blueprint best practices
- Miscellaneous Blueprint nodes

Blueprint Editor shortcuts

In the Blueprint Editor, we are going to work with variables a lot, so let's start with the shortcuts related to variables. When you drag a variable from the **My Blueprint** panel and drop it in the Event Graph, a submenu appears for you to choose either the **GET** or **SET** node. But, there are shortcuts to create **GET** and **SET** nodes. If you hold the *Ctrl* key and drag a variable to the graph, then the Editor will create a **GET** node. To create a **SET** node, hold the *Alt* key and drag a variable to the graph. The following screenshot shows the **GET** and **SET** nodes:

There is another way to create **GET** and **SET** nodes. If you drag a variable and drop it on a compatible pin of another node, then the Editor will create a **GET** or **SET** node depending on the parameter type. The next screenshot shows an example of the Score variable being dropped on an input parameter pin. If the pin is compatible, then the Editor will show a tooltip with a check icon and a label such as **Make B = Score**. This expression means that the **B** pin of the node will get the value of the Score variable. So, the Editor will create a **GET Score** node:

If you drop the Score variable on an output parameter pin, as shown in the following screenshot, then the Editor will show the **Make Score = ReturnValue** label, and it will create a **SET Score** node using the **ReturnValue** label of the other node as the input parameter:

The Blueprint Editor has an automatic type conversion system. To use it, drag a wire from the pin of one variable type and drop it on a pin of another variable type. The next screenshot shows that a tooltip appears to confirm that the conversion is possible:

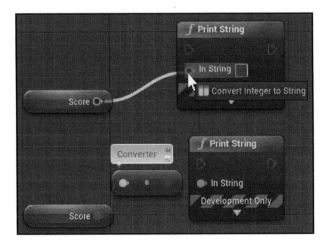

Another useful feature of the Blueprint Editor is that it is possible to change an existing node for another node that uses the same variable type without breaking the connections. There is an example of this in the next screenshot. **Player Health** and **PlayerStamina** are `float` variables. If you drag the **PlayerStamina** variable and drop it on the **SET Player Health** node, then the node will change to a **SET PlayerStamina** node and keep all connections:

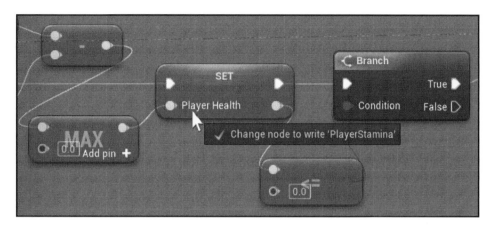

There is a shortcut to create variables based on the type of an input or output pin of a node. To do this, right-click on a data pin and select the **Promote to Variable** option, as shown in the following screenshot. This option creates a variable and connects it to the pin:

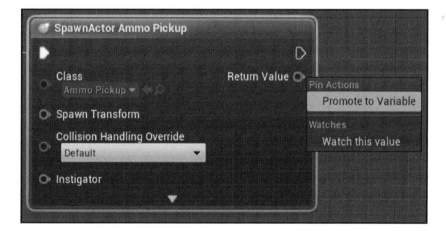

If you need to break all the connections of a pin, then hold the *Alt* key and click on the pin. You can move all the connections of a pin to another compatible pin by holding the *Ctrl* key, dragging the connections, and dropping them on another pin. This is very useful because you don't need to redo the connections one by one. In the next screenshot, all the connections of the **As First Person Character** pin will be moved to the **As Player Character** pin:

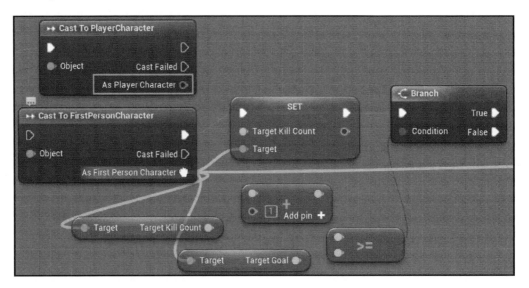

The Blueprint Editor offers several options for node alignment. To use them, select some Blueprint nodes and right-click on one of them to open a menu. **Alignment** is one of the options of this menu. The following screenshot shows the **Alignment** options that are available:

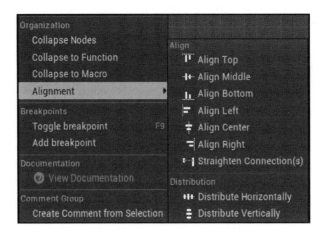

Most of the **Alignment** options are self-explanatory, but let's look at an example: **Straighten Connection(s)**. The next screenshot shows three nodes selected:

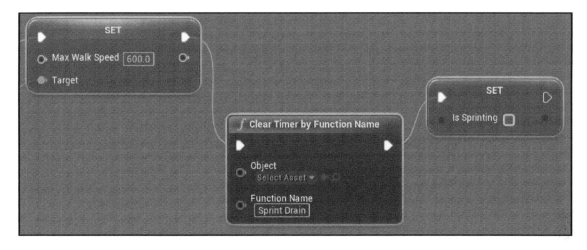

After applying **Straighten Connection(s)**, the nodes will be organized, as shown in the following screenshot:

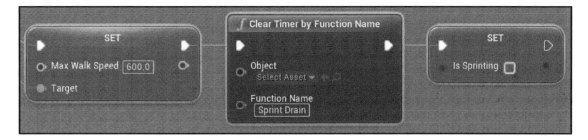

There are shortcut keys to create some common nodes in Blueprints. If you want to create a **Branch** node, then hold the *B* key and left-click on the graph. To create a **Sequence** node, hold the *S* key and left-click on the graph, as shown in the next screenshot:

Other shortcut keys are **F + left-click**, which creates a **ForEachLoop** node, and **D + left-click**, which creates a **Delay** node. These can be seen in the following screenshot:

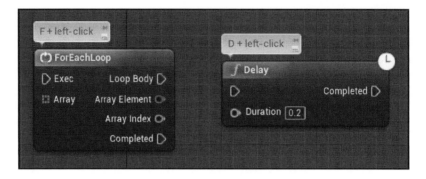

To create a comment box around some nodes, first select the nodes, then right-click on one of the selected nodes and select the **Create Comment** option from **Selection**, or you can just press the C key. The next screenshot shows a comment box that is labeled **More shortcut keys**. Inside the comment box, there are more examples of shortcut keys used to create nodes:

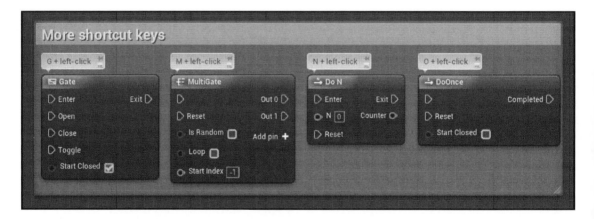

When you get used to some shortcuts, you will see how they speed up your work. Now, let's look at tips to help you build better Blueprints.

Blueprint best practices

In a project, you will deal with several Blueprint classes, and some of these Blueprint classes will be complex, with many nodes. The tips in this section will help you analyze your project and carry out some practices that will make your Blueprint classes more manageable. I separated these tips into two categories: Blueprint responsibilities and Blueprint complexities.

Blueprint responsibilities

When creating a Blueprint, you need to decide what its responsibilities will be. This refers to what it will do and what it will not do. You need to make the Blueprint as independent as possible. A Blueprint must be responsible for its internal state.

To illustrate the concept of Blueprint responsibilities, let's work with a simple example created for teaching purposes. In a game, the player is represented by the FirstPersonCharacter Blueprint. If the player collides with an Enemy Blueprint, then the player will die and an explosion effect will be spawned. The following screenshot shows the **Event Hit** that was implemented in the Enemy Blueprint:

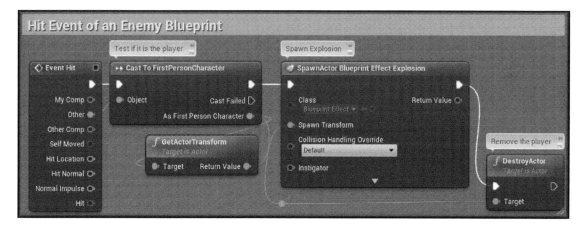

Next, you create another Blueprint that can also kill the player. So, you copy **Event Hit** and the nodes of the previous screenshot and paste them in the new Blueprint. Then, you create another different type of Enemy Blueprint and copy and paste **Event Hit** again. But, you decide to change the way the player dies. The player does not explode anymore, but a death animation is executed. However, to make this change in your game, you will have to search for all Blueprints that can kill the player and modify the script of all of them. This is a problem because you might forget one of the Blueprints, and the script may have frequent changes.

There is a way to avoid this type of problem. The script that defines how player deaths work must be implemented in the player Blueprint, which, in this example, is the FirstPersonCharacter Blueprint. The point is that the player Blueprint is responsible for the way the player dies. Let's redo our example, but now, we will create a custom Event named Death in the FirstPersonCharacter Blueprint, as shown in this screenshot:

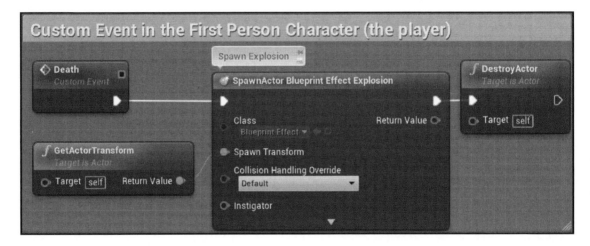

This way, if there are changes in the way the player dies, then these changes will need to be done only in the Death Event of the FirstPersonCharacter Blueprint.

When a collision occurs, the other Blueprints that can kill the player will just have to trigger the Death Event of the FirstPersonCharacter Blueprint. The following screenshot shows the new version of **Event Hit** of the Enemy Blueprint:

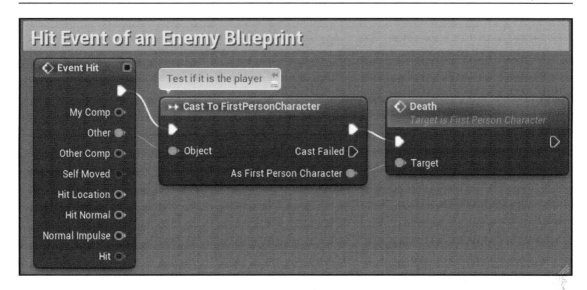

So, you can use Events and Functions to define how a Blueprint can communicate with other Blueprints. And if you need to send data between Blueprints, then it can be sent through input parameters.

Another topic related to Blueprint responsibilities is Level Blueprint. Each Level has its Level Blueprint, so if you create your game rules logic inside a Level Blueprint, then when you add another Level, you will need to copy and paste all Blueprint nodes to the Level Blueprint of the new Level. If your game rules logic changes, then you will need to modify all the Level Blueprints, and this can become a maintenance nightmare.

A Level Blueprint must be used only for logic and situations specific to one Level. A typical example is to put a hidden trigger on a Level. When the player overlaps it, an enemy is spawned in another room.

A better place to implement game rules logic is in a GameMode Blueprint class. The logic for other Actors should be implemented in Blueprint classes rather than being implemented in the Level Blueprint because instances of a Blueprint class can be added to any Level, so you do not need to copy and paste Blueprint nodes to use the same functionality in another Level.

Managing Blueprint complexities

A Blueprint Event Graph can become very complex and scary. When you open a Blueprint of this kind that was done by someone else, you wonder, *what's going on?*

Some practices and Blueprint tools will help you to manage the complexities of a Blueprint and keep it readable.

The most important concept that will help deal with complex Blueprints is **abstraction**. Abstraction is used to handle complexities by hiding low-level details, allowing the developer to focus on a problem at a high abstraction level without worrying about unnecessary details of other parts of the script.

In an Event Graph, there is a simple way to apply abstraction. You can select a group of nodes and convert them to a **Collapsed Graph**, **Function**, or **Macro**. To convert the nodes, right-click on the selected nodes. In the submenu that appears, within category **Organization**, you will see the options shown in the following screenshot:

Let's look at an example. The following screenshot shows some nodes selected. These nodes are responsible for resetting the sprint state of the player:

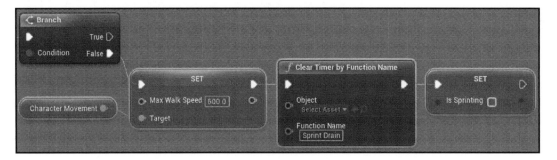

If we right-click on one of the selected nodes and use the **Collapse Nodes** option, then the Editor will create **Collapsed Graph**, which is represented by a single node. You can give a meaningful name to this node. The following screenshot shows the node named **Reset Sprint**, which represents **Collapsed Graph**. If you want to see or edit the nodes of **Collapsed Graph**, then double-click the collapsed node:

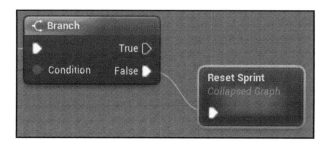

Only use collapsed nodes if the group of nodes is not going to be used in another place. If the same group of nodes is used in other places of the Event Graph, then you can use **Collapse to Macro**. And if you think that a group of nodes could be called from another Blueprint, then use **Collapse to Function**.

Now, let's imagine that you are opening a very complex Blueprint. But instead of seeing a giant graph of nodes, you see collapse graphs, Macros, and Functions with meaningful names. At least you will get an overview of what the Blueprint does. The complexities are there, but they are hidden, and you can look at the low-level details of a specific part when needed.

Another handy tool that can increase the readability of a complex Event Graph is a comment box. A comment box helps to identify a logic block. Its label stays visible when you zoom out of the Event Graph, and you can even change the color of comment boxes. The following screenshot shows an Event Graph zoomed out with three comment boxes:

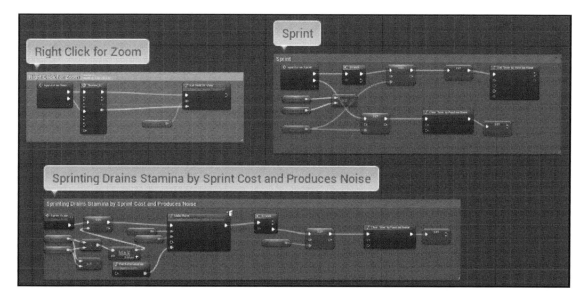

You can see a list of the comment boxes of a graph in the **Bookmarks** window, which can be accessed in the top menu **Window | Bookmarks**. The next screenshot shows the **Bookmarks** window:

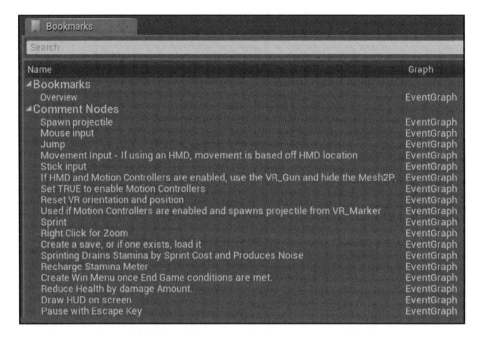

If you double-click an item in the **Bookmarks** window, then the Event Graph will be positioned in the associated location. You can create bookmarks to reference a location of the Event Graph by clicking on the star icon and giving a name to the bookmark, as shown in the following screenshot:

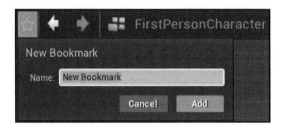

In the **My Blueprint** panel, you can see a list of the Events being used in the Event Graph, as can be seen in the next screenshot. Double-click an Event name in order to move the Event Graph to the position of the Event:

A complex Blueprint can have many variables. There are two variable properties named **Tooltip** and **Category**, which help you identify and organize variables. These properties are found in the **Details** panel of a variable, as shown in the following screenshot:

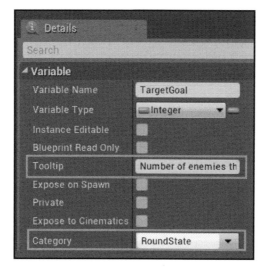

You can describe the purpose of the variable in the **Tooltip** property. It is shown when the mouse cursor is over the variable, as seen in the next screenshot. If the variable is **Instance Editable**, then it should have a tooltip so that the purpose of the variable is clear to the designer, who is using an instance of the Blueprint in the Level:

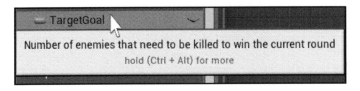

The **Category** property is used to group related variables. You can create categories or select an existing category in the drop-down menu. Variables are separated by categories in the **My Blueprint** tab, which you can open and close when you need it. This separation makes it easier to understand the variables of a Blueprint. The following screenshot shows a category named `Round State`, which has four variables:

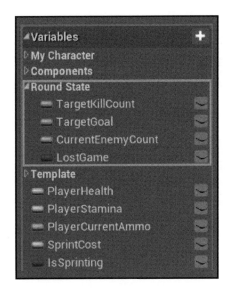

If you need to create variables that hold temporary values to help with more complex logic, then consider creating a Function. A Function allows the creation of **Local Variables**, which are only visible within the Function. When you are editing a Function, there is one more category for **Local Variables** in the **My Blueprint** panel, as shown in the next screenshot. Just a note: the values of **Local Variables** are discarded at the end of the Function execution:

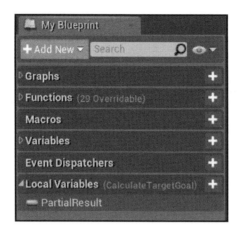

This section covers some best practices to deal with Blueprint responsibilities and complexities. We will now see how to use some interesting miscellaneous Blueprint nodes.

Miscellaneous Blueprint nodes

In this section, we will learn about some Blueprint nodes that can be very useful in certain situations.

These are the nodes covered in this section:

- **Select**
- **Teleport**
- **Format Text**
- **Math Expression**
- **Set View Target with Blend**
- **AttachToComponent**
- **Enable Input** and **Disable Input**
- The **Set Input Mode** nodes

Select

The **Select** node is very flexible. It can work with several types of variables for the index and for the values of options. The node returns a value associated with the option that corresponds to the index that is passed as input. The next screenshot shows the **Select** node:

To add more input option pins, click on **Add pin +**. You can set a pin type of **Option 0**, **Option 1**, or **Index** by dragging a variable reference or wire onto the pins. **Option 0** and **Option 1** can be of any type, but the **Index** type must be **Integer**, **Enum Boolean**, or **Byte**.

The following screenshot shows the **Select** node in use. There is an enumeration named **Difficult Level** that has the values of **Easy**, **Normal**, and **Hard**. The **SpawnBoss** custom Event will spawn a different class of **Boss** Blueprint, depending on the value of the **Difficult Level** enumeration variable. The option type in this example is Actor Class Reference:

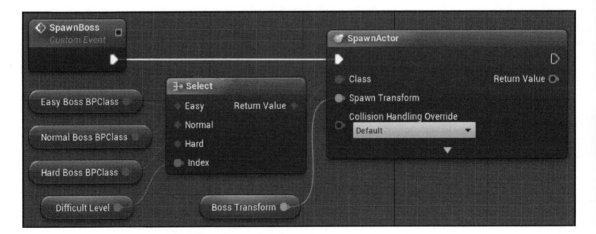

Teleport

The **Teleport** node moves an Actor to the specified location. The advantage of using **Teleport** rather than setting the Actor's location is that if there is an obstacle at the location, then the Actor is moved to a nearby place where there will be no collision.

The next screenshot shows an example using the **Teleport** node. There is a **BP Teleport Platform** Blueprint that has a reference to **Next Teleport Platform**. When the player overlaps **BP Teleport Platform**, they are teleported to **Next Teleport Platform**:

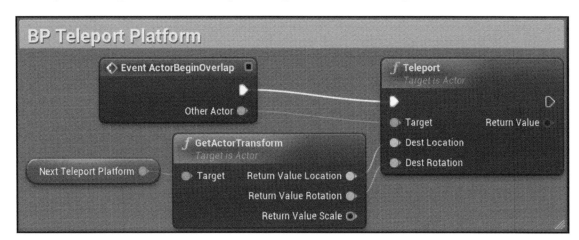

Format Text

The **Format Text** node builds a text based on a template text and parameters specified in the **Format** input parameter. To add new parameters in **Text**, use the { } delimiters with the name of the new parameter inside the delimiters. An input parameter is created for each { } delimiter found in the **Format** parameter.

The next screenshot shows the **Format Text** node being used to print the result of a round, with this template text: {Name} wins the round with {Score} points.:

An example output is Sarena wins the round with 17 points..

Math Expression

The **Math Expression** node is a collapsed graph created by the Editor, and is based on the expression typed in the name of the node. An input parameter pin is created for each variable name found in the expression. The **Return Value** output parameter is the result of the expression.

The following screenshot shows a Function named **Calculate Money Reward**, which uses a **Math Expression** node. The expression of the node is (PlayerLuck/5) * (EnemyHP/30):

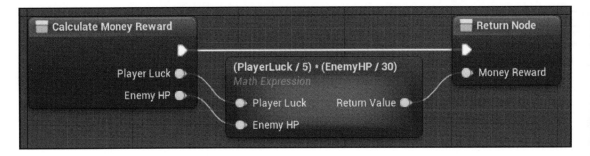

Set View Target with Blend

The **Set View Target with Blend** node is a Function from the **Player Controller** class. It is used for switching the game view between different cameras. The **New View Target** input parameter is the Actor to set as a view target, usually a camera.

The screenshot shows an Event of the Level Blueprint that is triggered when the player enters the treasure room. The **Set View Target with Blend** Function is used to change the game view to the camera that is in the treasure room:

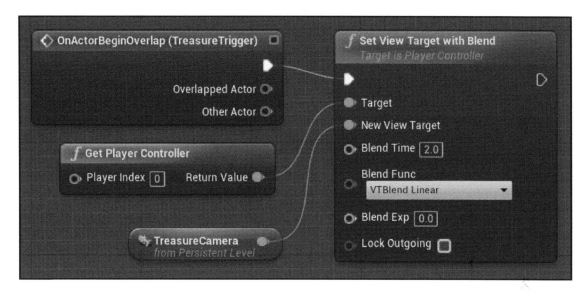

AttachToComponent

The **AttachToComponent** node attaches an Actor to the Component referenced in the **Parent** input parameter. The transformations of the **Parent** Component affect the Actor attached. Optionally, **Socket Name** can be used to identify the place where the Actor will be attached.

In the screenshot, the **EquipShield** custom Event uses the **AttachToComponent** node to equip a **Shield Actor** Component on a **Skeletal Mesh** Component. The **Skeletal Mesh** Component has a socket named LeftArmSocket, which is used to position the shield on the arm:

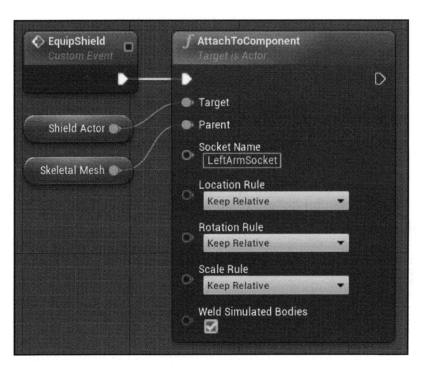

Enable/Disable Input

The **Enable Input** and **Disable Input** nodes are Functions used to define whether an Actor should respond to inputs Events such as keyboard, mouse, or gamepad. The nodes need a reference to the **Player Controller** class in use.

A common use of these nodes is to allow an Actor to only receive input events when the player is near the Actor. In the next screenshot, the **Enable Input** node is called when the player begins to overlap the Blueprint. When the player finishes overlapping the Blueprint, the **Disable Input** node is called:

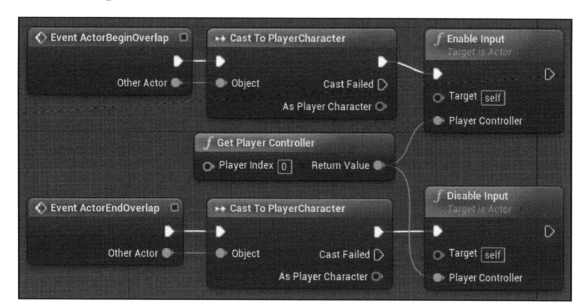

The Set Input Mode nodes

There are three **Set Input Mode** nodes that are used to define whether the priority in handling user input Events is with the UI or with the player input. These are the nodes:

- **Set Input Mode Game Only**: Only **Player Controller** receives input Events.
- **Set Input Mode UI Only**: Only the UI receives input Events.

- **Set Input Mode Game and UI**: The UI has priority in handling an input Event, but if the UI does not handle it, then **Player Controller** receives the input Event. For example, when the player overlaps a Blueprint representing a shop, a UI is displayed with options for the player to choose to use the mouse, but the player can still use the arrow keys to move away from the shop:

I recommend you get used to these miscellaneous Blueprint nodes. When working on a project, you will have to deal with some problems that can be easily solved with some specific Blueprint nodes.

Summary

In this chapter, we saw how to use Editor shortcuts to create variables in various ways, and how to organize Blueprint nodes using alignment tools. We also learned about some shortcut keys that are used to create specific Blueprint nodes.

Then, we looked at some Blueprint best practices to define Blueprint responsibilities and to manage the complexities of Blueprints.

Finally, we learned about some more useful Blueprint nodes. All these tips will help you to improve your scripts and build quality projects.

In the next chapter, we will explore the virtual reality template that is available in the Unreal Engine Editor.

Introduction to VR Development **16**

This chapter explains a number of **Virtual Reality (VR)** concepts and explores the VR template. As VR headsets have become more affordable, the number of users is increasing fast. There are demands for VR games and also for VR business applications. We will focus on the Blueprints of the VR template. This will be another opportunity to see Blueprint nodes being used in practice. You will be able to use some Blueprint concepts from this chapter in several other types of projects, so this is a useful chapter even if you do not have a VR headset.

Let's analyze the functionalities of the Pawn and Motion Controller Blueprints of the VR template. This chapter explains how to implement new objects that can be grabbed by the player using Motion Controllers, and we will learn about the Blueprint Actions used to implement teleportation.

These are the topics we will cover in this chapter:

- Exploring the VR template
- The Pawn Blueprint
- The Motion Controller Blueprint
- Object grabbing
- Teleportation

Exploring the VR template

Unreal Engine Editor has a Blueprint VR template that makes it easy to start experimenting with VR development. The following screenshot shows the creation of a project using the VR template. In **Project Settings**, choose **Mobile / Tablet** as the hardware, **Scalable 3D or 2D** as the graphical level, and **No Starter Content**. These settings were chosen because performance is essential in a VR application:

The following screenshot is from the start up map of the VR template and shows that there are two maps in the VR template with different types of locomotion. The first map contains an example of locomotion using the keyboard or gamepad, and the second map uses Motion Controllers for locomotion and interactions. In this chapter, we will use the second map, which is in the `VirtualRealityBP/Maps/MotionControllerMap` path. The letters **HMD** that appear in the screenshot mean **Head Mounted Display**, which is the VR display device:

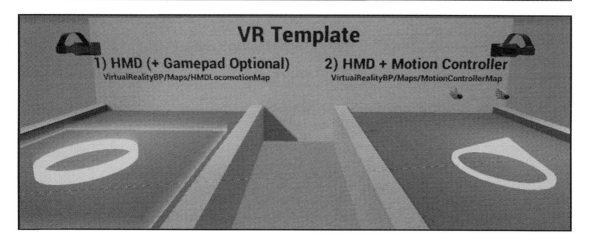

Open the `MotionControllerMap` level. If there is an HMD installed on your computer, then you can launch the Level in VR by clicking on the dropdown of the **Play** button and selecting **VR Preview**, as shown in the following screenshot:

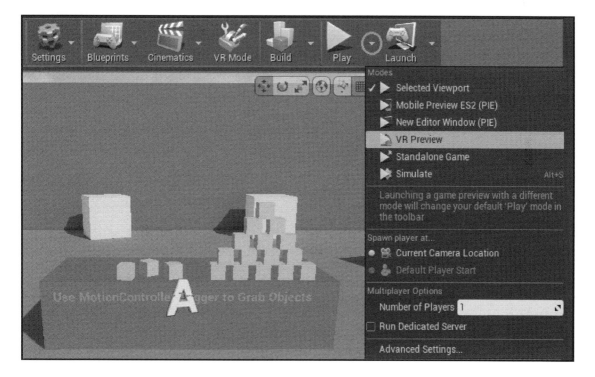

You can teleport to the level by pressing the touchpad, pointing in a direction, and releasing the touchpad. You can grab and move the boxes on the table by using the triggers of the Motion Controllers.

The VR template project is already set up for use in **OculusVR** and **SteamVR**. If you want to enable the use of other VR devices, then you need to open the **Plugins** tab on the **Edit | Plugins** menu and enable the VR device plugin, as shown in the next screenshot:

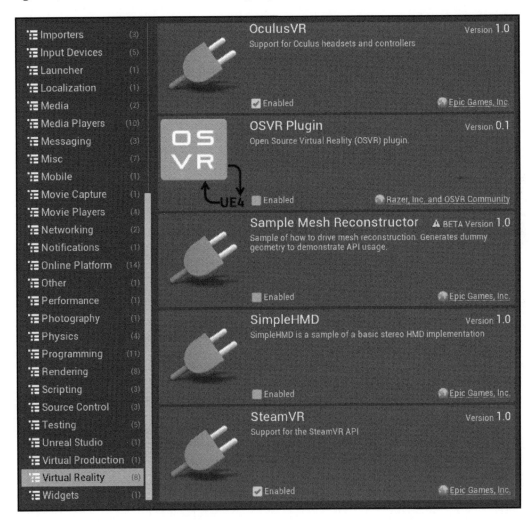

The Blueprints used in the template are in the `VirtualRealityBP/Blueprints` folder. Let's learn about how they work in order to make it easier to adapt them to our projects. Also, this will be an excellent opportunity to see practical examples of Blueprints.

The Pawn Blueprint

The Pawn Blueprint used in `MotionControllerMap` is `MotionControllerPawn`. This Blueprint represents the player in the level. Double-click it to open the Blueprint Editor.

The following screenshot shows the **Components** panel of the `MotionControllerPawn` Blueprint. Below **DefaultSceneRoot**, there is a Scene Component named `VROrigin`. The `VROrigin` Scene Component represents the tracking origin of the HMD and is used as a reference point to `Camera` and the Motion Controllers. Some HMDs use the tracking origin at floor level, while others use it at eye level:

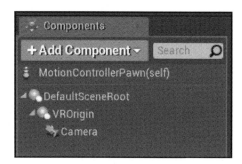

There is a Motion Controller Component that could be added as a child Component of `VROrigin`. However, the VR template created a Blueprint named `BP_MotionController` that contains the Motion Controller Component and possesses other features.

`MotionControllerPawn` has two variables of the `BP_MotionController` type, which reference the left and right Motion Controllers. The following screenshot shows these variables:

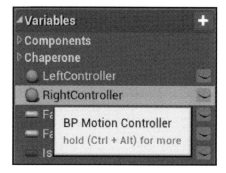

The instances of `BP_MotionController` are spawned in **Event BeginPlay** of `MotionControllerPawn`. The next screenshot shows the actions used to spawn **Left Controller** and attach it to the `VROrigin` component:

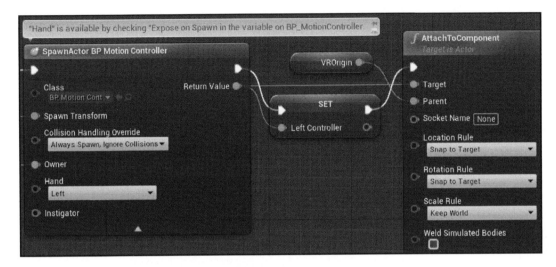

`MotionControllerPawn` is also responsible for handling the controller input for grabbing objects and teleporting. These two Actions will be analyzed in their respective sections.

There are many Blueprint Functions related to HMD. They are grouped in the **Input | Head Mounted Display** category, as shown in the following screenshot:

`MotionControllerPawn` works together with the `BP_MotionController` Blueprint to allow the user to interact with the world using VR. We will now see how the `BP_MotionController` Blueprint is implemented.

The Motion Controller Blueprint

Motion Controllers are implemented by the `BP_MotionController` Blueprint. Double-click it to open the Blueprint Editor.

Click on the **Viewport** tab to see a visual representation of the Blueprint, as shown in the following screenshot. The Motion Controller is represented by a hand Skeletal Mesh and has other visual Components that are used in the teleport:

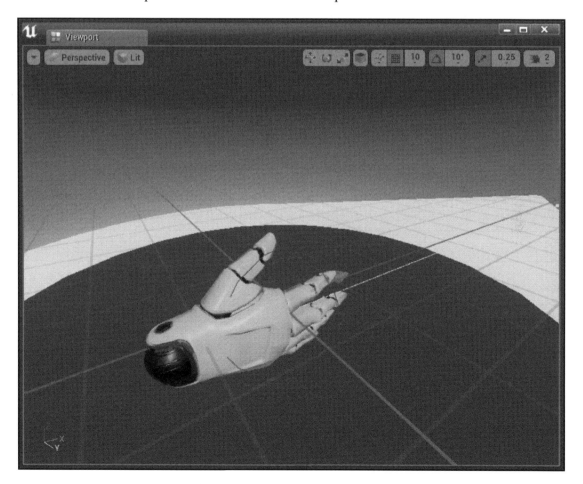

The next screenshot shows the **Components** panel of `BP_MotionController`:

Brief descriptions of the Components are as follows:

- **Scene**: The root Component.
- **MotionController**: The Motion Controller Component that tracks a Motion Controller device. When you move the Motion Controller device, the data of this movement is sent to the Motion Controller Component.
- **HandMesh**: A Skeletal Mesh Component of a hand.
- **ArcDirection**: An arrow Component used to indicate the direction of the teleport.
- **ArcSpline**: A Spline Component used to draw a curve representing the teleport movement.
- **GrabSphere**: A Collision Component used to detect whether the Motion Controller is overlapping an Actor on the Level.
- **ArcEndPoint**: A Static Mesh Component that stores the end location of **ArcSpline**.
- **TeleportCylinder**: A Static Mesh Component used to visually represent the target of the teleport.
- **Ring**: Another Static Mesh Component used to represent the target of the teleport visually.

- **Arrow**: A Static Mesh Component that indicates the rotation of the teleport.
- **RoomScaleMesh**: A Static Mesh Component visualized around the teleport target. It is only rendered if room-scale was successfully set up on the HMD.
- **SteamVRChaperone**: A Component used to map the playable area.

The Events related to the Motion Controller buttons are grouped in the **Input | Gamepad Events** category. The following screenshot shows the Events of the left Motion Controller, which are identified by **(L)**, and the same Events of the right Motion Controller, which are identified by **(R)**:

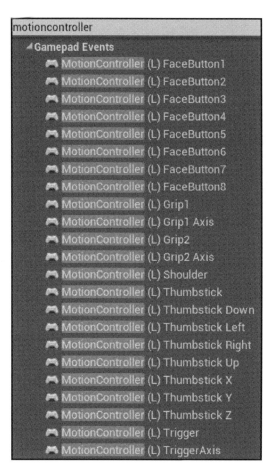

The VR template created Input Mappings for the **GrabLeft**, **GrabRight**, **TeleportLeft**, and **TeleportRight** Actions. They were associated with Motion Controller buttons, as shown in the following screenshot. The Input Mappings can be accessed via the **Edit** | **Project Settings...** | **Input** menu:

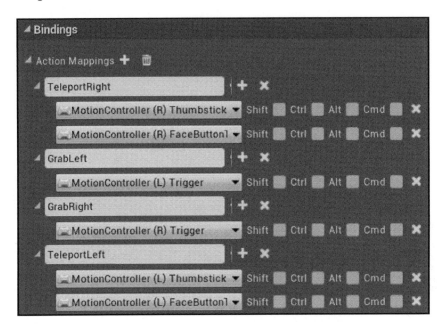

Now that we've learned about how the `MotionControllerPawn` and `BP_MotionController` Blueprints work, let's see how they are used to grab objects.

Object grabbing

In this section, we'll learn about how object grabbing is implemented. The following screenshot of the VR template shows the hand grabbing a cube object:

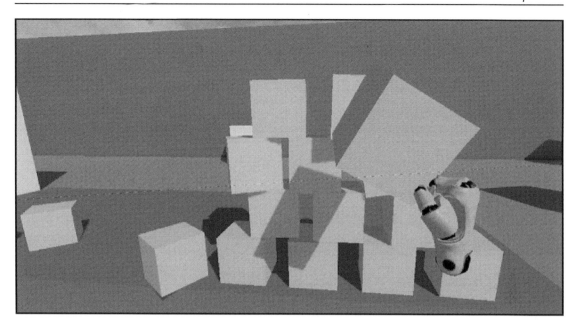

The VR template created **Blueprint Interface** named `PickupActorInterface`.
The **Blueprint Interface** only contains Function names and parameters and is used to share standard communication protocols between different types of Blueprints.

To create a **Blueprint Interface**, click the **Add New** button in **Content Browser**, and, in the **Blueprints** submenu, select **Blueprint Interface**, as shown in the following screenshot:

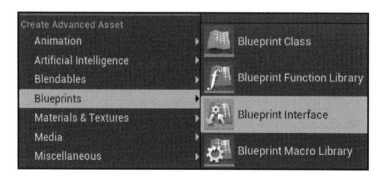

Double-click `PickupActorInterface`, which is located in the
`VirtualRealityBP/Blueprints` folder, to open the **Blueprint Interface** Editor. The next
screenshot shows that `PickupActorInterface` has two **Functions** named **Pickup** and
Drop. The **Pickup** Function has an input parameter named **AttachTo**, which is of the **Scene
Component** type:

We need to add `PickupActorInterface` to the Blueprint classes that can be grabbed by
the `BP_MotionController` Blueprint. To do this, click on the **Class Settings** button of the
Blueprint Editor. Then, in the **Details** panel, go to the **Interfaces** category, click on the **Add**
button, and select `PickupActorInterface`, as shown in the following screenshot:

When you add an interface to a Blueprint, it becomes possible to implement the interface Functions in the Blueprint. The next screenshot shows the Functions of `PickupActorInterface` in the Event Graph of a Blueprint:

You can check whether **Actor Reference** implements the interface by using the **Does Implement Interface** Function, as shown in the following screenshot:

Double-click BP_PickupCube, which is located in the VirtualRealityBP/Blueprints folder, to see how object grabbing was implemented in this Blueprint. The next screenshot shows **Event Pickup**. The **AttachTo** input parameter receives a reference to the Motion Controller Component of the BP_MotionController Blueprint. **Event Pickup** turns off the physics simulation and attaches the root Component of BP_PickupCube to the Motion Controller Component:

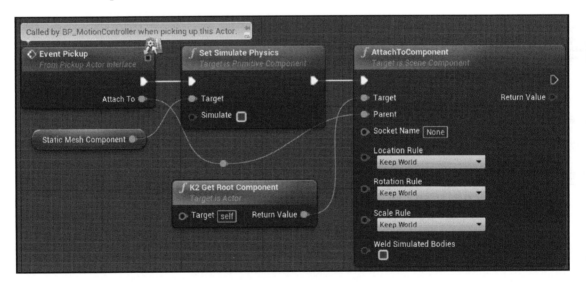

The following screenshot shows **Event Drop**, which turns on the physics simulation and detaches BP_PickupCube:

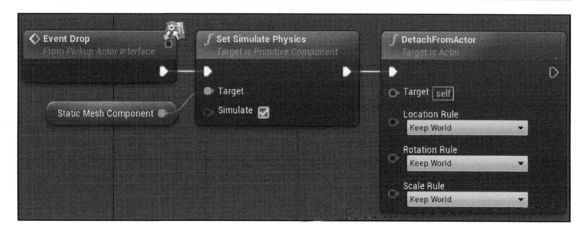

If you want to create another Blueprint that can be grabbed by the Motion Controller, then you need to add the `PickupActorInterface` interface to the Blueprint. Then, in the new Blueprint, you can implement **Event Pickup** and **Event Drop** with a different way of how an instance of this Blueprint can be grabbed by the Motion Controller.

Object grabbing starts when the player triggers the **GrabLeft** or **GrabRight** Events. These Events are implemented in the `MotionControllerPawn` Blueprint. The next screenshot shows the **GrabLeft** Event. When the trigger is **Pressed**, the **Grab Actor** Function is called, and when the trigger is **Released**, the **Release Actor** Function is called. Both Functions can be found in `BP_MotionController`:

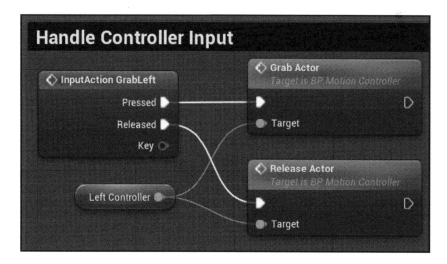

The following screenshot is from the **Grab Actor** Function of BP_MotionController. The **Get Actor Near Hand** Function of BP_MotionController returns the nearest overlapping Actor that implements PickupActorInterface. The reference to the Actor returned from the **Get Actor Near Hand** Function is stored in the **Attached Actor** variable and is used to call the **Pickup** Event that will attach it to **Motion Controller**:

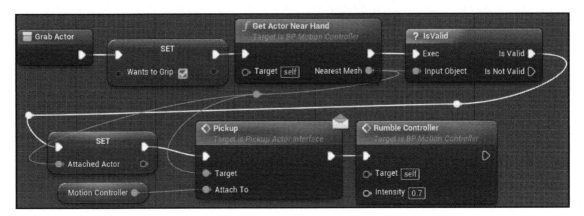

The **Release Actor** Function of BP_MotionController calls the **Drop** Event of the attached Actor and resets the variables used when an object is grabbed, thereby finishing the grab movement.

Teleportation

In this section, we'll go through the main Events and Functions used in the teleportation. The next screenshot of the VR template shows when the teleport is active:

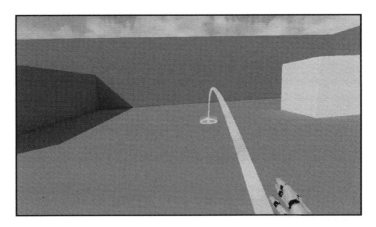

Teleportation starts when the player triggers the **TeleportLeft** or **TeleportRight** Events by pressing the thumbstick of the Motion Controller. These Events are implemented in the `MotionControllerPawn` Blueprint. The next screenshot shows the **TeleportLeft** Event. When it is **Pressed**, it activates the teleporter arc of **Left Controller**, and disables the teleporter arc of **Right Controller**, because only one can be active. The player points to the desired location, and when they release the thumbstick, the **Execute Teleportation** Event of `MotionControllerPawn` is called to perform the camera effect and teleport the player:

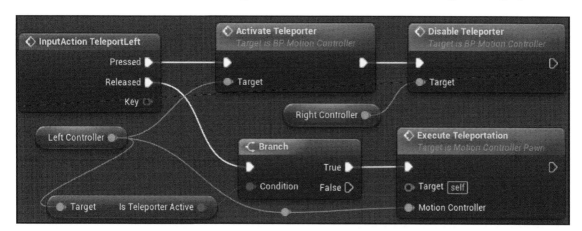

In the **Activate Teleporter** Function of the `BP_MotionController` Blueprint, the Boolean variables, **Is Teleporter Active** and **Visibility** of **Teleport Cylinder**, are set to **True**, as shown in the next screenshot. The rendering of the teleport arc is done in the **Tick** Event if **Is Teleporter Active** is **True**:

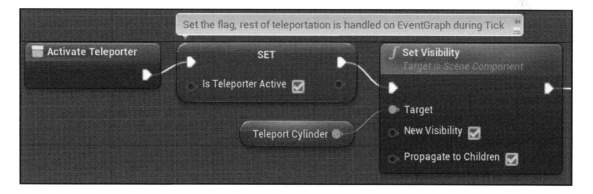

The **Disable Teleporter** Function of the `BP_MotionController` Blueprint resets the variables used in the teleportation and hides **Teleport Cylinder**.

The **Tick** Event of `BP_MotionController` is complex because it deals with the animation of the hand Skeletal Mesh and handles the teleportation arc. The next screenshot shows some Actions of the **Tick** Event, which are related to the teleportation arc. The **Clear Arc** Function resets the variables used by the last rendering of the arc. If the **Is Teleporter Active** variable is **True**, then the **Trace Teleport Destination** Function is called to calculate the points that will be used in the **ArcSpline** Component to render the arc:

We have analyzed the main elements used in the VR template, so now, it will be easier to understand more complex parts of the VR template. If you want to learn more about VR development, then I suggest that you access the Epic Games documentation about VR development: `https://docs.unrealengine.com/en-US/Platforms/VR/index.html`.

Summary

In this chapter, we explored the VR template, which is a simple way to start experimenting with VR development. We saw that the main functionalities of the VR template are divided between the `MotionControllerPawn` and `BP_MotionController` Blueprints.

We learned about the concept of the **Blueprint Interface** and saw how to use it to create new Blueprints that can be grabbed by a Motion Controller. We analyzed the implementation of object grabbing and teleportation in order to be able to adapt them to our projects.

We have reached the end of the book, but this will be the beginning of a new journey for you and your projects. Start by creating some simple projects to practice the knowledge you learned in this book and gain experience. Then, find a complete Unreal Engine project, open it, and try to understand how Blueprints were used. Epic Games has some complete projects available as learning resources.

I wish you great success.

Other Books You May Enjoy

If you enjoyed this book, you may be interested in these other books by Packt:

Unreal Engine Blueprints Visual Scripting Projects
Lauren S. Ferro

ISBN: 978-1-78953-242-5

- Set up Unreal Engine and all of its foundational components
- Add basic movement to game objects and create collision mechanism
- Design and implement interfaces to extend player interaction
- Create a dynamically filling inventory system along with a UI to interact with it
- Add audio effects based on triggered events to various parts of the game environment

Unreal Engine 4.x Scripting with C++ Cookbook - Second Edition
John P. Doran, William Sherif, Stephen Whittle

ISBN: 978-1-78980-950-3

- Create C++ classes and structs that integrate well with UE4 and the Blueprints editor
- Discover how to work with various APIs that Unreal Engine already contains
- Utilize advanced concepts such as events, delegates, and interfaces in your UE4 projects
- Build user interfaces using Canvas and UMG through C++
- Extend the Unreal Editor by creating custom windows and editors

Leave a review - let other readers know what you think

Please share your thoughts on this book with others by leaving a review on the site that you bought it from. If you purchased the book from Amazon, please leave us an honest review on this book's Amazon page. This is vital so that other potential readers can see and use your unbiased opinion to make purchasing decisions, we can understand what our customers think about our products, and our authors can see your feedback on the title that they have worked with Packt to create. It will only take a few minutes of your time, but is valuable to other potential customers, our authors, and Packt. Thank you!

Index

Printed in Great Britain
by Amazon

55212539R00217